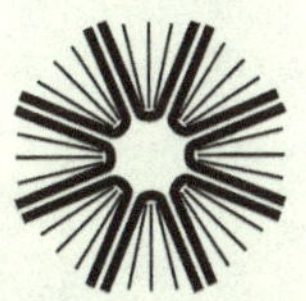

I08355I0

George Orwell's Elephant & Other Essays

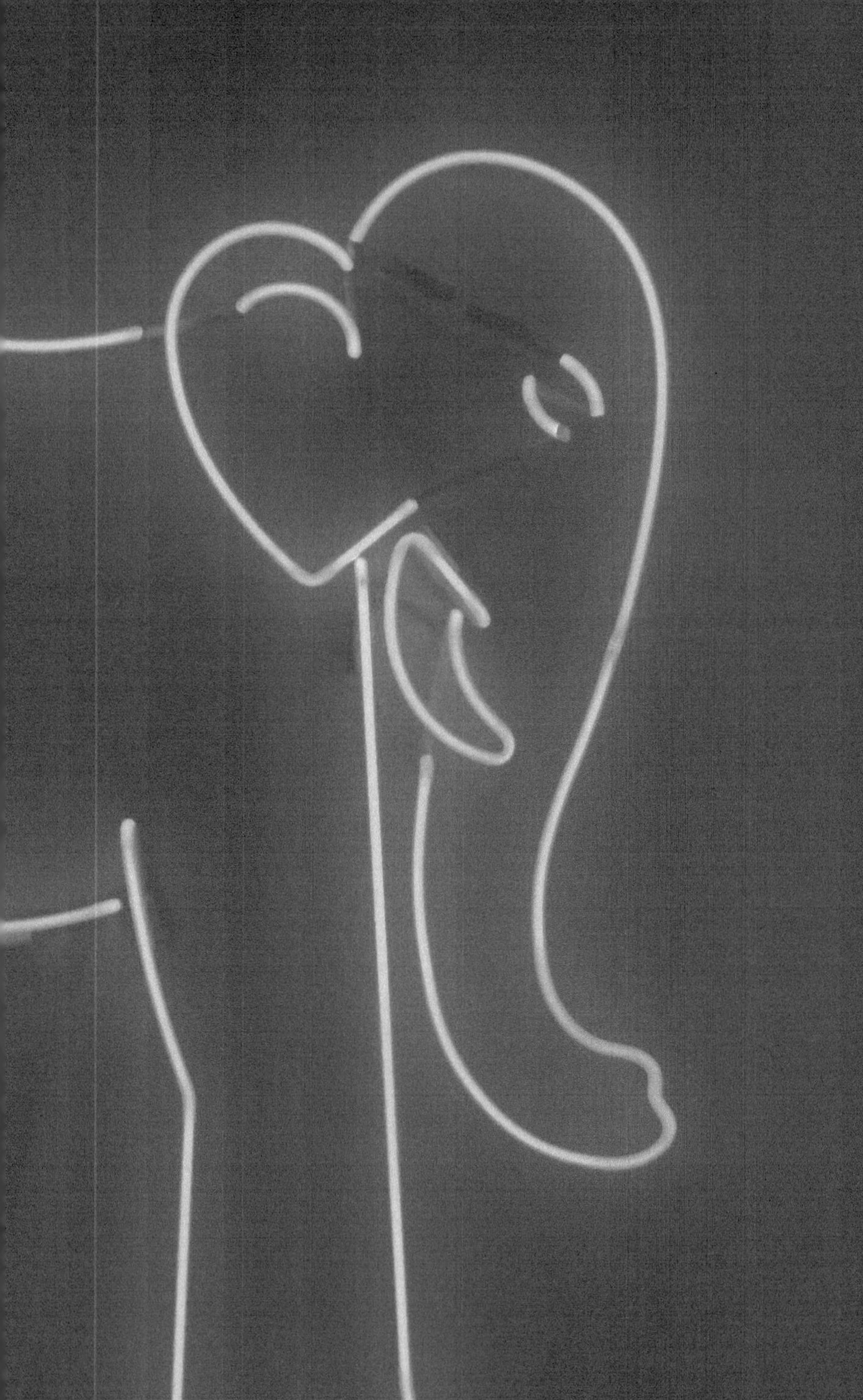

GEORGE ORWELL'S ELEPHANT & OTHER ESSAYS

SUBHASH JAIRETH

GAZEBO BOOKS SUMMER HILL 2024

Gazebo Books
PO Box 375
Summer Hill
New South Wales 2130
Australia
gazebobooks.com.au

First published 2024

The publication of this book has been assisted by artsACT.

National Library of Australia
Cataloguing-in-Publication Entry
Author: Jaireth, Subhash
George Orwell's Elephant & Other Stories
First edition
ISBN 978 0 6456337 9 5

Cover and interior design by Mountains Brown Press.

Cover and interior image: Euan Heng,
Elephant, 2007, neon, 120 x 99 cm,
Art Gallery of Ballarat collection

To Hamish, Miles, and their Dearest Oma

Car toutes les choses du monde conservent des souvenirs, d'elles-mêmes et des autres. Le grand livre du monde s'ouvre et se déploie comme un palimpseste à plusieurs épaisseurs, écrites en plusieurs langues et souvent effacées en partie.

(For all things in the world hold memories, of themselves and of others. The great book of the world opens and unfolds like a palimpsest of several thicknesses, written in several languages and often partially erased.)

... les choses autour de nous écrivent autant et meme mieux que nous – elles lisent même parfois –, de sorte que savoir consiste à déchiffrer les milles et un codes sous lesquels les choses, inertes ou vivantes, ont gravé, d'elles-mêmes et sur elles-mêmes, en soi et pour soi, leurs languages propres.

(... the things around us write as much and better than we do – they even read, at times – so that knowledge consists in deciphering the thousand and one codes with which things, inert or living, engraved their own languages, by themselves and on themselves, *en soi et pour soi.*)

– Michel Serres
Ecrivains, savants et philosophes font le tour du monde

Contents

George Orwell's Elephant

'Did you really shoot the elephant?' I imagine asking him.

'I did,' he says. 'Perhaps,' he adds after a pause.

Perhaps. I repeat the word a few times and realise that the story I want to tell has to begin with it.

Why perhaps? Why did he add this word? Why not a yes or no? Why this prevarication?

He is a writer I admire for his honesty and courage.

A writer steadfast in the pursuit of truth, ready to expose lies and deception, but most of all, eager to reveal the brute force of power and its companions: the fear and trickery of words.

The pseudonym he had adopted could also have been an act of trickery. He was Eric Arthur Blair when he shot the elephant in Burma, but by the time he wrote about it he had become George Orwell.

Why a new name? What was he trying to hide? A second self, a mask, or just a hide-out like the Barnhill on the Jura island in the Inner Hebrides where he wrote the famous *Nineteen Eighty-Four.*

He wasn't a happy man. This is the overwhelming impression I get from his biographies, books and essays. Unhappy, indignant, insolent.

•

In July 1998, I walked on the southern bank of the Orwell River that flows through the Suffolk city of Ipswich. Initially I had not planned to go to Ipswich because my interest was focused mainly on Raydon, a little village, fifteen kilometres south-west of Ipswich.

Raydon is the birth place of Proby Cautley, the main protagonist of a book I was working on. Cautley arrived in India in 1819 to serve as a military engineer with the East India Company. He was the principal designer and supervisor of the five hundred and fifty-kilometre-long Upper Ganga Canal, hailed to be one of the longest irrigational constructions in British Colonial India. The canal was officially opened in 1854 and became fully functional in 1857, the year of the Indian Mutiny against the company.

Cautley left India a few weeks after the opening. He had by then spent thirty-five eventful years in India, building and supervising irrigational works and collecting fossils of megafauna in the sediments of the Siwalik Hills through which the Upper Ganga Canal had to be cut.

The villagers living around Roorkee, the Indian town, where Cautley had established his head office, still hold fond memories of the English Sahib.

For an area ravaged by droughts and famines, the canal was a divine gift from Cautley who in the eyes of the villagers was as mighty and generous as any Hindu god.

Cautley was one of those Englishmen who happily

carried what Kipling has described as 'the white man's burden'. Orwell neither liked the term nor the people who fitted that description. For him, most, including himself, were racist agents of the empire.

In Raydon, the priest at Stratford St Mary Chapel, where Cautley had been baptised, suggested that I should visit Ipswich County Library because it might have some archival material about Cautley. I followed his advice and worked in the library for a couple of days.

One day, I met a Burmese Buddhist monk there. We were standing in a queue near the reference desk waiting for our turn to collect books and documents we had requested. 'Thant San,' he had said, introducing himself. He was tall and slim and looked much younger than his age, which I would find out later from his letters. What caught my eye was a little vertical cut on his left cheek not far from his upper lip. Each time he smiled, and he smiled often, a ripple ran over it.

He heard my name and said, 'You must be good with languages.' The prefix *su* in my name means 'good' and the word *bhash*, 'language.'

'No, I am not,' I said. 'I am lazy and slow.'

'But isn't it the tortoise that always wins the race?' He asked. You are very kind, I wanted to say. 'There are no tortoises in Mr Orwell's *Animal Farm*,' he said.

'And no goats either,' I added.

'He loved goats and kept a couple when he was in Burma,' Thant San said. 'He also adored elephants, their largeness which they carry with grace and humility.'

Did he really shoot an elephant in Moulmein? I wanted to ask him.

In the late afternoon we went for a walk in the Christchurch Park. The late summer sun was warm, the wind soft and moist and the air smelt of pollen and flowers. There were chestnuts, oaks, pines and limes. An old Indian Horse Chestnut that stood alone surrounded by a lush carpet of grass caught our eyes as we neared a large pond. We sat on the bench near the pond not far from a luscious Canadian birch which within a few months would turn glowing yellow.

'Isn't the birch beautiful?' Thant San asked.

'It is,' I said. 'It reminds me of my days in Moscow.'

I soon found out that Thant San had read almost everything written by Orwell and had come to visit places where Orwell had lived and worked. He mentioned that he had been to Motihari, a little Indian village in the foothills of the Himalayas, where Orwell was born in June 1903.

Like me, Thant San suffered from bronchitis and carried with him a Ventolin puffer. 'The pollen isn't good for me,' he said and asked me if I was interested in travelling to Wallington, to see The Store, the house where Orwell wrote his essay about the elephant. I told him that I wasn't sure because I had to go through some material waiting for me in the British Library in London, the material a kind librarian had dug up for me. He wrote down on a piece of paper the day he would be going to Wallington and said that he would wait for me outside the Baldock Station at around eleven o'clock.

Before saying goodbye, Thant San said something remarkable. 'Mr Orwell didn't like Buddhist priests,' he said, 'and would have gladly driven a bayonet into the guts of someone like me.'

I know the words I had wanted to tell him, for I had read Orwell's essay several times, underlining each time the stark and hateful words Thant San had mentioned. The most irritating thing for Orwell was the way the young Buddhist monks jeered Europeans like him.

'Mr Orwell felt guilty after shooting the poor elephant,' said Thant San, 'but I doubt if he would have felt any remorse for killing one of us.'

I heard his voice quiver. He turned his face away and when he looked again in my direction, I noticed that the smile on his face wasn't able to mask the sadness he seemed to have been carrying inside him.

I remember clearly the final words Thant San had said before we parted: 'Mr Orwell is a very good writer and I like him as a writer. But I don't know if he was a kind man. Perhaps he was. We all are or try to be. Maybe some of the time. I am hoping that by visiting places where he lived and worked, I would be able to get a glimpse of a kind and caring man inside Mr Orwell. I hope I can.'

•

In the library in London I busied myself researching Cautley, reading reports, notes and most importantly a few of his hand-written letters. I would have loved to get hold of more letters from him and to him mostly because I wanted to find out if, like Orwell, he had a dark side.

After returning from Ipswich I had resolved that I would try to empty my mind of Orwell and focus on Cautley. I failed.

Each night I walked to my hotel, Orwell walked with me, whispering to me in his croaky, raspy voice, urging me to dig deep about Cautley.

'Your Proby was different but not by much,' I would hear him say, then laugh, his laugh interrupted by the coughing of a chain smoker.

Two days before the trip to Wallington I was caught in the rain. It was quite late at night, and as I hurried to leave the library, I forgot to pick up my umbrella from the cloak room. The rain was heavy and the wind freezing cold. It blew off my beanie and I got thoroughly wet. The cold and fever that followed kept me in bed for three days.

I wrote a letter to Thant San apologising for not being able to join him on the trip to Wallington. I posted the letter to an address in Glasgow where he was planning to go after Wallington. In Glasgow he was staying at the Buddhist Centre from where, he had told me at our last meeting, he would undertake a pilgrimage to the Barnhill on Jura.

Often on my way to the British Library I would walk along Gower Street, on the north-western end of which stands the red cruciform building of the

University College Hospital. In January 1950 Orwell was admitted to a private ward of this hospital to give him some relief from tuberculosis that had become menacing. The treatment didn't work and on January 21 he died. His body had withered from the disease and as Gordon Bowker notes in his biography, he looked totally emaciated. He passed away at around two-thirty in the morning from a massive haemorrhage; 'an artery in the damaged wall of his lungs had ruptured and he was suffocated'.

One late afternoon I stopped at the hospital to look for the ward on the ground floor. I didn't want to go inside so I stood outside one of its large windows to peep inside.

'Don't be silly,' I heard Orwell whisper. 'It's a room like any other room. Nothing there to see and find. Nothing.'

I lingered for a few moments, looked around, and after a couple of pigeons had darted off the porch bearing a tall flag-less post, and flew past me, I decided to walk away.

That night Orwell spoke to me in my dream, describing the last few minutes of the dying elephant: 'Finally, I fired two remaining shots into the spot where I thought his heart must be. The thick blood welled out of him like red velvet, but still he did not die. His body did not even jerk when the shots hit him, the tortured breathing continued without a pause. He was dying very slowly and in great agony, but in some world remote from me where not even a bullet could damage him further.'

Orwell died alone in the ward, in agony like the elephant he said he had shot not once but several times; some shots fired to quicken the death and bring the animal relief.

'Never tell me,' he writes in *Shooting an Elephant*, 'that the dead look peaceful. Most of the corpses I have seen look devilish.'

Devilish. I prefer tired and tormented. That's what death does to humans and animals, even to animals we think and believe we kill humanely.

A week after recovering from my cold I decided to go to Sutton Courtenay, where in an English churchyard Orwell is buried. Like his two names, Orwell, writes Bowker, had two funerals. The one for George Orwell, the writer, was 'pompous, formal, unsubtle and dark'. It took place in Christ Church in Albany Street, and was '... attended by a large if disparate congregation'. The second, '...funeral of Eric Blair took place in the quiet village of Sutton Courtenay, with just four people and the pall-bearers present...'

It took me an hour to reach the village after travelling by train and then catching a bus. The bus dropped me at the George & Dragon pub, a few metres from the All Saints Church in the greens of which the remains of Eric Blair rest in a grave. The day was Wednesday and at around eleven in the morning there was no one around except for an old man sitting on a bench. That day too was relatively warm and sunny, and I hoped that it would stay that way for a few more hours.

It didn't take me long to find the grave. As I had read in books, it stood on the side of an alley along which a grove of English yews had been planted. I first saw the gravestone of David Astor, because it was a little taller than the rest and then noticed the straggly rose bushes near the one I had come looking for. Orwell loved roses. There was an 'Albertine' rose he had planted in front of the cottage, in the little Hertfordshire village of Wallington, where he would live several happy and unhappy years with his wife Eileen Maud Blair (née O'Shaughnessy), who also adored roses.

Eileen died in March 1945 from uterine cancer, alone in a hospital in Newcastle. She was six months away from marking her fortieth birthday. Orwell was in Paris and didn't know how seriously ill she was. In September that year, a few days before Eileen's fortieth birthday, Orwell visited her grave and planted a polyantha rose on the grave.

The roses on the straggly bushes on Eric Blair's grave were also polyantha, at least when they were first planted.

As I stood in front of the gravestone reading the simple inscription, it was the roses which coaxed my mind to recall the grave of Eileen. The inscription on her gravestone is also simple but a little longer: 'Here lies Eileen Maud Blair wife of Eric Arthur Blair Born 25th September 1905 Died March 29th 1945'.

Eileen was his wife and so Eric Blair found his name on her gravestone. Perhaps that's what Eileen had wished. It was naïve of me to imagine Eileen's name on

Eric Blair's gravestone and yet my mind wanted her name to be there, right next to Eric's.

Is this because I am convinced that although it was a short, nine-year marriage, the support of Eileen was critical for Orwell to keep working and writing? Most biographers acknowledge the role she had played in the making of *Animal Farm*.

That it wasn't a happy marriage, especially for Eileen, was clear to them both and I appreciate the honesty with which Orwell admitted it. 'It wasn't an ideal marriage,' he said. 'I don't think I treated her very well sometimes.'

The word 'sometimes' makes me uneasy. I would have replaced it with 'most of the time'. To live with Orwell wouldn't have been easy. He was, as Bowker writes, 'one of the great misfits of his generation, an outsider who made idiosyncrasy his hallmark'. Eileen was different; she 'believed in his great gifts and potential and was prepared to suffer with him'. In Eileen he had found a wife who showed 'readiness to be self-effacing and to keep a home for him'.

Orwell was a misfit like his alter-ego John Flory, the tragic hero of the *Burmese Days*. The inscription Flory wished for his fictional grave was humble and precise: 'John Flory Born 1890 Died of Drink 1927'. And he wanted the words to be engraved not on a stone but carved 'on the bark of some great peepul tree above [his] head'.

There aren't any peepul tress above Orwell's head. What we see instead is a grove of evergreen yews, the red fruit of which is poisonous because of the seed. Astor, the English newspaper owner, who also published Orwell, planted the grove in his honour.

The gravestone, battered by rain, snow and wind, had aged and yet it appeared solid like most stones, but muddied, stained and chipped, asking to be touched. And I touched it. It was moist and cold. On its flat top I found several coins, amongst which were a few Russian kopeks, an Iranian rial, a couple of Indian rupees, an Australian two-dollar coin, and a German mark. But what caught my attention was a Burmese 50-kyat coin.

'Thant San,' my mind whispered. He must have come here. Of course he must have. But I doubted if he was the one who had left the coin because the green and blue stains from the bronze coin had streaked down the stone, showing that it could have been sitting there for many years. However, the thought that Thant San had come here kept nagging and soon I spotted something that my mind found sufficient to convince me that the idea wasn't so far-fetched. Tied neatly on one of the branches of the straggly roses, I saw a triangular prayer flag. The saffron flag was small and appeared shy, unwilling to show itself. I believe that it would have remained unspotted by most visitors. I saw it because I was looking and wishing for it to be there.

'Thank you, Thant San,' I said and stepped back from the grave.

•

'In Moulmein, in Lower Burma, I was hated by large numbers of people.'

This is the line with which Orwell opens his essay about the elephant.

In Moulmein, people hated him, and he hated them with all the fury he could muster. And he hated himself for hating and being hated.

Each bullet he had fired at the elephant was in rage at himself and at them, but it was only the poor beast that was killed.

No, I am wrong. With the elephant a part of Orwell also died.

Orwell was sent to Moulmein, nowadays known as Mawlamyine, in 1926. The post of a sub-divisional police officer in the town was the highest position of his brief career in the Indian Imperial Police Force. 'The only time in my life,' he writes explaining the opening line in the essay, 'that I have been important enough for this to happen to me.'

He had arrived in Burma in June 1922, a few weeks before celebrating his nineteenth birthday. The following four years in Burma were maddening. Bowker writes that 'soon after arriving in Burma he realised that he had made a great mistake.' Bowker's assessment is supported by Orwell's confession that in the 1920s, 'few able men went east of Suez if there was any way of avoiding it'. Emma Larkin (a pseudonym) in her book *Finding George Orwell in Burma*, writes that Orwell considered his time in Burma as 'five boring years within the sound of bugles'.

His stay in Moulmein could have been happier, for it was the town where his mother Ida Mabel Limouzin had grown up as a child, and it was the town where Ida's mother, Theresa Catherine Halliley, still lived in a large house on one of its main streets.

Orwell's grandmother Theresa had died in 1925, a year before he came to Moulmein, but Orwell did meet her on his earlier visits to the town. Bowker notes that Theresa was 'an interesting woman who had said to have "gone native", adopting native Burmese dress and having native Burmese friends.' But unlike Orwell who had learnt Hindustani, Burmese and Karen, Theresa had not bothered to speak Burmese in the forty years she had lived there. Her behaviour Orwell would write later was 'typical of the ordinary Englishwoman's' in the colonies.

In Moulmein he also met other members of his mother's family: his uncles and aunts, and cousins. One of them was Kathleen, the daughter of his uncle Frank and his Burmese wife or mistress Mah Hlim.

The house the family lived in was called 'Franconia'. It stood in the trendy riverside area of Salween Park. In 2014, Larkin did search for the house but couldn't find it. However, she was able to locate a street with a sign that read Leimmew-zin, 'the nearest Burmese pronunciation of Limouzin'. Twelve years later, Richard Eilers, an English journalist, visited Moulmein, and a local historian helped him find the site. The house, he was told, had been destroyed in the bombing during the British-Japanese war. What remained on the site was an 'impressive gate and high walls'.

The British Library's archives hold an old map of the Moulmein River and its approaches. On this 1936 map I see the river and its sprawling delta. On its eastern bank, not far from its junction with the two other rivers, the Darebuak and the smaller Ataran, I spot the town of Moulmein.

The main street follows the bank, mimicking its meandering shape. Most public buildings are on the main street whereas residential houses stand close to the river bank. The street running along the bank was called the Strand Road. On the map I see the post office, the hospital, and the famous Chaitlan or Kyaikthanlan Pagoda. In the east the city is bordered by a narrow ridge on which stand several tall pagodas rising above the forest canopy. The map doesn't show the police headquarters but it's quite likely that it was situated not far from the court house.

In the archives of the library I also discovered several photographs of nineteenth-century Moulmein. One of them is by Samuel Bourne, the English photographer who spent years in India and Burma photographing people and places. In 1868, he also visited the Upper Ganga Canal and took a few remarkable photographs of it.

His 1870 photograph of Moulmein was taken standing outside the Kyaikthanlan Pagoda. One of the limestone columns of the pagoda fills the left side of the photographs. The rest of the space shows a panoramic view of the town, the river, and beyond it the hazy outlines of the Gulf of Martaban and of the ranges to its west. Interestingly, in the photograph I also see the large building of the Moulmein jail. Orwell's headquarters would have been quite close to the jail and it's likely that he frequently visited the building.

The photograph that I found most intriguing was that of the Strand Road. It was taken in the 1890s by Henry Watts and Frederick Skeen, two of the many popular colonial photographers of their time. On the left side of the photograph I see a stone wall marking the river embankment. Most of the space, however, is taken by a wide street on the right-hand side of which stand residential houses with fences, a few street lights, and some palm trees. But what attracts me most is the figure of an Indian man in his *dhoti*, a dark coat, and a white *pagri*. He reminds me of the *mahout* Orwell mentions in his essay.

The captions of some of the photographs provide succinct descriptions of the town Orwell lived in, in 1926. One of them reads as follows:

> Moulmein, the chief town of the Mon State, lies on the coast of south-east Burma at the mouth of the Thanlwin (Salween) river where it meets the Gulf of Martaban (Mottama). It developed as a colonial town between 1827 and 1852, when it was the administrative capital of British Burma. During this period, it became a major centre for the export of teak and remains an important

seaport for coastal shipping. A number of shrines and monasteries like the Kyaikthanlan Pagoda (referred to in Rudyard Kipling's poem 'Mandalay') were built on a ridge of hills running north-south in east Moulmein, commanding a view of the town and river.

Elephants were important in the economy of colonial Burma. The city was full of domesticated elephants and there were stables of ten to twelve animals rented out to haul timber and other goods. It is possible that the elephant Orwell had shot was from the stable of a timber company, and therefore quite valuable. Orwell in his essay writes that after the shooting some younger Europeans in the town expressed their displeasure at the killing of the elephant. In their opinion 'it was a damn shame to shoot an elephant for killing a coolie.'

Very little is known of Orwell's life in Moulmein. We don't know the house or its address but Bowker suspects that like most Europeans in Burma he could have lived with a Burmese mistress whom he passed off as a maidservant.

After the shooting, Orwell was ordered to leave Moulmein and he moved to Katha, a remote town in Upper Burma. Bowker like many other biographers suggests that it was a punishment not just for shooting an elephant belonging to an influential timber company but also because Orwell had become an embarrassment to authorities in Rangoon, having offended in other ways against the code of the pukka sahib, perhaps talking out of turn or involved in some scandal similar to that between Flory and Ma Hla May.

George Stuart, a railway engineer in Moulmein who knew Orwell, remembers that he saw Orwell pacing and loading his belongings before he left for Katha. They included 'a lot of farmyard creatures, like hens and ducks and so forth which happened to escape on the platform and caused quite a commotion'.

George Stuart was at the club in Moulmein when Orwell after 'being informed that an elephant had gone must [out of control], causing great havoc and killing its mahout, immediately called for a gun and set off in an old Ford car to deal with the matter'.

The shooting of the elephant brought a premature end to Orwell's stay in Burma and on 12 July 1927, less than a year after the incident, Orwell left Burma. Five months later, in December 1927, he resigned from the Indian Imperial Police Force.

His departure from Burma was quick and final, but Burma, especially the memory of its people and the way they smelt, remained with him till the very last months of his life.

Larkin mentions Orwell's notes for his novella, *A Smoking Room Story*, which he was planning to finish and publish soon after *Nineteen Eighty-Four*, his last book. The novella was set on a ship sailing from Burma back to England.

•

Orwell began writing his essay about the elephant in The Stores, the cottage he was renting in Wallington.

After visiting Wallington, Thant San had sent me a brief note with a few sketches of the cottage and the surrounds. The packet also contained a map of the little village he had bought at a local shop that showed the location of the cottage and the barn that Orwell had turned into the Manor Farm of Willingdon in *Animal Farm*.

Thant San mentioned that he saw a blue car parked in the driveway of the cottage and couldn't bring himself to walk in to have a look. He lingered in front of the house only for a few minutes, moved back and sat down on the lawn across the street to make a quick sketch. He also didn't go inside the barn, deterred by the heavy metal gate. 'But I left a yellow ribbon tied to the lowermost railing of the gate. It's tiny and I am certain no one will see it and my indiscretion will remain unnoticed.'

He wrote that he enjoyed sitting near the duck pond, watching the sheep grazing in the farm across the fence, imagining how Mr Orwell would have sat at the same place feeding his goat Muriel.

I smiled after reading about the ribbon. It reminded me of the saffron prayer flag I had seen tied to the roses on Eric Blair's grave.

Orwell began working on the essay soon after his wedding on 9 June 1936. He toiled hard and it took him less than sixteen days to finish and send it to John Lehman, the editor of an anti-Fascist literary magazine, *New Writing*.

A few weeks earlier, he had mentioned to Lehman that he was thinking of writing a 'sketch' about shooting an elephant but wasn't sure if 'there was anything anti-Fascist in it'. The idea, he said, 'came back to me very vividly the other day and I would like to write.'

Bowker suggests that it was probably 'Kipling's death, and mulling over what he had seen in the north,' on his trip to Liverpool, that could have 'stirred memories of his time in Burma'.

Orwell confronted the elephant in 1926 and he wrote about it ten years later. Did he keep notes of the incident or did he rely solely on his memory?

Neither Bowker nor any other biographer of Orwell mention anything about notes for this or for his other equally powerful essay about a hanging Orwell is said to have witnessed in a Burmese prison. In the essay *A Hanging*, Orwell describes the execution of 'a Hindu, a puny wisp of a man, with a shaven head and vague liquid eyes'. The essay was published in 1931 in the magazine *Adelphi*. The author of the essay is Eric Blair and not George Orwell, a name he would adopt a few years later.

Most readers find the two essays compelling because of the precision with which they relate the story. The prose is crisp and bare and comes close to the 'window-pane-like prose' he aimed to master. 'I am trying to find a style,' he once explained to Michael Sayers, a young Irish poet with whom he shared an apartment, 'which eliminates the adjective.'

There are adjectives in *Shooting an Elephant*, but they aren't overused. The Latin and foreign words, which he would also start to avoid, are also rare. This makes the description direct, almost unmediated. Perhaps it's the immediacy of description, and the first-person voice Orwell adopts, which convinces us that the story is not merely believable but factually true.

Orwell doesn't shy away from expressing his feelings about the despotic nature of imperial administration in the colonies and about the role he, as a police officer, plays in it. His honesty and the confessional tone of the essay helps him to win our confidence and we soon begin to sympathise with him, ready to assure him that we understand his situation; that, like him, we didn't want the elephant to die but it died because it had to, because such things, however cruel, do happen; that we all have our roles to play and our duties to perform. We are disappointed that the poor beast had to be killed but we are impressed by the expression of guilt and remorse and are prepared to forgive him. We are even willing to laud him for the care he took to reduce the pain the animal would have endured.

Writers, if they are good, seduce us. Orwell isn't merely good; he is a genius. But like all seductions, this too has limits. Soon its hold on us wanes and we begin to ask questions.

Orwell had first-hand experience of the brutality with which the British imperial government in Burma ruled and therefore it wasn't difficult for him to describe the 'tiny incident' in such a way that it complied with the anti-Fascist theme of the magazine.

He makes his intentions clear in the very first lines with which he introduces the incident:

> One day something happened which in a roundabout way was enlightening. It was a tiny incident in itself, but it gave me a better glimpse than I had had before of the real nature of imperialism – the real motives for which despotic governments act.

Orwell is aware of the part he plays in the despotic government. As a police officer he is its symbol and its agent. Through him the power is imposed on the hapless people in the colonies. However, what infuriates him most is his inability to defy the power:

> For at that time I had already made up my mind that imperialism was an evil thing and the sooner I chucked up my job and got out of it the better. Theoretically – and secretly, of course – I was all for the Burmese and all against their oppressors, the British. As for the job I was doing, I hated it more bitterly than I can perhaps make clear. In a job like that you see the dirty work of Empire at close quarters. [...] All I knew was that I was stuck between my hatred of the empire I served and my rage against the evil-spirited little beasts who

> tried to make my job impossible. With one part of my mind I thought of the British Raj as an unbreakable tyranny, as something clamped down, in *saecula saeculorum*, upon the will of prostrate peoples; with another part I thought that the greatest joy in the world would be to drive a bayonet into a Buddhist priest's guts. Feelings like these are the normal by-products of imperialism; ask any Anglo-Indian official, if you can catch him off duty.

'Poor Orwell,' I say as I read the above passage and smile. He wants me to believe that he is just a little cog in the wheel of oppression; a petty officer who is merely following orders. He wants to rule judiciously and kindly, he tells me, but the people over whom he rules make his job difficult, forcing him to do things he doesn't wish to.

The passage, however, reminds me of the sorrowful look on Thant San's face. The real target of Mr Orwell's bullets wasn't an elephant, I imagine him saying, but monks like him.

Orwell often wished to kill the monks but to shoot an elephant wasn't his intention:

> As soon as I saw the elephant I knew with perfect certainty that I ought not to shoot him. It is a serious matter to shoot a working elephant – it is comparable to destroying a huge and costly piece of machinery – and obviously one ought not to do it if it can possibly be avoided. And at that distance, peacefully eating,

the elephant looked no more dangerous than a cow. I thought then and I think now that his attack of "must" was already passing off; in which case he would merely wander harmlessly about until the mahout came back and caught him. Moreover, I did not in the least want to shoot him. I decided that I would watch him for a little while to make sure that he did not turn savage again, and then go home.

But at that moment I glanced round at the crowd that had followed me. It was an immense crowd, 2,000 at the least and growing every minute. [...] I looked at the sea of yellow faces above the garish clothes – faces all happy and excited over this bit of fun, all certain that the elephant was going to be shot. They were watching me as they would watch a conjuror about to perform a trick. They did not like me, but with the magical rifle in my hands I was momentarily worth watching. And suddenly I realised that I should have to shoot the elephant after all. The people expected it of me and I had got to do it; I could feel their 2,000 wills pressing me forward, irresistibly. And it was at this moment, as I stood there with the rifle in my hands, that I first grasped the hollowness, the futility of the white man's dominion in the East.

Here was I, the white man with his gun, standing in front of the unarmed native crowd – seemingly the leading actor of the piece; but in reality I was only an absurd puppet pushed to and fro by the will of those yellow faces behind. I perceived in this moment that when the white man turns tyrant it is his own freedom

> that he destroys. He becomes a sort of hollow, posing dummy, the conventionalised figure of a sahib. For it is the condition of his rule that he shall spend his life in trying to impress the "natives," and so in every crisis he has got to do what the "natives" expect of him. He wears a mask, and his face grows to fit it. I had got to shoot the elephant. I had committed myself to doing it when I sent for the rifle. A sahib has got to act like a sahib; he has got to appear resolute, to know his own mind and do definite things. To come all that way, rifle in hand, with 2,000 people marching at my heels, and then to trail feebly away, having done nothing – no, that was impossible. The crowd would laugh at me. And my whole life, every white man's life in the East, was one long struggle not to be laughed at.

Orwell didn't shoot. It was the crowd of yellow faces that shot the elephant. Although it was his finger that pulled the trigger, the force that pushed the finger was the collective will of the crowd. He was just a puppet, a helpless English sahib.

'You are right,' Mr Orwell, I hear Thant San say. A mere *nimitta-matram*, a Sanskrit word that means an 'instrument'. You were just following orders.

In the essay, the narrator wants us to believe that he shot and killed the elephant, but does this really imply that Eric Blair, the police officer in Burma and the author of the piece, killed an elephant? Normally, it should but most biographers doubt whether Eric Blair did indeed shoot an elephant.

Similar doubts are raised about Orwell witnessing a hanging in Burma, which he describes in his other essay. Bernard Crick, an English political theorist, who was commissioned by Sonia Orwell, the second wife of Orwell, to write Orwell's biography, notes that there are reasons to doubt whether he witnessed hangings in Burma:

> Did he witness a hanging at all? The old hands feel fairly certain it would not have been part of a young ASP's duties; but he could have watched a hanging if he had asked. The tale does not make clear what the narrator is doing. Orwell told a friend, Mabel Fierz, sometime in the early 1930s, and also told his housekeeper, Susan Watson, in 1946, that 'it was only a story' — this after they had praised it and tried to get him to talk about it. And a year later he said the same to his sister. Yet not only did he write in *The Road to Wigan Pier* that 'I watched a man hanged once; it seemed to me worse than a thousand murders,' but he repeated this to readers of *Tribune* in 1944: 'I watched a man hanged once. There was no question that everybody concerned knew this to be a dreadful, unnatural action.' There could have been another hanging which he witnessed and *A Hanging* could be, indeed, a brilliantly artful short story. His denials could have been simply to stop unwelcome and morbid conversations, for he disliked talking about his work, even his past work.

Is *Shooting an Elephant* also an 'artful short story'? Some biographers believe it to be. D. J. Taylor writes in *Orwell: The Life*, that

> ambiguity also hangs over *Shooting an Elephant* – full of intent, densely realised description, but incapable of being fixed to a particular date or locale, and referred to only once, and that indirectly, elsewhere in Orwell's writings. (Elizabeth in *Burmese Days* is 'quite thrilled' when Flory describes 'the murder of an elephant he had perpetrated some years earlier'.) George Stuart claimed to have been at the club in Moulmein when the message about the rogue elephant came through, prompting Orwell to borrow a rifle and set out in pursuit, but this memory of the episode may not have been wholly accurate. … Another of Orwell's contemporaries thought that he remembered a report of the incident in the *Rangoon Gazette*, and indeed there is such a report, dated 22 March 1926. However, the protagonist was not Orwell but Major E.C. Kenny, subdivisional officer at Yamethin, who shot an elephant that had killed a man five miles east of the Tatkon township 'to the delight of the villagers.'

'Did George Orwell shoot an elephant?' asks Gerry Abbott in an article. I like the way he tries to answer the question. He reproduces Orwell's essay in full, with a brief introduction that ends with the words:

> To me, Orwell's description of the great creature's heartbreakingly slow death suggests an acute awareness of wrongdoing, as do his repeated protests: 'I had no intention of shooting the elephant … I did not in the least want to shoot him … I did not want to shoot the elephant.' Though Orwell shifts the blame on to the imperialist system, I think the poet did shoot the elephant. But read the sketch and decide for yourself.

Yes, each of us has to decide for ourselves. The story in the essay is persuasive enough for us to believe that the narrator shot and killed the elephant. Does it matter if he was Eric Blair or George Orwell or someone else?

Strangely it does and doesn't.

I can imagine what Thant San would say: 'Mr Orwell killed the elephant because he wanted to kill one. The desire to kill is, in a sense, the same as the killing itself. They both corrupt us. They both denude the human in us although there are only a few on the earth who haven't thought of killing one or the other living creature. To kill and be killed is the natural way of being in this world.'

•

I know the Sanskrit word *nimitta-matram* from my reading of the poem *The Bhagavad Gita*. It appears in verse number 33 of chapter 13. As a fifteen-year-old boy I was able to recite most of the poem from memory.

Now my knowledge of Sanskrit and of the poem has waned but the significance of the story it tells hasn't.

To kill or not to kill is the question that Arjuna, the warrior prince, asks in *The Bhagavad Gita*. A question to which he hopes Krishna, his friend and charioteer, would find a convincing answer otherwise Arjuna wouldn't fight and kill and thereby disgrace himself in the eyes of his gods and his kith and kin.

Most historians believe that *The Bhagavad Gita* was a later addition to the Indian epic *Mahabharata*. It recounts the story of the 'great war' between two groups of cousins and their armies that took place sometime around 900 BCE. For centuries, the story was told and retold by professional bards and performers and attained its present form between 200 BCE and 200 CE. The epic, as we know it now, comprises over 80 thousand verses and a few prose passages.

The linguistic analysis of *The Bhagavad Gita* reveals that the Sanskrit used in the verses was of much later provenance than the main text of *Mahabharata*. It is believed that the oral version of *The Bhagavad Gita* was in circulation during the later centuries of the first millennium BCE, and the written text appeared sometime between the second and third century CE.

On the first day of the eighteen-day war, Arjuna, the chief warrior of the Pandava clan, one of the two groups of cousins, asks Krishna to drive the chariot to the front of the army line so that he can look at his enemies. Krishna obliges but Arjuna soon discovers that the enemies he is going to fight, and kill, are his close and distant relatives, his teachers and mentors, and his friends. Dejected, he lays downs his arms saying: 'My limbs sag, my mouth feels parched, my body quakes, and my hair stands on end.'

In the following seventeen dialogues Krishna attempts to persuade Arjuna to fight. Krishna, however, isn't an ordinary charioteer; he is also one of the many incarnations of the Hindu god Vishnu. Hence, his conversation with Arjuna turns into an exposition of basic Hindu philosophy and ethics.

Krishna says to Arjuna that he should fight and therefore be ready to kill because 'the wise do not lament either the dead or the living'. The wise know that 'there was never a time when either I, or you, or those rulers of men did not exist. Nor will there ever be a future when all of us cease to exist.' Whatever takes birth or dies, argues Krishna, is just the body whereas the soul, immortal as it is, remains unharmed. The body is mortal and therefore to grieve for it is neither wise nor beneficial.

Arjuna should fight, says Krishna, because the battle he has been asked to participate in is righteous. His enemies, although they are his cousins and friends, are impure, sinful and corrupt and therefore it is his duty to take up arms against them.

Arjuna should fight, says Krishna, because he is a proud Kshatriya, a warrior, and therefore, it is his dharma to take up arms and attack. Krishna urges Arjuna to 'perform the action prescribed for him, because it's better to act than to be inactive'. To fail to act according to one's code of conduct, argues Krishna, is naturally and morally wrong.

Arjuna should fight, says Krishna, believing that he is acting 'in the spirit of sacrifice, free from any form of attachment,' and without 'an eye on its fruit'. He shouldn't worry about winning or losing, living or dying. By keeping himself detached from his action he would be able to set himself 'free from the good and evil consequences' resulting from it.

Arjuna should fight, says Krishna, because it's what the gods have willed. The fate of his enemies and his own is prearranged. Being evil, his enemies have to die, and die they will. Krishna says:

> I am Time, the destroyer of the worlds, matured, and occupied now in destroying the world. Even were you not here, all the warriors, standing variously arrayed in different armies, shall be no more. Therefore, arise and obtain glory. Conquering your enemies, enjoy a flourishing kingdom. I myself have already killed these earlier. Become merely the instrument, O Savyasācin [Arjuna].

As expected, Arjuna gives in. Krishna is persuasive; his logic flawless. 'My ignorance has been destroyed,' he says to Krishna, 'and I have got back my memory through your grace O Krishna. I shall be steady, freed of doubt. I shall do what you have stated.'

You have been duped Arjuna, I say. Duped and forsaken.

Unfortunately, Arjuna isn't the first or the only person hoodwinked by sweet talkers who hold the reins of power. We have encountered them too often in history and many more will show up in the future, for the weakness to let ourselves be duped is universal. We are morally weak, always looking for excuses and scapegoats.

Was Orwell one of them?

'Perhaps he was,' I hear Thant San speak. 'Mr Orwell simply followed his dharma; the dharma of a police officer.'

'What if he had driven a bayonet into the guts of a monk?' I ask.

'Is a monk any different from an elephant?'

'I don't know,' I mumble, evading the question, because the answer, whichever way I look, seems perilous.

•

'I've always been good with animals,' Orwell had once said to Susan Watson, the housekeeper he had asked for help in looking after Richard, his fifteen-month-old adopted son. Taylor in his biography of Orwell uses these words as a caption to a well-known photograph of Orwell feeding Muriel, the goat, at Wallington. This was in response to her compliments on his upbringing of the young boy.

Orwell loved animals and liked to have them with and around him. 'Most of the good memories of my childhood,' he writes in his autobiographical essay, *Such, Such Were the Joys*, 'are in some way connected with animals.'

On his posting in the Burmese town Insein, he is known to have kept 'goats, geese, and ducks'. It was the same in Moulmein where he was called on to confront a runaway elephant.

In the cottage in Wallington where he lived with Eileen, the couple had a productive vegetable garden with fruit trees, and many animals. After the wedding they temporarily inherited Hector, the family dog and 'to keep Hector company they acquired a little sandy cat, some chickens and finally that goat, which was christened Muriel after one of George's Limouzin aunts'.

In the Orwell Archive of the University College London Library there is a photograph which shows Orwell milking a goat. In the photograph I also see a Burmese man, who is described in the caption as 'a local servant'. He is sitting on the other side of the goat holding the rope and the harness around its neck. His left hand is under the goat assisting Orwell to squeeze its teats. I find this photograph more fascinating than the one with Muriel but strangely I haven't come across it in any of the many biographies of Orwell.

In July 1937 when Orwell returned from the Spanish Civil War to resume his stay in Wallington, he and Eileen acquired a few more animals. Hector, the dog, returned to Orwell's family and was replaced by a black poodle which they called Marx. They also brought in a second goat who received the name Kate, after Orwell's aunt. By the time they left the cottage they had more than thirty chickens.

In Marrakech, where Orwell and Eileen had travelled in September 1937 for Orwell to convalesce after his first prolonged bout of tuberculosis, they kept chickens and goats. Villa Simont, the stone house they had rented, was located in an orange grove not far from the foot of the Atlas Mountains. To make themselves feel at home they started a small vegetable patch near the house.

After Eileen's death in 1945, Orwell moved to Barnhill, a remote and deserted farmhouse on Jura to stay and work in isolation. This was to be his ideal summer home. The old greystone house, notes Bowker,

> stood like some Bleak House, eerie and inhospitable. At other times, bathed in sunlight and lapped by blue water, it offered a more welcoming prospect. Although it was poor farming land the island was rich in wild life – red deer, wild goats, rabbits, rats and snakes in abundance, and teeming with birds – just the place for the solitary naturalist to ramble and observe while being close to the heath-like, boggy surface of earth and the unpredictable elements.

Soon he was joined by his younger sister Avril and Richard, his young son. The life was hard but that's what Orwell enjoyed, producing most of the food at the farmhouse. Supply from the small vegetable garden was supplemented by fishing and shooting of rabbits and ducks. They also had a cow and a few chickens.

Orwell had always enjoyed hunting but at Barnhill, the hunter and the naturalist re-emerged with new vigour. Now he could go on long walks, sleep under the stars and take off on lonely fishing expeditions. As Bowker notes, Orwell kept 'a meticulous diary, recording changes in the weather, the fluctuating mood of the sea, the progress on his garden, the flora and fauna observed and the state of the fuel supply.' The writing wasn't forgotten. Often, he retired to the large attic room and shut himself in to read and write. His fingers clattered the words of *Nineteen Eighty-Four* on the typewriter placed on an untidy desk, sitting near the window looking out on to a bay of pitch-dark water lapping the shore.

The naturalist and the hunter sat in him amicably, but hunting, as most biographers note, also revealed the darker side of his attitude towards animals. An attitude that combined 'a strong love of them with an equally powerful hunter's urge to destroy them.' Like many children, he had, in his childhood, enjoyed blowing up toads with a bicycle pump, cutting up wasps, and smashing birds' eggs. 'The best way to catch eels,' he once told the young boys he had been asked to tutor, 'was to blast them with shot guns.'

He loved guns and had bought his first Salon Rifle at the age of ten. He was drawn to hunting instinctively but 'his hunting instinct,' notes Bowker, 'had more than a trace of cruelty about it – a compensation, perhaps, for strongly suppressed sadistic feelings towards humans.' Bowker recounts a story he had heard from Bill Dunn, Avril's future husband, about an incident involving a snake:

> He, Avril, young Richard, and I went for a picnic to Scarba ... Well, the first live thing we met on stepping ashore was an adder. Eric put his foot on it, just behind its head. I expected him to bash it with the other foot or a stone or stick or something, but surprisingly he deliberately took out his penknife and opened it and slit the snake from top to bottom. He degutted it and filleted it.

Sayers, the young Irish poet with whom Orwell shared an apartment, noticed that 'there was something inside him which was repellent and dangerous'. Orwell, he writes, was aware of his darker side and struggled to keep it repressed because often it only needed a little trigger or provocation to erupt. It didn't matter then if the target was an animal or a human being. His fury was uncontrollable.

One of the victims of Orwell's fury was Rayner Heppenstall, a writer and a friend, who shared an apartment with Orwell. In his memoir *The Four Absentees*, Heppenstall describes the ugly incident. One late Sunday night Heppenstall arrived heavily drunk. Orwell asked him to calm down but Heppenstall took a swing at him and Orwell responded by hitting him with his shooting stick:

> There stood Orwell, armed with his shooting stick. With this he pushed me back, poking the aluminium point into my stomach. I pushed it aside and sprang at him. He fetched me a dreadful crack across the legs and then raised the shooting stick over his head. I looked at his face. Through my private mist I saw in it a curious blend of fear and sadistic exaltation.

Heppenstall fell on the floor and 'saved himself from a final crack across the head by parrying it with a chair before passing out.'

Heppenstall published the account some twenty years after the incident and five years after Orwell's death. However, the break in their friendship was temporary, and after a few years they made up and remained friends.

In his biography of Orwell, Crick notes that 'the account written some twenty years later raises the same kinds of problems as Orwell's own autobiographical writings. The incident certainly occurred, as Mabel Fierz confirms, to whom the battered Rayner retreated the next morning.'

I am ready to believe that the incident did happen; however, what interests me more is the fear that Heppenstall saw on Orwell's face. Why fear? Fear of what? Of himself? Of his own aggression?

That this wasn't an isolated event is confirmed by a similar incident that occurred in Rangoon in November 1924. There on a railway station platform Orwell vented his fury on a Burmese boy. Dr Htin Aung, a former vice-chancellor of the Rangoon University, was a schoolboy in 1924 and witnessed the episode. He described the ugly clash in a lecture he gave in 1969 at the Royal Central Asian Society in London. In Larkin's book I find a brief account of what he saw. In this case Orwell's anger was roused by a bunch of boisterous schoolboys messing around on the platform. One of the boys

> accidently rolled under the Englishman's feet and caused him to tumble heavily down the stairs. The Englishman jumped up furiously and raised his cane to smack the boy on the head. At the last minute he checked himself and instead the cane came down on the boy's back. The boy and his friends, including Htin Aung, were angry at the unnecessary violence. The stationmaster told them the Englishman's name was Eric Blair.

A fictional version of the incident appears in the *Burmese Days*. The attacker in Orwell's novel is Ellis, an English timber merchant who assaults a jeering Burmese boy and renders him blind.

The rage that simmered inside Orwell during his stay of five and a half years in Burma is palpable in the novel and the two essays he wrote about Burma. Strangely, the source of rage and its target are the same: the insolent young boys and Buddhist monks. However, this doesn't mean that Orwell spares himself. He is terribly angry with himself.

Christopher Hollis, a friend of Orwell at Eton, met him in Burma. In his book *A Study of George Orwell*, Hollis recounts the conversation he had with his friend at a dinner. Hollis is surprised that Blair [Orwell] showed 'no trace of liberal opinion'. The conversation leaves him in no doubt that Blair 'was at pains to be the imperial policeman, explaining that these theories of no punishment were all very well at public schools but that they did not work with the Burmese.' Blair, the policeman, was convinced that 'such people were unfit for liberty, especially the Buddhist priests against whom he thought violence was wholly desirable merely because of their sniggering insolence.'

Bowker in his biography of Orwell also describes the incident at the Rangoon platform and concludes that 'the intense remorse Orwell felt about his actions as a policeman – his abuse and beating of Burmese servants and prisoners to which he later confessed,' brought about a transformation that forced him to question his place and role in Burma.

I remember the sadness on Thant San's face when he talked about the hate and anger Orwell displayed for the young Burmese. Does Thant San know about the remorse Orwell felt for his actions? I hope he does because it should bring him some comfort. The sceptic in me, however, wants to know if the remorse was genuine. I hope Thant San is more gracious, forgiving, and kind. I doubt if I am.

•

Five years after my trip to Ipswich I received a small packet from Thant San.

It contained a saffron ribbon, an old black-and-white photograph of the Rangoon railway platform with the year 1930 scribbled on its back, a photocopy of a page from one of Orwell's essays, and a brief typed note from Thant San's niece.

I looked at the photograph of the railway platform and it didn't take me long to imagine that like Dr Htin Aung, Thant San might also have a personal connection with the incident on the platform. Why not? That might explain the urgency with which he wanted to get inside the mind of Mr Orwell.

The photocopied text was from Orwell's essay *Looking Back on the Spanish Civil War*. I know the essay. It is included in the *Penguin Essays of George Orwell*, the book that carries on its cover a photograph of Orwell sitting at his desk and writing. The photograph was taken in Marrakech.

I opened the book and found the page, the photocopy of which I had received in the packet. I wasn't surprised that the paragraph highlighted on the photocopy had also been underlined by me in the book.

The highlighted section forms the final part of the paragraph that begins with the lines: 'Early one morning another man and I had gone out to snipe at the Fascists in the trenches outside Huesca.' What follows next is a brief description of Orwell's encounter with a Fascist soldier:

> At this moment a man, presumably carrying a message to an officer, jumped out of the trench and ran along the top of the parapet in full view. He was half-dressed and was holding up his trousers with both hands as he ran. I refrained from shooting at him. It is true that I am a poor shot and unlikely to hit a running man at a hundred yards, and also that I was thinking chiefly about getting back to our trench while the Fascists had their attention fixed on the aeroplanes. Still, I did not shoot partly because of the detail about the trousers. I had come here to shoot at 'Fascists'; but a man who is holding up his trousers isn't a 'Fascist', he is visibly a fellow creature, similar to yourself, and you don't feel like shooting at him.

As I read the text, I notice that I have underlined the last sentence twice and have also jotted an exclamation mark on the margin.

In Burma, Orwell didn't want to shoot and kill the elephant but did. In the trenches in Huesca he didn't want to shoot at the Fascist and didn't. He didn't because the Fascist appeared to him like a fellow creature, similar to himself.

'So, we have found the kind man in Mr Orwell,' I wanted to say to Thant San.

'Perhaps we have,' I heard him reply.

•

The brief note from Thant Sant's niece said that her uncle passed away six months ago. The death was sudden and quick and was caused by a massive heart attack. Uncle had asked me, she wrote, to send you three books from his library. Two are by Mr Orwell and the third is a book of poetry, *The Wasteland* by T.S. Eliot. She said that she had posted the parcel and I should receive it in the coming few weeks.

It took me weeks to find peace after the sad news. I hadn't lost a friend, because we weren't friends, but I had lost a companion with whom I had established an imagined fellowship of thoughts and feelings. A wanderer with whom I had traversed the landscape of Orwell's writing, criss-crossing the topography of Orwell's mind and emotions, one of the places on which was Burma. Burma had made the person Orwell had become and Burma was the land without which he wouldn't have turned out to be the writer we admire. And yet we had only just begun to get a glimpse inside his enigmatic self, much of which would remain shrouded in mystery.

In the essay *Why I Write*, which Orwell would have written shut up in the attic room at Barnhill, I find words that resonate with me. I believe Thant San, like me, would have found some consolation in them:

> I see that I have made it appear as though my motives in writing were wholly public-spirited. I don't want

> to leave that as the final impression. All writers are vain, selfish and lazy, and at the very bottom of their motives lies a mystery.

There lies in all of us a mesa of mystery and it would be gracious on our part to let it remain unvisited, untouched, unsoiled.

With Head and Heart to the Rock (Uluṟu)

Unable to sleep, I step out of the bed and go to the balcony. The cold hits. The body shivers and I notice a strange hum in the air, as if someone is plucking the string of a large cello. A loud snap pizzicato that Bartók would have loved.

I like the hum although it creates a sense of alarm. I want to know its source, its cause.

I look and notice the Rock in the distance. Slowly the calmness descends. The Rock is humming, a voice whispers. And the stars too, I want to add.

In the darkness the Rock appears light, its solid body reduced to lines on a canvas. The silhouette reminds me of Mark Rothko's *Black on Black*, which I once saw in Madrid's Reina Sofia Gallery. The force with which the blackness of the two blacks pulled me in that afternoon is indescribable. I felt as if I was being asked to walk and disappear inside a black void.

The pull of the Rock I experience now is similar but more sentient and therefore more real. I know that I am not looking at an image and that tomorrow when the first light of the new day dawns, the Rock will stand before me large, solid and luminous.

Luminous it is even now, and my mind persuades me to imagine that the Rock is snoring, tucked cosily under the sheet of a starlit sky spread over it with blissful abundance. The four-day moon shines hesitantly as if trying not to spoil the show. I see the Southern Cross just above where I assume the spine of the Rock is. I have always liked the relatively smaller orange star that sits at the top of the cross bar more than the larger blue star, the Acrux, which is at its foot. To the left of the Southern Cross, I notice the pointers, the two stars which define the foot of Centaurus. I look hard to spot the head-like shape of dark nebula, the Dark Emu. I can only delineate an oval form and nothing more. I am a novice, I console myself. I need patience to see dark spaces without getting distracted by the bright stars which stream along the Milky Way. In it I locate Canis Major, the Great Dog and Sirius, its brightest star.

Meanwhile the Rock sleeps and as my eyes get used to the darkness and I overcome the attraction of stars I begin to notice the wrinkly fissures running down from the spine. The initial silhouette-like appearance starts to acquire shape, volume, and mass.

Not far from the balcony stand tall river red gums. I hear the birds stir and a branch falls on the ground. My concentration fades. The mind wants to move away from the Rock. Enough, it seems to say. Enough for now.

Tomorrow the quest will begin. Hanna and I will spend three days walking around the Rock, getting to know it, up close, touch its wrinkly granular surface and let the red dusty crust stain our hands.

•

Barry Hill begins the introduction of his book, *The Rock: Travelling to Uluru*, by recounting a brief conversation with Tony Tjamiwa, one of the traditional owners of the land.

Tjamiwa tells Hill about his opinion on the work of Bill Harney, a celebrated bushman who became the first ranger at the Rock. Harney's travelogue, published in 1964, has long been thought to present a reliable account of Aboriginal beliefs about the Rock.

'Bill Harney didn't know anything,' Tjamiwa tells Hill. He wasn't 'from around here'. He was 'a fish,' and 'a crocodile,' meaning that he had spent most of his life in Northern Australia and not in the desert with the desert people.

Tjamiwa is convinced that Harney got it all wrong because he 'wasn't from around here'. To understand the significance of Uluṟu for Aṉangu, you have to be either an Aṉangu person yourself or to have lived with them for a considerable time. 'Harney said what he wanted to say about the Rock,' he explains to Hill. 'Now it's time for the Aṉangu to say what they want to say.'

The warning in Tjamiwa's words is loud and clear and it is directed at outsiders like me, and yet I want to write about the Rock. I won't tell stories the Aṉangu own, and I won't silence their voices. I'll speak only about me and my encounter with the Rock as a geologist and a writer.

In his book Hill very rarely uses the name Uluṟu. It is the name of a deceased elder, he argues, and hence to utter it out loud is inappropriate. His preference is to call it 'the Rock' and I like his choice. It pleases the geologist in me. I find the simple name most befitting because it brings in to focus the first thing we see when we look at it: it's solid rockiness. For millions of years the Rock has stood tall surrounded by sand dunes and mulga playing its role in the creation of a unique ecological landscape.

It is this rocky solidness with which most of us begin our encounter with the Rock. But to overlook what the Rock has become as a result of various encrustations of history that have come to grow around it is also foolhardy. The name Uluṟu is part of that history. It is needed because it rubs off, albeit partially, the colonial name which still lingers, and it is needed also because Aṉangu and other indigenous Australians have started using it as one of the symbols of their enduring survival.

For Aṉangu and their ancestors the Rock is 'an Aboriginal place with much Aboriginal law (*Ananguku ngura nyangatja, Anangu Tjukurpa tjutatjara*)'. They have lived here for thousands of years following their law and looking after it. This is a place where their Tjukurpa manifests itself in land, people, plants and animals; a place where time past is ever present, and the present is always impregnated with time future.

This simultaneity of time existing within and around the Rock also creates a simultaneity of spaces. The Rock embodies in itself different places, the traces of which can be discovered and described. These places are physically real and metaphorical, and the two, the physical and metaphorical, feed off each other, reinforcing their presence.

Like this essay, most stories, oral or written, are predominantly linear and successive. Can one rely on them to portray the simultaneity of spaces which inhabit places such as the Rock? Does this mean that I should stop writing this essay?

I am reminded of Jorge Borges's story *The Aleph*, in which the narrator is confronted with a similar problem. How can I describe the Aleph, he asks? 'It's a place,' he explains, 'where, without admixture or confusion, all the places of the world, seen from every angle, coexist.' He knows that whatever he is going to write is successive because language is successive. Like all writers he feels helpless, naming his predicament as 'the beginning of every writer's hopelessness'. But like all astute writers, Borges does find a way out of the conundrum and it is quite simple and pragmatic. He makes his narrator confess that he will describe 'the Aleph as best as he can, hoping that he would be able to capture something of it'.

I find solace in the words of Borges's narrator and like him I say to myself that I should also try to do my best and hope that I would be able to grasp something of the Rock. To give up isn't an option. Write I must because only by writing will I be able to make some sense of my enchanted attachment to the Rock.

•

The formal title of the map is long: it tells the readers that on this map they will find the 'route travelled, and discoveries made' by William Gosse who in 1873 led an exploration expedition for the South Australian Government. However, what interests me more is the name printed in a rather small size under the title. The name is that of Edwin S. Berry. He was Gosse's second-in-command and his sole cartographer and draftsman and he sketched the well-known, sphinx-like drawing of the south-western side of the Rock.

I know the south-western side well. I have walked past it several times and I have seen it in many photographs. But none of them is able to capture the giant, animal-like shape that I see on Berry's sketch. In it the Rock appears like a mammoth squatting amongst the bushes. It has turned its head to the viewer revealing its half-opened mouth, an oval-shaped cave. Once I decide that it looks like a mammoth my mind easily finds its graceful spine running all the way to its large posterior. This mammoth, unlike all mammoths I have read about, has zebra-like stripes along its side, their shape enhancing a large depression just below the spine. The sharp line with which Berry has drawn the boundary between the light and the dark or shadowed parts seems unreal, but it indicates that Berry would have sketched the Rock when the evening sun was going down behind his left shoulder.

Berry saw the Rock as if it was a giant animal and portrayed it as such in his drawing. Hill, travelling to the Rock almost two hundred years later, will describe it as a whale: 'What a sight! All of sudden, while you are gazing across the undulating dunes, it surfaces on a crest, out of the trough of a wave with the bulk of a whale. You look again, and it's gone.' As if to reinforce his point Hill places Berry's sketch on the facing page.

Gosse's description, on the other hand, is simple, almost matter of fact. He is an explorer with the eye of an amateur scientist but even in his account I can hear undertones of wonderment. Here is his entry dated 19 July 1873:

> Camp in Spinifex Sandhills. Barometer 28.12 in, wind south-east. Continued same course, in direction of the hill, over the same wretched country. The hill, as I approached, presented a most peculiar appearance, the upper portion being covered with holes or caves. When I got clear of the sandhills, and was only two miles distant, and the hill, for the first time coming fairly in view, what was my astonishment to find it was one immense rock rising abruptly from the plain; the holes I had noticed were caused by the water on some places forming immense caves. At 34 miles reached the foot; only found enough water to replenish our

> bags, but none for the camels—they seem very thirsty, though only twenty-four hours since they had water. No sign of a creek on this (the north) side; the water runs into large shallow basins, about 100 yards from foot of rock. The good country extending for two miles round the rock. I have named this Ayers Rock, after Sir Henry Ayers.

Gosse describes walking through the 'wretched country' dotted with spinifexes, and 'timbered with mulga, native poplar and acacia bushes', then reaches the immense rock and finds an abundance of water around it. The presence of water changes his mood: the 'wretched country' turns into 'good country', extending for a couple of miles around it.

The Rock he has named forms the highest hill in sight, and he can't resist the desire to climb to its top. On Sunday, July 20, he begins the ascent and succeeds in reaching the summit after much effort. From the summit he sees the rock like a trained geographer. 'This is a high mass of granite,' he notes, 'the surface of which has been honey-combed, and is decomposing, 1,100 feet above surrounding country, two miles in length (east and west), and one mile wide, rising abruptly from the plain.'

The Rock is given a geological name and its dimensions are assessed and recorded. Most impressive for him is its height, towering above the sandhills. That the Rock isn't granite, but a layered body of sandstone, arkose, and conglomerate, will become clear to him later and he will alter his description on Berry's map.

Standing on top of the Rock he is able to look far and wide, and record whatever he sees and name all that is yet to be named:

> Seeing a spur less abrupt than the rest of the rock, I left the camels here, and after walking and scrambling two miles barefoot, over sharp rocks, succeeded in reaching the summit, and had a view that repaid me for my trouble—Kamran accompanied me. The top is covered with small holes in the rock, varying in size from two to twelve feet in diameter, all partly filled with water. Mount Olga is about twenty-mile west. Some low ranges and ridges west-north-west, one of which I think must be McNicol's range; part of the lake visible, bearing north Mount Conner 96°, and high ranges south-east, south and south-west, with sandhills between. The one south-east I have named after His Excellency Governor Musgrave; and a high point in same bearing 141°, Mount Woodroffe after the Surveyor General.

Naming prominent landforms is as important as describing them. He names them to allay his anxiety because by naming them he would make them appear more familiar, friendly, and, perhaps, more homely. But he names them also to please his patrons, the people of power and authority. By acknowledging their power, he also flaunts his own authority: the authority of an ardent explorer. Like a writer he turns places and the people after whom they are named into characters in his story. The debt he may have acquired is paid back with interest, and favours he could have received are returned with respect.

Once he has satisfied his benefactors, he is free to name features and places at will. On his track around the Rock he finds a spring coming from the centre of the rock pouring down steep gullies into a large deep hole at the foot of the rock. 'This,' he notes in the diary, 'I have named Maggie's Spring.' He doesn't know or doesn't want to know that the Aṉangu name for the waterhole is Mutitjulu. They would have told him if he had time or inclination to ask. He didn't and was possibly keen to find a name of his own. Who was Maggie? We don't know.

Gosse also names a well after his Afghan cameleer Kamran. His name is mentioned several times in Gosse's diary and in each of the entries Gosse praises Kamran's skill and resourcefulness. Kamran is successful in locating a water well and Gosse is pleased by his success. In the entry dated 26 July 1873 he writes: 'King's Creek. Barometer 28 in; wind east. Travelled to three miles past native well, which I have named "Kamran's Well". Sufficient water for wagon horses and camels.'

Gosse likes Kamran and takes him to climb up the Rock with him, admiring the ease with which Kamran negotiates the climb over the slippery rock. 'How I envied Kamran his hard feet,' he records. 'He seemed to enjoy the walking about with bare feet, while mine were all blisters.'

There is very little known about Kamran, except that he was one of the three Afghans Gosse hired to accompany him on the expedition. The two others were Jemma Kahn and Allanah. Gosse had also brought with him 'a Peake black boy'. We know him by the name 'Moses'. Like Kamran, one of the main tasks of Moses is to look for water. On Tuesday 2 September, Gosse comes across a 'gum creek with plenty of water' and names it Moses Creek.

A month earlier (Tuesday 29 July), he had named a little hill not far from his camp at Maggie's Spring, Allanah's Hill. The only person to miss out is Jemma Kahn. Why?

Reading Gosse's diary I keep wondering whether he told the cameleers or the 'black boy from Peake', that he was naming places after them. Did he seek their consent, and did they consent? Nobody knows. It's quite likely that he used their names without their knowledge or permission. He was leading the expedition and they were working for him and therefore it was in his power to do whatever he felt appropriate.

Of all the names given by Gosse, Moses Creek is most intriguing. At a camp near the Peake in South Australia, he finds a 'black boy' and names him Moses. It's possible that the boy belonged to one of the clans of the Arabana people living in the area, and he definitely had his own name. Gosse would have deemed unnecessary to find out. He liked the boy and his skill in hunting for food and finding water. That's why he named one of the creeks after the boy.

With one simple act Gosse erased two names: the name of the boy and that of the creek. The boy has passed away, but the name given to him endures, archived in the database of Australian geographical names. Each time I read the name of the creek I am forced to think about the young Arabana boy and his people. I wonder if his descendants know about the creek named after one of their adventurous ancestors.

Berry's map, on which places named by Gosse are recorded, is often called a route-map. It shows the route travelled by Gosse's expedition with dates and camp sites. Along the route, the map also portrays the nature of the land with the help of cartographic symbols distinguishing mountain ranges, hills, lakes, creeks and water holes. However, the area depicted on the map is restricted to the route itself suggesting that whatever is shown on the map has been seen by Gosse or other members of his expedition. It is, thus, an eye-witness record of the journey. The extent of extrapolation beyond what has been seen is limited and intrusion of imagination is, as far as possible, avoided.

Looking at the map I am surprised by the number of times the word 'water' appears on it. It reflects the principal objective of Gosse's expedition: to describe and evaluate the land in terms of its suitability for farming. Hence it was necessary to give an account of the availability of water, timber, vegetation and soil. Gosse's letter to the Honourable Commissioner of Crown Lands and Immigration that opens the report succinctly summarises his evaluation of the land proximal and distal to the Rock:

> The country to this point is chiefly sandy soil, densely timbered with mulga (a name given to small trees found numerous in the interior of Australia, a species of genus acacia, belonging to the natural order leguminosæ), or stretches of spinifex sandhills. In the vicinity of the lake the sandhills are higher, and very few small patches of mulga, nothing fit for occupation. I found a spring at Ayers's Rock—the first permanent water seen since leaving Alice Springs, but the good country is very limited, not more than thirty square miles.

The conclusion is clear: 'the good country' for farming, is very limited, not more than thirty square miles. However, focus on the suitability of land for farming does not blind him from describing, although briefly, interesting observations about the indigenous inhabitants in the area:

> This seems to be a favourite resort of the natives in the wet season, judging from the numerous camps in every cave. These caves are formed by large pieces breaking off the main rock and falling to the foot. The blacks make holes under them, and the heat of their fires causes the rock to shell off, forming large arches. They amuse themselves covering these with all sorts of devices,

> some of snakes, very cleverly done, others of two hearts joined together; and in one I noticed a drawing of a creek with an emu track going along the centre.

His cursory interest in the lives of the indigenous people is soon overtaken by the feeling of wonder the Rock evokes in him. 'This rock,' he notes, 'is certainly the most wonderful natural feature I have ever seen. What a grand sight this must present in the wet season; waterfall in every direction.'

Yes, it is, Mr Gosse, I want to say for I have seen the Rock washed by torrents of rain. Then standing not far from it I wasn't able to decide which of the two was happier, the rain or the Rock; the two quite keen to share each other's delight and spread it to all the living and the non-living around.

•

The guidebook sat for many years on one of the bookshelves in my office. It was given to me by Alistair Stewart, one of its three authors.

In 2014 as I packed up my things before leaving the job, I gave away most of my books and journals. One of the books that I brought home was the guidebook.

My neighbour across the street borrowed it and took it on his trip to the Rock. It was returned to me a few weeks later, a little battered and dusted but undamaged. He apologised for the red dust stains on some of the pages which wasn't necessary because the stains had made the book special, as if it had been blessed by none other than the Rock itself.

There is a beautiful geological map of the area in the book, a revised version of an older map finished in 1963. The book is lavishly illustrated with photographs and sketches. Together they summarise geological history of the Rock and the surrounding area. A brief introduction outlines the main objective:

> The spectacular shapes of Uluru (Ayers Rock) and Kata Tjuta (The Olgas) dominate the surrounding desert and are the culmination of geological events stretching over hundreds of millions of years. It is the description of those events – the telling of the geological story – which we attempt in this book.

In recounting the geological history of the Rock, the authors don't overlook the stories of Pitjantjatjara and Yankunytjatjara people. They aren't explicitly told but their significance is acknowledged:

> Tjukurpa is the word used by the Anangu to describe the laws that give meaning and order to all aspects of life. The Tjukurpa provides explanations for the origin of life and all living things as well as features of landscape. Archaeological research suggests that there has been human settlement in this region for at least 22,000 years although the initial settlement was evidently much earlier. The science of geology is similarly based on sets of rules, but interpretation

of the origin of landscape and its features is very different from those of the Tjukurpa.

I like the word 'different'. It opens a space in which two dissimilar practices of knowledge (geological and Tjukurpa) can exist side by side, challenging and enriching each other.

The book tells the readers that the Rock is not one single entity but layers of sediments which were deposited in the near-shore area of a geologically very old sea. The sediments were lithified to form a layer of arkose, a type of sandstone, made up of sand and pebble-size fragments of a particular mineral composition. It also notes that the sediments were buried under the surface, endured heat and pressure and were then brought up by geological forces after which they were subjected to continuous erosion for over three hundred million years.

The present monolith-like shape of the Rock rising above the sand dunes has resulted from prolonged erosion in the area. The action of wind, water and heat created cracks, crevices and caves. They also turned the rock red, the colour of iron-bearing minerals. The fresh rock, untouched by erosion, '… is light to dark-grey, greenish or pinkish-grey.'

An important aspect of most geological studies is to give rock formations names so that they can be correlated across regions making it possible to write their geological history in relation to other regions. The sediments that form the Rock are called Mutitjulu

Arkose whereas slightly younger rocks which make Kata Tjuṯa are known as Mount Currie Conglomerate. These rock units are part of a larger rock formation belonging to the Centralian Basin.

The studies also show that the folded layers of the Rock extend to the depths of three to five kilometres beneath the surface. Similarly conglomerates that one sees at Kata Tjuṯa extend at least five and a half kilometres beneath the surface. It is also suggested that the rocks at these two places were formed during the Cambrian period around five hundred and forty million years ago but under slightly different conditions. If the sediments that now make up the Rock were deposited in alluvial fans of rivers and streams emptying into the sea, the geologically younger conglomerates at Kata Tjuṯa were deposited in '… an extensive network of braided river channels carrying vast numbers of boulders along with pebbles, sand and mud.'

In addition to the geology map of the area as seen on the present-day surface, the book also includes a solid-geology map which shows interpreted distribution of rocks beneath the sands and other geologically younger rocks. The interpretation is portrayed in a series of slices or cross-sections drawn as block-diagrams to illustrate the shape and size of rocks beneath the surface. A trained geologist can read these maps independently of the text and decode its geological history. Non-geologist readers on the other hand can look at the maps and get some idea of how the story described in the text unravels spatially.

Robert Frodeman, writing on the scientific method used by modern-day geology, argues that geology is a historical and narrative science. Its main task is to solve an inverse problem which involves understanding the history of a geological object in order to explain its presence here and now. This is what the book and maps try to accomplish by reconstructing millions of years-old history of the Rock and the region.

Gosse, who led an expedition on behalf of South Australia's Surveyor General, explored, mapped and described the area in order to evaluate how sustainable the land was for farming and pastoral activities. This book has no such objective; its main aim is to present geological evolution of the Rock for readers with no, or minimum, geological knowledge. Perhaps this is the reason it discusses in some detail the appearance of the Rock, exploring differing ideas on the origin of the caves, waterholes and parallel ridges and ribs on its surface.

The book describes how the Rock has been able to generate around it a special type of biological region containing a vibrant assemblage of plants and animals. Such regions require water and the Rock because of its size, particularly its elevation above the surrounding dunes, and its composition, helps to accumulate water. The studies show that the area around the Rock has an abundance of surface- and ground-water.

'The sand layers and other sediments,' the book explains, 'are the main aquifers in this area and now supply the water for Yulara. The water is slightly salty and has to be desalinated before use.' Based on the information on water holes it suggests that 'the water table is 25 metres deep near Kata Tjuṯa but shallows to 12 metres at Yulara Airport. The groundwater eventually flows underground into Lake Amadeus.'

As I read this description, I recall the words of Robert Layton, an anthropologist who worked in the area in the late nineteen seventies. Paddy Uluṟu, now a deceased Aṉangu elder, told him stories of Wanampi, the water snake who created *wanapitjara*, the springs and other lakes in the area. Recounting these stories, Layton notes:

> The *Wanampi* are a class of legendry beings who carry water underground from one available source to another. One *Wanampi* made Britten-Jones Creek as he crawled north from Musgrave Ranges, diving below the sandhills, where the creek fades out and re-emerging at *Katiti* (Bobby's Well), on the shore of Lake Amadeus.

Hill in his book also refers to Layton's description and adds that during his conversation with Layton, Paddy Uluṟu drew concentric circles on the sand showing location of lakes and then explained that Wanampi had dug out the ground with a stick to create lakes.

In Hill's book I find a slightly different account of the role ascribed to Wanampi. Based on the stories researched by Hill, the permanent home of Wanampi is near Kata Tjuṯa:

> *Wanampi* is a mythical giant serpent. *Wanampi* is not like the totemic beings of Tjukurpa time, as he has not created any of the topography of the land but remains the same today as he always was. Mount Olga is the permanent home of a dangerous, highly coloured *wanampi*. *Wanampi* live and guard waterholes. During the wet season this Kata Tjuta *wanampi* lives in the waterholes, on top of the mountain, but during the dry season he resides in a waterhole in the Gorge at Kata Tjuta. If these dry up he retreats inside the rock itself. A wind blows constantly in Olga Gorge, sometimes gently at other times like a hurricane. This is the breath of *wanampi* when angry. Anangu will not light a fire in the area or drink from the waterhole.

Wanampi, the water snakes, live and guard waterholes and depending on the season carry water from one source to another: form mountain tops to springs and lakes. As a geologist I find the story intriguing but believable because they sound similar to the stories I have heard from hydrogeologists working in the area. On their maps I see geologically old channels filled with permeable sediments. These are the channels along which water travels from source areas, such as the Rock, to various springs, water holes, and lakes. On the map, the channels look like trails of a snake-like creature borrowing underground. But the significance of the wanampi story can't be overlooked because it reminds us that the sources of water are guarded by Wanampi and we need to be judicious in using it.

One of the few permanent water sources in and around Uluṟu is the Mutitjulu Waterhole. Paddy Uluṟu calls it holy: 'this is my great ceremony, my great camp with its holy tree [Ngaltawata, the ceremonial sacred pole] and *mutitju* [cave] on this side is holy. Ayers Rock is holy. I am Uluṟu and these things are mine ....'

The presence of water has made the Rock and the waterhole special. They are places of shelter and refuge, the sites where ceremonies are performed, where stories are told and enacted, and where memories are stored for safekeeping so that they can be retrieved and remembered when required. They are also special because they have been consecrated by memories. The association between the two, the sites and memories, is the lifeline for the clan to endure and flourish. Life without ceremonies and law can't be sustained and this is why the sites acquire unique power and meaning often described by the word 'spiritual'.

Layton in his book recounts the words of a young Kikingkura man with whom he visited the Rock. Pointing to a cliff face of the Rock the young man said, 'that's a rock, but that has got to have something else, because that's got all those old men's memories inside.'

The sacredness which Paddy Uluṟu associates with the Rock is different from what T. G. H. Strehlow, the son of a pastor, experiences when he visits the Rock in 1935:

> The Rock was reached at last, the goal of my boyhood dreams—the shadow of a great rock in a weary land,

> and how welcome it was. All hushed tonight. Only the moon is shining down upon the great black of rock—and one feels that the land of God is indeed near. It is like the great silence of eternity. And nearby lies the body of a dead man; and the body has brought us hither to this vast pile that shall endure long after our own bodies will be dim, scattered dust, known to no man, forgotten by all save God alone who moulded them first even as He fashioned this great Rock, that sleeps tonight in a still moon-dream.

Standing on the land in the shadow of the Rock he begins to feel that the promised land is not far because the Rock is one of God's unblemished creations. The source of its unworldly beauty is God and it is God who has made the Rock sacred.

In contrast, for Paddy Uluṟu the sacredness of the Rock is nothing but worldly. It is sacred because of the way it stands in the world here and now, as it always was, and more importantly, it will always be because it is inseparably tied up with his everyday life and the life of his ancestors. In the Rock he sees and reads Tjukurpa, which he has inherited and looks after.

Tjukurpa, the Aṉangu believe, manifest physically in Tjukuritja, the features of landscape they live with and within. These are the places where ceremonies are performed, where law is practiced and maintained and where life is lived and endured. The Rock hosts several such sites and one of them is the Mutitjulu Waterhole.

In a YouTube clip I watch Barbara Tjikatu, one of the traditional owners of the land, tell the Tjukurpa of its creation. She sits near the site and speaks pointing out features of the Rock and the waterhole:

> This is Mutitjulu, and here is the story and Tjukurpa of Kuniya, the sand python coming. Kuniya, the sand python, see just over there, she is moving across, descending this way. She left her eggs a short distance away, and came across just over there, coming across, you can see her over there, coming across there. Doing her ritual dance as she comes closer, moving across there. From over there she got earth, from the ground and put in on herself in preparation. She was becoming enraged and challenging for a fight because of what had happened to her nephew and she, Kuniya the sand python, struck the Liru. In this way: see how it is over there, up above.

Compared to the Tjukurpa of Kuniya, the geological story about the waterhole sounds bland. The waterhole, I find in the guidebook, is located near the sharp southern face of the Rock marked by the presence of a major fracture. Some large fissures running off it would have facilitated intensive erosion of the Rock creating deep gullies, one of the largest of which is Mutitjulu. The waterhole sits in a permanent pool hosted by a depression carved by water flowing off the top of the Rock and its slopes, producing 'spectacular series of beautifully sculptured plunge pools'.

Although I am captivated by the Tjukurpa of Kuniya, the geologist in me can't ignore the geological story explaining the making of the waterhole. The two stories are salient in their own way and therefore the best option for me is to let them stay together in my mind complementing each other, forcing me to think about the unusual ways by which we make sense of the reality which we encounter and create for ourselves. Like shards of coloured glass in a home-made kaleidoscope I used to play with as a child, the two stories have the potential to create novel visions of my understanding of the Rock.

•

I first saw an image of the *Cockatoo Dreaming* in the exhibition catalogue *Desert Country* authored by Nici Cumpston and Barry Patton and published by the Art Gallery of South Australia. I went to see it again after I had started working on this essay.

I walked out of the gallery disappointed. In the catalogue I felt at home with the painting although it was a copy. The large format of the book allowed me to look at it from different angles. I placed the book flat on the floor and looked at it from above, standing close to it. I also made it stand upright on one of my bookshelves to look at it as I would have seen it hung on the wall of the gallery.

In the gallery it seemed crowded by other paintings. Their presence created a visual haze that appeared to interfere with my view. Although I am accustomed to looking at art works in galleries and have trained myself to block out other objects, on this occasion I failed.

It felt as if the painting wanted me to look at it differently. I would have liked it to be placed on the floor of the gallery and gaze at it walking around it. It would have been even better if the painting or its projection had covered the whole floor, allowing me to walk on it.

Is this because I have convinced myself that this painting is a map, and like any other map I should be able to walk with my eyes and fingers taking any of the many routes available to me? Is this because the geologist in me wants to impose my obsession with maps on the painting? It wants me to look at this painting as a map-painting: a map that has the aesthetics of an artwork and a painting that is imbued with the knowledge and precision of a map.

Bill Whiskey Tjapaltjarri, the text in the exhibition catalogue notes, 'was born at Pirupa Alka in the southwest of the Northern Territory near Pirrulpakalarintji outstation, about a hundred kilometres west of Uluṟu.' He and his wife were *ngangkari* (traditional healers). 'He received the name Whiskey because of his bushy whiskery beard – a potentially misleading title for a teetotaller.'

He painted the rockholes near Kata Tjuṯa several times. This is the place around which he had grown up. He knew the place, living on it and with it. The knowledge he had of this place was bodily, intuitive, unmediated by the noise of ideas and thoughts. Whatever thoughts he had were perhaps formed by and expressed in the stories he was told, and he himself told. Walking and telling of stories happened together, complementing each other, merging like tributaries of life, lived and imagined. When he discovered painting, it became a natural extension of walking and telling stories. Now he could paint and walk without walking and tell stories without words. Painting became a cartography of his wanderings and wonderings about his place, his country. *Cockatoo Dreaming* could have been the result of these wanderings. It was his story walked, told, and painted only by him.

Because I am acquainted with the iconographic language used in the painting, I feel secure and confident with what I see, read and hear in it. This is why I readily accept the story in the painting as explained in the exhibition catalogue: 'The frenzy of white dots … represent the feathers' of the cockatoo. 'The large concentric circles depict rockholes made during the fight,' between the cockatoo and the crow, 'as well as dependable sources of fresh water used by his family group.' The dotted lines extending from the circles, Bill Whiskey explained, 'are the tracks around the rockholes that we follow when we travel in and out.' The coloured dotting that forms patchwork fields represents 'the flowers that grow in the different seasons, the flowers and bush tucker.'

Bill Whiskey describes the painting almost like a map; for him it is a map that helps to locate sites where food and water can be found, a map that tells people how to reach those places.

In a convoluted way the painting reminds me of the 1873 route map I see in the record of Gosse's exploration, who fastidiously mapped the presence of water, soil, trees (timber), flowers, birds and other animals. But the significance of this similarity is outweighed by a vital disparity: a disparity stemming from the two ways of living in and with the land.

The disparity becomes clearer to me when I read in the exhibition catalogue about Bill Whiskey's visit to his country:

> Bill Whiskey pointed out the features in the landscape formed during this epic fight: a brilliant white rock is the cockatoo, a hill is the eagle's nest protectively overlooking the cockatoo, white stones around the area are the cockatoo's scattered feathers.

Gosse, the explorer, as we know, was keen to name landscape features after his patrons and assistants. With each new name he erased histories lived by the indigenous peoples in the area.

In *Cockatoo Dreaming* the names mentioned by Bill Whiskey belong to an entirely different symbolic system. Cockatoo, eagle, and feathers aren't proper nouns similar to the ones Gosse selected for naming but simple common nouns. The naming here isn't associated with the act of laying a claim on this or that feature as Gosse had intended. The rock becomes a cockatoo and the hill an eagle's nest. There is no disunity or division between the world of the animate (animal and human) and the inanimate (rocks, water hole and hill). All are different and yet one, living with and for each other. This is what the belief system expressed in Tjukurpa proposes and this is what is valued, respected and followed by the Aṉangu.

•

In September 2015, Rosario López, a Colombian visual artist and photographer, went to see the Rock and Kata Tjuṯa. A year or so earlier she had created a sculptural ceramic piece of the Rock for an exhibition of her work in Colombia. She was fascinated by the Rock and by the stories of political and cultural tension associated with its presence. She wanted to look at it as an outsider but also wanted to inhabit the place and feel its presence. She has always been interested in 'looking at the landscape from above', she writes in the exhibition catalogue, 'to observe Earth's elevation and the way it changes colours as far and wide as my eyes can see.' The Rock was perhaps the right place to satisfy this urge. Standing alone, tall and mighty, dwarfing the flatness of red soil and sand spotted with mulga, it provides the most fitting landscape for her to inhabit, and experience the 'primary idea of the horizon'.

She took photographs of the Rock, KataTjuṯa and the surrounding landscape, showed them to the traditional owners of the land and to the authorities in the National Park Office and gained their approval to exhibit them. They weren't ordinary photographs.

They reveal the melancholic splendour of the Rock; so incredibly large and so alone. The star-lit sky draping over it emphasises its languid presence. It also 'establishes boundaries fragmenting the landscape.' The photographs she brought with her also became the starting material for sculptures and an installation she created at the ANCA (Australian National Capital Artists) studio in Canberra.

The exhibition *Unfolding Memories* opened in the Australian National Capital Artists gallery in May 2016. It featured an installation of 45 sculptures, framed sculptures and photographs. I saw the installation on the night it was opened and went again to have a closer look a few days later. Luckily for me there wasn't anyone else in the gallery at that time and I was able to walk through the installation at my own pace without disturbing anyone else. I walked and it felt as if I was stepping on the surface of a map as well as on the landscape that had been mapped. For a moment I thought I had turned into Suarez Miranda, the fictional writer of the *Travels of a Prudent Man* created by Borges in the story *On Exactitude in Science.* In his story, Borges describes how in an unnamed empire, dissatisfied by the imprecision of existing maps, 'the Cartographers Guilds struck a Map of the Empire whose size was that of the Empire, and which coincided point for point with it'.

The map I was walking on, created by López, felt precise, but the precision it showed was of a different order; it wasn't based on one-to-one correspondence between the image and the real world it was aiming to portray, but on the emotional engagement it was able to produce. It instantly aroused the memory of my walks near the Rock a few years earlier. The memories were not only stirred and provoked again but they acquired a new significance. It felt as if I was tracking the walks as a different person; as if I was walking in the footsteps left behind by López.

On the floor of the gallery there were white, greyish to yellowish-white, skin-like encrustations. The surface of the encrustations was puckered, showing crests and vales. They were pocked with orifices reminding me of the pores, cavities and crevices I have seen on the Rock. There were little stones hung from the ceiling. They swayed like pendulums.

Their swinging reminded me of the wind that blows in and around the Rock. But they also became a metaphoric measure of time endured by it, prompting me to believe that the Rock wasn't just a spatial landform but also a repository of past time. I realised that no walk is ever only spatial. Time passes as we walk, and we too pass in time and with time, getting older and stepping closer to the moment of our own disappearance.

That the skin-like encrustations were white and not hematite red didn't trouble me because the geologist in me knows that under the red skin, the Rock is really grey. The red colour indicates the duration of time the Rock has interacted with the wind, the water, and the sun.

As I negotiated the narrow space between slices of the 'skin' and 'flesh' of the Rock I also felt that I was looking at them from above – as if I was flying over it like a bird, experiencing the plan-view so enjoyed by indigenous painters. It reminded me of Lopez's words in the catalogue, recording her fascination with the aerial views of the landscape: 'from above, landscape becomes a great horizontal surface enclosed by a winding line that separates a strip of matter that we refer to as land.'

In the catalogue she also describes the process by which she produced the encrustations. It required a close and sustained involvement of her body.

> I start my sculptural process, by throwing a certain amount of clay upon a table trying to spread it several times in the same direction. The flat clay surface gathered the body's gesture … and … replicated the stroke produced by my body.

The clay sheet so produced became the foundation from which she created the skin-like encrustations. To achieve this, layers of synthetic resin and plaster were condensed on the clay surface resulting in a surface potted with orifices similar to the pores, cavities and crevices one sees on the Rock as well as Kata Tjuṯa.

The installation Lopez has created represents an emotional cartography of the Rock and the land around it. It maps her feelings for them, and the mapping is precise because it is able to evoke similar feelings in the visitors who stand and look at it or walk around it.

Standing face to face with the installation, my imagination leaves geographical features of the Rock behind and begins to delve into the world of emotions the Rock arouses in me. I begin to participate in the emotional cartography which produces my own map, a map which captures my experience and my feelings.

•

'Are you writing something about Uluṟu?' I remember Hanna asking me on our bike ride around the Rock. 'Yes,' I had answered. 'One of your meandering essays or stories, I suppose,' she had said.

Most of my essays tested her patience because they never quite reached a final point, deferring indefinitely the possibility of a narrative closure. She was also weary of the way they played with facts, mixing them with fictional, or, what I prefer to call, imagined events and details.

'And it is, as always, going to be about you,' she had said, to which my response was an awkward smile.

On that warm late afternoon day in May 2014, when the sky was bare but for a few streaky strings of cloud, the light soft and hazy and breeze smooth like the well-rounded polished pebble of quartz I had picked on the track where we had stopped for a drink, I didn't tell her that I had been writing this essay-like piece for close to fifty years.

In 1976, a friend, a student in my Geology course in Moscow, gave me an Australian postage stamp. This was to thank me for helping him with his chemistry assignment. Bisman Harahap was an avid collector of philatelic material showing rocks, mountains, rivers, and other interesting landscapes. He inherited the passion for collecting stamps from his grandfather, a trade-union leader in Indonesia.

The stamp which Bisman gave me had an image of Ayers Rock. 'This is the most interesting rock in Australia,' he had said, 'and I hope I am lucky enough to see it one day.'

A few weeks later when I got a chance to go to the library at the Indian High Commission in Moscow, I looked in the Encyclopedia Britannica to find out more about the rocky heart of Australia. I have in my files two pages of notes written in a mixture of Russian and English, because back then my Russian was a little better than my English.

Over the years the files have accumulated hundreds of other items about the Rock and the region around it. They include maps and travel brochures, images of paintings and other artwork, photographs which include images of polished slabs and wafer-thin sections of the Mutitjulu Quartzite, given to me by Alastair, my geologist friend and one of the co-authors of the guidebook. There are bilingual dictionaries of Pitjantjara and Yankunytjatjara words and audio-recordings of ABC's *Word-Up* program about several indigenous languages.

One of the most interesting of these items is a compact disc titled *Uluru*, with fourteen pieces of solo cello written for David Pereira and performed by him. The disc, produced by Tall Poppies Records, was released to mark the tenth anniversary of the ceremony of handing over the Rock to its traditional custodians. It also has a recording of Pereira's own composition, *The Great Rock*.

I remember one early afternoon in August 2015, when Pereira played the piece for me twice. We were sitting in his studio in Murrumbateman, near Canberra. First, he played to illustrate different sounds – humming drone, strumming, plucking and striking – he had used in the piece and then he played the whole composition, lasting close to six minutes. The piece includes a brief movement in which he has to whistle and strike the strings with the bow at the same time. It's the wind, I imagined, running through and playing with the Rock, the mulga and the sand dunes around it.

It reminded me of the wind Hanna and I had encountered standing near the Rock. There is a set of steep fractures on the north-eastern face of the Rock, which slice it open to the wind and the water. It is the place where the Kantju Gorge weaves its way through. That late afternoon in May 2014, the wind rolled out of the gorge, scrubbing the pitted surface of the Rock and whizzed through the leafy bloodwoods and red gums.

We had stopped near the gorge lured by a pair of *mittiti*, crimson chats, we had spotted. They seemed to have disappeared inside the gorge, leaving in the air a crimson trail of their presence. We waited to hear them call and they called, chattering at a high pitch. 'Did you hear?' I remember Hanna asked. I definitely had but before I could reply the wind came gushing out from the gorge.

I don't know if it was the wind or the crimson chats but driven by a weird urge, I took my shoes off and stepped on the track leading towards the opening of the gorge. I didn't go more than a couple of hundred steps inside and turned back. By then the wind had subsided, replaced by a soft breeze, cool and moist, and smelling of mint from *karingana*, the striped mint bush. The sandy, gritty track hurt my feet first but soon they got used to the discomfort and my first steps, taken gingerly, turned in to a more confident gait. As I ambled back, I noticed marks of my footprints on the track. Before putting on my socks I brushed my soles with my hands and noticed how they were stained by the reddish, brownish dust. The indented soles had cracks marked with a few little beads of blood.

Back at the hotel I said to Hanna that I had merely wanted to touch and feel the ground under my feet.

In his book *The Wild Places*, Robert Macfarlane mentions that before felling trees the Chinese woodsmen of the T'ang and S'ung dynasties would bow to them and offer promise that they would be used well. I am not sure if geologists like Alastair had done something similar, but I had deliberately left my pick-hammer at home, and any desire to use it to break a piece of the Rock never materialised. I was content just to pick up loosened rocks, touch and examine them before placing them back.

I was also glad that I was able to leave the footprints of my briefest of walks on the dusty, gritty track, and the track had reciprocated by marking its own presence on my soles and hands. The footprints won't last for more than a couple of hours, but their memory, and the memory of our transaction, will definitely endure.

•

In the visitor guide to the Uluṟu-Kata Tjuṯa National Park I read the rather sobering words of Kunmanara, one of the traditional owners of the land:

> The tourist comes here with the camera taking pictures all over. What has he got? Another photo to take home, keep part of Uluru. He should get another lens – see straight inside. Wouldn't see big rock then. He would see that Kuniya living right inside there as from the beginning.

Hanna and I had also gone to the Rock as tourists, but I didn't have a camera with me, and I didn't take photos. I saw whatever I was able to, and let my mind help me remember what it wished to.

I am not certain if I was able to engineer the special lens Kunmanara suggests but I believe that I am slowly learning to see and hear the way he wants us to. The trick is to allow the mind to look through an imaginary pair of binoculars and keep switching between the close-up and long-shot views of the world we live in.

I am fortunate that I have the comfort of seeing and reading what others before me have looked at and responded with. My view of the Rock is both illuminated and clouded by their views and ideas. If this is a handicap, so be it because this is the predicament we have to live with, and the consolation, if there is any, comes from the thought that that's how the act of learning has to begin and continue. Each time I talk and write about the Rock, I find myself engaged in a dialogue with other voices.

One of these many voices is that of Tony Tjamiwa, the same voice with which I began my current dialogue with the Rock. I am glad that Hill opens his wonderful book with Tjamiwa's words because they remind us about learning the law:

> … straight in the heads and straight in the hearts, that's how they learnt their Law. No pens, no typewriters. And some parts of the Law they would never put in a typewriter.

'Yes,' I say to him, 'Yes with the heart and head I have tried to reach the Rock.' I hope in the process I have learnt something about the world in which it stands and more importantly something about myself. I hope I have.

Like a Stranger in Delhi

'Is this the right place?' I ask the driver of the three-wheeler.

'Of course, Sahib,' he replies and smiles, and then stops, noticing how disappointed I look.

It was a mistake to come here. I should have listened to my younger brother who tried to convince me that it wasn't such a good idea to go out looking for a place that might not be there anymore. But I decided to take a risk, and here I am, feeling lost and betrayed; betrayed by the map I had in my mind; a map that doesn't match the geography I see in front of my eyes.

I take out my notebook and unfold the map I have brought with me, on which I find the cross I had marked to indicate the place I was looking for. It should be here, I say to myself, perusing the map and the busy street I am standing on.

It should be here, but it is not.

Meanwhile the driver waits, and then, without prompting, walks up to the tea shop at the corner of the street. I watch him talk to the *chaiwallah*. They chat and look, every now and then, in my direction. After a few minutes the driver returns with *paan* in his mouth, chewing loudly.

'Everything over here has changed, Sahib,' he spurts out. 'New houses, new buildings, new shops.' Then, just to console me, he adds, 'We forget, Sahib, we all forget. Do you have the right address? Please check again.'

'I have,' I say and show him my notebook and the map. He looks at the cross on the map, bemused. I draw his attention to the railway line on the map and then point towards the rail track I see in the distance, explaining that the street and the house I am searching for were located not far from them.

The driver watches and listens seriously and says, 'Sorry, Sahib,' then smiles, not sure if he should.

Before getting back on the three-wheeler, I look around once more and after a few brief moments ask the driver to take me to Rajouri Garden Station on the Delhi Metro line.

'Really sorry, Sahib,' the driver says, makes a quick U-turn in the busy traffic, blowing the horn loudly, his right arm raised, and we drive on.

The air smells of dust and urine. It's hot and noisy. Like a foreigner, I feel out of place, out of sorts.

'You'll get used to it all in a couple of days,' my brother will say later that day, to cheer me up.

Luckily, it's quieter at the station. Before entering, my backpack is checked, and I have to walk through a body scanner followed by frisk search.

The train arrives on time. The coach is clean and not crowded. I sit and look outside the window as the train runs on overhead tracks crossing over one of the many slum colonies.

The contrast between what I see inside the coach and outside isn't new to me, but it still hits me hard.

No, I won't get used to this. I won't.

•

I have come to Delhi after a gap of six years. Before that I used to visit almost every year, mostly to see Ammiji, my mother. She passed away five years ago, in September 2006. The phone call came late at night, but it took me a few days to get a visa and book a ticket. By the time I arrived in Delhi Ammiji had been cremated.

A day later, my brother and I went to the burning ghats on the eastern bank of the Yamuna River to collect her ashes. We were given a small red cotton bag with her ashes, which we carried the next day to Haridwar, the holy city in the foothills of Himalayas, to release them in the waters of Ganga.

After the ritual, supervised by a Brahmin priest, we went to a man, a record-keeper, who sat cross-legged on a cushioned floor in his little office surrounded by hundreds of clothbound notebooks. 'He keeps the birth and death records of our clan,' my brother whispered.

The man asked me if I needed a chair, seeing me struggle to sit on the ground cross-legged.

'We are all getting old,' joked my brother. Old, stiff, and cumbersome, I wanted to add.

This was my second visit to this place. In 1968, a few days after I had turned eighteen, I had come here with Ammiji and my elder brother to inform the record-keeper about the passing away of my father, who had died six months earlier in an army hospital in Bombay.

He had cancer and it took less than ten months for the dreaded disease to end his life.

I asked him if he remembered my last visit.

'Of course not,' he replied. 'You must have met my father,' he explained. 'I wasn't even born then. My father passed away last year, not of illness but old age. A good death, as they say. Very peaceful, Sir, utterly peaceful.'

Ammiji too died of old age but struggled in the last few years with one ailment or another, complaining about the burden of an unsettled and troublesome widowhood that had gone on for long, very long – forty years.

•

In August 1978 when I returned to India after spending more than nine years in Moscow, the first thing Ammiji had said to me was that I had changed, that I wasn't an Indian anymore, and that she shouldn't have let me go abroad at such a young age.

It took her a few years to reconcile with the fact that going to Moscow was neither bad for me nor for her. I got good education, learnt a new language and was ready to start a job with a decent salary. While I was away, she didn't have to worry about me and could focus on my other two brothers, far more resourceful and enterprising than me.

'But you don't look happy,' she often complained. '"He is born old, this middle one of ours", your father used to tell me, and I agree, old and worried; all the time worried. He wanted me to keep an eye on you, concerned that you would renounce the world and turn into a *sadhu.*'

No, I haven't become a *sadhu,* I want to say to her now, but I do feel out of place. Not always but often. Even the Australian passport and driver's licence I carry aren't enough to make me feel grounded. They merely suggest that I am no longer an Indian as I once used to be, when I was young.

'You are funny,' my brother laughs, 'acting like a tourist.'

It's because of the silly passport, I want to reply.

My brother is right. I have definitely started behaving like a tourist. I have a Lonely Planet guidebook to Delhi in my bag, and I also carry a stack of other maps, which include five that show India and most of the neighbouring countries. They are beautiful maps, printed on separate sheets by Nelles Verlag, a German publisher.

The inside front cover of the Lonely Planet guidebook contains a map of Delhi. I like it too, its simple, almost cartoonish look. In the past, first as a schoolboy, and later as a young academic, I had found the city familiar and homely. Often it felt like a big town, too chaotic to be contained within the limits of a map. On the Lonely Planet map, Delhi looks like a city. It has a shape, a structure, rationality defined by a neat pattern of straight roads, roundabouts, and green patches of boulevards, parks and gardens. The meandering blue outlines of the River Yamuna painted along the eastern margin of the map makes the city picturesque.

•

There is a Sadar Bazaar shown on the map. It is one of the main markets of Old Delhi, located on the western end of Chandni Chowk, the principal street of Shahjahanabad, the Delhi of the Mughal emperor Shahjahan, who willed to build the Taj Mahal in Agra. But the Sadar Bazaar of my childhood is different. It is not visible on this map, for it sits behind the rectangular box that lists 'places to stay' and 'other places of interest'. My Sadar Bazaar is in the cantonment of Delhi, or Delhi Cantt as it is commonly known.

Like Delhi, almost all large Indian cities inherited cantonments, the colonial military stations, built like fortresses with checkpoints and armed guards in place of walls. They were generally situated between five and ten kilometres from the main city. In the 1880s Winston Churchill visited India and stayed in the cantonment of Secunderabad in southern India, which housed at least twelve thousand men. Like other Indian cantonments, their main role was to keep an eye on the neighbouring twin cities, which contained, to use Churchill's words, '… all the scoundrels of Asia'.

Most streets in the main cities were renamed after Independence, but in the cantonments Mall Roads and Church Roads have somehow kept their names. Large parade grounds and lavish officers' messes have also survived. In many, the old colonial Sadar Bazaars still function as main markets. The cantonments were designed and laid out like camps. Their grid-like geometry and an ordered pattern of barracks and bungalows were, and remain, quite distinct from the unrestrained muddle and hodgepodge of the main city. I know the contrast well because most of my childhood had been spent in cantonments.

In the mid-1950s my father served as a junior officer in the army, and we stayed in the cantonment of Delhi. Our barracks were located close to the edge of the cantonment, not far from the railway lines, the same lines I see on the Lonely Planet map. I remember going to the railway lines with my friends. We would place an ear on the line to hear the rattling sound of the wheels of approaching trains. Sometimes we would put a thick nail on the line and wait for the train to pass. The nail would be flattened into a thin shiny plate. We valued these nails because we used them in our colourful wooden spinning tops.

One of our favourite trains was the Frontier Mail that came from Bombay. It ran three days a week and was hardly ever late. We waited for it to whiz past. The goods trains were slow, graceful and leisurely. I would run along the track waving to the guard who sat in a chair in his special compartment and waved back and smiled. I remember one guard particularly well because of his thick black moustache and khaki pith helmet.

One late evening in June, during our school holidays, we found the naked body of a young woman near the railway lines. The wheels had cut the body into three pieces. The head had been dragged away for a few metres, and her long black hair was smeared in dried crusty blood. We saw the body and ran away sick and scared, and hardly ever went to the railway lines again.

•

In 1638, Shahjahan had decided to move the capital from Agra to Delhi. It took around thirty years to build the new city. The Red Fort stood majestically on top of an elevated plateau on the western bank of the River Yamuna. From there looking south-west one found an equally majestic Jama Masjid, the main mosque, with its two minarets built of vertical strips of red sandstone and white marble, and three white onion-shaped domes.

'At one o'clock in the morning,' reminisced Emily, the daughter of Sir Thomas Metcalfe, the English Resident of the East India Company in Delhi in the 1840s and 50s, 'looked out of my palanquin, and saw in the glorious moonlight the minarets of Jama Masjid … the wonderful red walls that surround the city and I felt I was really going home.'

Emily was enchanted by the Delhi of the Mughals. It had also captured the heart of Emily's father, who was perhaps the most influential man in Delhi at that time. The Mughal empire was falling apart and everyone knew that power was really in the hands of the East India Company, which had gained respect and authority by ushering in a period of peace and stability in a city that, for over half a century, had been ravaged by scores of Indian and foreign invaders.

During his stay in Delhi, Sir Thomas Metcalfe commissioned local artists to paint the scenes of his beloved city. He wrote captions to the paintings and added detailed notes about people and places. The book came to be known as the Dehlie Book. Like the natives, Emily and Sir Thomas Metcalfe called Delhi, 'Dehlie', its true Hindustani name. It is hard to know when and how the Hindustani 'Dehlie' was replaced by the English Delhi. A slip of the tongue, perhaps, or an innocent spelling mistake?

•

Ali Mardan Khan, Shahjahan's chief supervisor of construction, had repaired and extended old canals to bring water to the city. One small canal ran through the middle of Chandni Chowk, one of the two main boulevards in the city. However, by the end of the eighteenth century the canals had dried up and it was Sir Charles Metcalfe, the elder brother of Sir Thomas, who had them reopened in 1820. It is said that as water once again gushed through the canals, the Dehliewallahs greeted its coming with flowers.

Along each side of Chandni Chowk stood two-storied houses with tiled roofs and light wooden balconies in the front. The ground floor was commonly occupied by shops, with the families of the merchants living on the second floor.

Robert Minturn, who drove in a buggy through Chandni Chowk sometime in the 1850s, found the natives seated on magnificently caparisoned elephants painted with bright colours around the eyes and on the trunk. He saw people riding milk-white horses with tails dyed scarlet. There were bailees, the two-wheeled bullock carts with bright canopies, and palkees, the palanquins, and there were graceful English phaetons or buggies, drawn by well-groomed Arab steeds.

In Susan Gole's book *Indian Maps and Plans* I find two nineteenth-century street maps of Chandni Chowk. The street, the canal and the trees are shown as seen from above, as a bird would have seen them. Most modern maps employ this technique of projecting the seen onto a horizontal surface. However, in these particular maps, the houses along the street have been drawn as seen from the front. One can clearly see the tiled roofs of two- and three-storey houses, their arched windows and triangular canopies. Two viewpoints, two modes of seeing and showing, have been juxtaposed in these maps. The cartographer is not satisfied merely to fly over the street but wants to get down and walk along it. He is reluctant to reduce these beautiful buildings into squares, rectangles and circles. In nicely calligraphed

Persian he has inserted the names of buildings, squares and fountains. I adore these maps. They are far more interesting than the walking tour maps inserted in the Lonely Planet guide. They make you feel as if you're walking on the street and stopping to look and marvel.

One of the maps also shows old Kotwali, the police station, in front of which, in 1857, the corpses of three princes, two sons and one grandson of the last Mughal emperor, Bahadur Shah Zafar, were displayed on a cart. The 1857 sepoy mutiny had unsettled the East India Company. It began doubting its hold on power, outraged at the humiliation it had suffered at the hands of the disorganised mutineers. It is believed that, in revenge, the army of the company razed more than one third of the city; almost the whole of the native population, estimated around 130 thousand, was evicted. The Hindus were allowed to come back a few years after the mutiny but the hostility toward the Muslims continued for several years.

After the recapture of the city, a serious debate about its future ensued in the press and within official circles. One newspaper wanted to destroy the city to demonstrate the invincibility of British power. A suggestion was made that the Red Fort be levelled to give way to Fort Victoria. Lord Egerton wished to flatten Jama Masjid and replace it with a cathedral. Fortunately, the Secretary of State ignored these radical proposals, but all buildings within a 500-yard radius of the Red Fort, other than the Hindu temples, were cleared. The Jama Masjid was turned into an army camp, only relinquished in 1862 on the condition that no political meetings be held there. Scores of gallows were erected in the city and public hangings became commonplace. Sir Theophilus Metcalfe, the joint magistrate of Delhi, nephew of Sir Thomas Metcalfe and cousin of Emily, headed special commissions for the trials of the natives. It is said that his victims were often hanged from the charred beams of his own house.

•

Mirza Ghalib, one of the greatest Urdu poets, came to Delhi in 1810 as a young boy and made Delhi his own. It is hard to imagine Delhi without him.

Ghalib rented a number of houses not far from Chandni Chowk. One afternoon in August 1993 my friend and I went looking for the house where he had lived. My friend knew the area well; for years his father had worked as a cashier in a sari shop a few hundred metres from Chandni Chowk, and the family rented a house on Nai Sarak, one of the more recent streets that joined it from the south.

There is a letter Ghalib wrote to the son of one of his Hindu friends in which he describes the house:

> There was only Machia the courtesan's house and two by-lanes between us. Our big mansion is the one that now belongs to Lakhmi Chand Seth. I used to spend most of my time in the stone summer-house near the main entrance. I enjoyed flying my kite from

the roof of a house in one of the lanes nearby and to match it against Raja Balwan Singh's.

Ghalib liked to write letters and wrote them well. They paint a vivid picture of nineteenth-century Delhi. He, like most people of his time, didn't quite know what to make of the presence of the British in Delhi. He appreciated and valued the renaissance which the political stability brought in by the East India Company had initiated in the city. The city now had a college, a press for printing both in Persian and Urdu, and a number of newspapers. His first Urdu collection appeared in 1841 and was sold out immediately to be reprinted again after a few years. In 1842 he was offered a professorship in Persian in the Delhi College but declined presumably because the English Secretary to the Government of India did not come out to greet him when he went to see the Secretary for the interview.

In spite of this overt fascination with the Company and its rule, he was reluctant to displease his Mughal patrons by appearing to be too willing to adopt alien ways.

His response to the 1857 mutiny also shows a similar ambivalence. He did not know which side to support or condemn, but one thing is sure – he detested the looting, violence, and carnage that followed the mutiny. Ghalib wrote a book, *Dastanbuy*, a diary-like record of the traumatic events. Most commentators believe that the book was far from a spontaneous account of the days before and after the mutiny. Ghalib, the experts agree, wanted to please the English. Like most people of his time, he believed they were going to rule forever. The introduction in the book does not leave any doubt about his motives. I have 'eaten the bread and salt of the British,' Ghalib notes, and 'from my earliest childhood I have been fed from the table of these conquerors of the world.' His letters to his friends, however, describe the events differently. In them he is quite critical of the way the victorious army of the Company unleashed a wave of terror in the city.

We found the street where Ghalib is known to have lived but couldn't locate the house. We asked a few people for help but failed again. One young boy who worked in a teashop took us to a house next to the Excelsior Cinema and left us there. An old guard at the cinema told us that the cinema used to be part of a big mansion owned by Hakim Ahsanullah Khan, the personal physician of the last Mughal emperor. Ghalib was a close friend of the physician and lived not far from his mansion. 'Where?' we asked the guard a number of times. 'God only knows,' the man replied and smiled.

A year later, in the book *Mansions at Dusk: The Havelis of Old Delhi*, I found photographs and description of the mansion. In 1857 it had been ransacked by an angry mob of sepoys. It was reclaimed by the Hakim after the mutiny and rebuilt. The book contains a photograph of the dilapidated inner courtyard of the mansion with the caption: 'the picture shows the pitiable condition of the *daalan*, the courtyard, where it is said Ghalib loved to sit while composing his verses.'

Ghalib's student, poet Hali, notes that Ghalib

> often used to compose verses at night, under the influence of wine. When he had worked out a complete verse, he would tie a knot in his sash, and there would be as many as eight to ten knots by the time he retired to bed. In the morning he would recall them, with no other aid to his memory, and would write them down.

•

In the introduction to *Mansions at Dusk*, Varma writes:

> There is something hauntingly sad in a once beautiful city crumbling away. Shahjahanabad is such a city and it is being destroyed at a relentless pace. Handsome buildings of considerable historicity are demolished routinely. Carved ceilings in wood are ripped off for firewood. Marble stepped wells are cemented to build godowns. Intricately worked stone pillars are junked to create space for lathes. Gateways and arches, *baolis* and *jaffries*, pillars and panels, seen today, are gone the next.

As I walk along Chandni Chowk I begin to understand the intensity of this lament. The city scares me too, with its chaotic traffic, overcrowded streets, stench of overflowing sewers, and webs of wires and cables draping the crumbling façades of old buildings. The whole place has been turned into a maze of shops, storehouses and wholesale markets. The trees, parks and gardens have disappeared. The fountains have dried. Chronic scarcity of water and electricity plagues the city. The air is heavy with dust, smoke and acrid fumes. They hurt your eyes and squeeze your lungs. In the forty-degree heat, dust sticks to you like a thick paste. The city is crumbling under its own weight. A giant taking its last breath, wasting away slowly and steadily, and there is nothing one can do about it.

What is it that I want from Delhi? Is nostalgia getting the better of me and of people like Varma? Nostalgia for a past we have never lived but have only read about? Do we want the old city, or at least parts of it, to be restored and transformed into a museum-city? I find myself thinking about Tallinn, the capital of Estonia, a city I visited a number of times in the mid-1970s, spending hours walking through its medieval centre.

In Varma's book I find a photograph of Begum Samru's mansion. The front façade, which faced the Chandni Chowk, was dominated by eight Corinthian columns crowned with carved entablatures and a flat roof laced with a railing of stone balusters. The front wall had six large, triangular headed windows with rectangular panes. You had to walk over one of the two symmetrically placed, curved balustraded steps to reach the portico. Green-coloured *jaffries*, the lattice work of bamboo, partially covered the building. The rear façade was even more impressive, with nine double Corinthian pillars and a flat roof with balustraded railing culminated in a pitched roof with triangular gables, and intricately carved arched heads over the windows. The mansion stood within a beautiful garden and the long drive to it from the Chandni Chowk was lined with cypresses.

'To live means to leave traces,' writes Walter Benjamin, the famous Jewish-German writer and literary philosopher. The present-day photograph of the *haveli* in Varma's book shows the traces well. Past living has turned it into a bricolage, a conglomerate of debris and fragments. The Corinthian columns of the front façade have survived. So have bits and pieces of the balustraded railing of the flat roof. A faded inscription, 'Lloyds Bank Limited', on top of the façade is partially blocked by a huge white and blue hoarding advertising Orient ceiling and table fans. A slightly smaller signboard for the Central Bank of India hangs right underneath. A larger hoarding for the same bank with the name written both in English and Hindi is nailed across three columns. To its right is the red billboard of Oriental Agencies. A faded and tattered brownish *jaffry* has replaced Begum Samru's green *jaffry*. A row of pigeons is sitting on the roof. But the most intriguing aspect of the building is the way it has been squashed, compressed and preyed upon from all sides. Small and large buildings have grown on and around it. Poles with telephone and power cables run across it. The place where once stood the imposing steps is occupied by a house, on the roof of which I can see a garbage dump: a discarded tyre, several small and large cardboard boxes and sacks full of refuse.

The mansion is now called Bhagirath Palace and houses a wholesale market for electrical appliances. One of the largest in Asia, the people in Chandni Chowk say proudly. My friend took me there a number of times. He was in the process of building his house in the suburbs and was hunting for cheap electrical fittings.

Looking at this building I understand why my friend bursts into laughter when I show him a picture postcard of Tallinn and tell him about a fifteenth-century bakery where even now one can go and buy a freshly baked loaf of bread.

•

Traumascapes is the title of a book by Maria Tumarkin, a Russian-speaking Jewish-Ukrainian writer now living in Australia. In the book she tells the story of places marked by pain, violence and loss. So marked, these places turn into sites of collective guilt, shame, and resilience. To visit them is harrowing but not to visit, a moral failure. They ask for our silence when we are there but demand that we speak about them after we have walked away from them. To hide them is impossible, but to hide away from them unviable, a betrayal of our own humanity.

Let me take you to one such traumascape in Delhi.

To go there we'll have to find the Turkman Gate, one of the fourteen original gates in the walled city of Shahjahanabad. It stands in the southern part of the wall, helplessly trying to outlast the onslaught of urbanisation. The gate, or whatever remains of it, leads us to one of the oldest and colourful bazaars in Delhi, the Bazaar Shah, famous for its ivory carvers, embroiders, silver and coppersmiths. At the corner of a paved courtyard next to the gate stands a charming little mosque. The bazaar and the area adjacent to it are one of those rare parts of Delhi where a majority of the population is still Muslim.

In April 1976, during the dreaded years of what has come to be known in India as the Emergency, the Delhi Development Authority began an intensive program of slum clearance. The plan was to demolish most of the so-called unauthorised settlements, and to transform the capital into a beautiful garden city. The demolitions in the Turkman Gate area began on 14 April, but five days later, at around 10.30 a.m., a crowd of a few thousand people came and stood in the way of the advancing bulldozers escorted by the police. The police charged with canes and then resorted to tear gas, but unable to control the situation decided to open fire. The official sources reported three deaths although eyewitness accounts spoke of heaps of bodies, including those of the policemen, being loaded onto trucks. Most of the courtyard and the houses in and near it were destroyed. The people were rounded up, pushed into trucks and taken to remote settlements, east of the Yamuna River and dumped in vacant plots with no drinking water and no other amenities.

It is said that up to ten thousand people were forcibly evicted from the area.

The main driving force behind the project of beautifying Delhi was Sanjay Gandhi, Indira Gandhi's youngest son. He entertained scant respect for democratic processes, and earnestly believed that a certain amount of brutality was essential to bring order and discipline.

The protestors at the Turkman Gate, however, had one other important reason to stand in the way of the advancing bulldozers and policemen. They were no doubt angry at the authorities for demolishing their houses, but they were more enraged at the way their bodies, individual and collective, were being interfered with. With the declaration of the Emergency, the family planning program, which in India was primarily a plan to control the growth of population, gained unprecedented momentum. A part of the bureaucracy sincerely believed that what India needed was a sustained and well-targeted policy of compulsory sterilisation. Like all such government-driven programs, it also attracted bureaucrats who, in order to please the Prime Minister Indira Gandhi and her son, became overzealous in achieving the outcome. But the Muslims, perhaps justifiably, saw in the program a sinister attack on their faith and way of living, a well thought out plan of the Hindu lobby in the Government to destroy them.

Since the declaration of the Emergency a number of sterilisation camps had begun operating in the area. The newspapers reported that often demolition gangs were joined by medical squads, which systematically sterilised people, old and young, married or unmarried, with or without their consent. The people whose houses were destroyed were often told that sterilisation would drastically improve their chances of getting a small residential plot in a new suburban settlement.

As I write about these tragic events my mind begins to secrete an entirely different set of images from my childhood. Although I can easily blame my memory for leading me astray, I have to confess that I also enjoy the surprises my memory springs on me.

A few hundred metres from the Turkman Gate, across one of the busiest roads in Old Delhi, stretches a relatively open space called the Ramlila Ground. Each year the ground hosts the climactic performance associated with the Dusserah festival.

Dusserah and Diwali are the two most significant Hindu festivals spread over a period of three to four weeks in October and November each year. For about ten days amateur theatre groups enact scenes from the epic Ramayana. The final act of these performances includes the ritualistic slaying of the ten-headed Ravana and his two brothers. This pivotal moment of the show also celebrates the victory of Rama and his rag-tag army led by Hanuman, the monkey god. The slaying is followed by the burning of effigies of Ravana and his brothers.

In October 1955, my parents decided to take my brothers and me to the show. I was five then, and although I didn't want to miss the colourful spectacle, I was also apprehensive of the ear-shattering noise of the firecrackers.

I remember clearly how my *Mama*, the younger brother of my mother, had raised me onto his shoulders to let me have a look at the effigy of the ten-headed giant that swayed and swooned in the wind; the thick ropes that held him and his brothers upright moaned and groaned, filling my heart with awe and wonder.

Although Ravana has become an archetype of the most hateful demon in Hindu mythmaking, I have, for no apparent reason, developed a strange empathy for him. I find him more audacious and charming than Rama, the warrior god. The spectacular death of Ravana, brought about by deceit and heavenly design, saddens me; I see in him a hero, fallible and mortal like humans. I know that the narrative logic of the story in Ramayana demands that he be slayed because only sacrificial killing can grant him nirvana. Hence the evil deeds ascribed to him have a purpose: the aim is to bring him closer to his ultimate demise and escape from the perpetual cycle of birth and death.

But on that evening in 1955, perched on the shoulders of my uncle, I was preoccupied by just one thought: to get through and, if possible, to enjoy the deafening fireworks without panic. Soon I heard the loud sound of the conch shells followed by the beating of drums announcing the arrival of the auspicious moment. The actor who played the role of Rama stood erect on a chariot, waiting to release his fiery arrow. In the blink of an eye the arrow whizzed through the air and hit the clay figure of a monkey fixed on a wire. The monkey caught fire and whirred along a cable stretched towards the belly button of the ten-headed Ravana. The epic tells that Ravana had a pitcher of nectar hidden inside his belly. The pitcher had to be destroyed and drained to kill him once and for all.

The monkey hit the belly; a red tongue of fire jumped out, and with a bang the effigy caught fire. The fire spread to his brothers and they also burst into flames beginning the thunderous explosion of numerous firecrackers. This is when, in spite of all my intentions to be resolute, a strange terror gripped me. To remain seated on my uncle's shoulder became impossible. I slid myself off and rushed to my mother to hide behind her back, burying my face in her sari, shutting my eyes and ears as tightly as possible.

'What a silly boy,' she said after the fireworks had stopped, and smiled. 'Come here,' she whispered and gave me a hug, wiping off my tears with her sari.

•

The Ramlila Ground is located at the north-eastern margin of British Delhi. Edward Lutyens, who was the principal designer of the new city, had suggested that this seventh incarnation of Delhi could be called Georgebad or Marypore. I am glad that the British Government settled for a more sedate and simple name: New Delhi.

In her book *Stones of Empire*, Jan Morris, describes the project as '… the last and most calculated of British civic creations … quixotic and certainly extravagant'. Lutyens, who had earlier designed the Hampstead Garden suburb in England, wanted to create a garden-city. Its shape, notes Morris, was roughly hexagonal and was conceived to be built around three focal points: in the west the Government Centre which included the Viceroy's House, the Secretariat and the Legislature building; in the east a ceremonial plaza and a junction of roads around the Arch of India; and in the north a shopping and commercial centre called Connaught Circus constructed as a circular colonnade. The three formed a triangle similar to the Parliamentary Triangle in Walter Burley Griffin and Marion Mahony Griffin's Canberra.

The Viceroy's Palace was to be the heart of this new capital of Britain's Indian Empire. The site for the palace was selected by Lord Hardinge, the then Viceroy who, one fine Delhi morning in 1912, rode with Lord Hailey, the then commissioner of Delhi, galloping across the plain to a hill:

> From the top of the hill, there was a magnificent view embracing Old Delhi and all the principal monuments

> situated outside the town, and the Jamuna winding its way like a silver streak in the foreground at a little distance. I said at once to Hailey, "This is the site for Government House", and he readily agreed.

The Viceroy's Palace sat on the hill at the apex of a ceremonial parade called the Kingsway. Like the famous Champs-Élysées (but twice as wide), the processional way led to the Arch of India. This east-west axis was cut across by another wide road called Queensway, running north to south. The space in between the two axes was enmeshed with a network of straight roads interrupted with Canberra-style roundabouts. Green lawns ran along on either side of the main axis roads, punctuated with water-filled ponds and fountains and surrounded by orderly rows of eucalyptus and casuarina.

The New Delhi of Lutyens was conceived and built as an orientalised modern city of the empire. It was marked by an ample use of red sandstone, the main building material of the Delhi of the Mughals and by other 'traditional' architectural elements such as stone *chattris* or canopies, stupa-like domes with miniature elephants, and above all, by *jaalis*, the pierced-stone screens. One of the several *chattris* stands on the Kingsway, a few hundred metres from the Arch of India. It used to house a statue of King George V. After India was granted independence in 1947, it was decided to remove the statue and replace it with a statue of Mahatma Gandhi. However, to this day the canopy remains empty. It is rumoured that the committee appointed to run the competition for selecting the statue wasn't able to settle on the winning entry.

However, most colonial and imperial names of buildings, streets and squares were changed without much delay; the Viceroy Palace became the Rashtrapati Bhawan (President's Palace); the Kingsway and Queensway were changed to Rajpath (the State Avenue) and Janpath (People's Avenue) respectively; and the Arch of India became the India Gate.

The emptiness of the canopy is hardly noticed by people these days. The Kingsway, on which the Viceroy used to come out in his ceremonial carriage driven by twelve beautiful horses, nowadays hosts the Republic Day parade held on 26 January each year.

As a schoolboy I was often taken on picnics to the India Gate. We would play around the fountains, and if we had money, hired a boat from the boating club to go rowing on the ponds, navigating carefully through a crowd of lotuses and lilies. In the spring we flew kites and played cricket. The heat and dust of Delhi summers were hard to endure. The situation was made worse by frequent shortages of electricity and water. The possibility of having a decent shower became a cherished dream. Perhaps that is why this unbelievable plenitude of water near the India Gate appeared to us so otherworldly.

•

In the *Practice of Everyday Life*, Michel de Certeau, a famous French philosopher and critic of language and the practice of living, explores metaphorical equivalence between walking and speaking. 'Walking,' he notes, 'is to the urban system what the speech act is to language. Walking [in a city] affirms, suspects, tries out, transgresses … it speaks.'

As I write and read this essay, I also begin to retrace my walks in the city. My walking, writing and reading have thus created a map for you to read and walk with. However, the walks you would undertake would also traverse the mindscape of my memories. In a way I have opened before you a map of my mindscape.

I have often wondered how a map, almost like a book, opens ways to other maps. As if one map contains within itself all other maps. As if one on its own is insufficient, and only the adjacency of other maps or at least its ability to create a desire to see other maps, gives it a semblance of completeness.

Maps, like stories, *de*-scribe and *in*-scribe places. Through them places are assimilated, owned and disowned, longed for and belonged to. My essay doesn't read like a travel story, but it is still impossible to imagine and write it without walking in Delhi. My walking and writing have created a poetic geography, the geography of my memories, which like Christo and Jeanne-Claude's installations, wrap over the literal geography of the city of my childhood.

•

Maps also store memories, attaching them to places. Each time one looks at them the memory lights up. It doesn't matter if it's the finger that is tracing the route on the map because with the finger the whole body walks, dragging the capricious mind along. It's the mind that brings along words and images and the memory so retrieved is reinvented.

Benjamin demonstrates this interplay of memory, remembering and writing in the essay *A Berlin Chronicle*. Like Benjamin's Berlin, my Delhi has been, inadvertently 'adorned with incomprehensible, capricious frills of imagination'.

This is the reason that the Delhi I am remembering, walking in, and writing about has also turned into an imagined topography. It is imagined but not imaginary because it feels real, its reality grounded in actual experience, mine and that of others whose stories I have tried to recall.

But maps, like memories, are dated. A time comes when a fissure opens between what is remembered on a mind-map fails to match the real geography. This is what happened to me when I went looking for the old house of my childhood. It disappeared from the real geography but resisted vanishing from the topography of my mind-map.

As I write about my Delhi, I also realise that my memory has played tricks on me. Why is it that I am only able to recall certain things and only certain aspects of people and places? For example, I remember clearly the cold January day my father took us to the

Republic Day parade at the India Gate in New Delhi. I remember the eight-feet tall soldier Bahadur Singh, the star attraction of the parade that year, the stocky Sikh bandmaster in the bagpipe band of the Sikh regiment, his bright turban with a yellow patka (cotton band), and his radiant staff, but can't recollect anything about the rest of the band members. I even fail to remember the face of my young *Massi*, the younger sister of *Ammiji*, who was with us that day.

The most vivid of the memories that have stayed with me, however, is the horrific image of *Ammiji's* blood gushing out from her forehead. During the parade a minor stampede had started just behind us. The wooden benches on which we were sitting came crashing down. The first-aid people escorted *Ammiji* to an army medical van to see if she needed stitches.

I remember those stitches. Whenever she came to put me to bed at night and to tell me a story, I would ask her about the scar and the number of stitches the doctor had to put in to stop the bleeding.

•

The maps on which our memory draws places and routes to reach them are not flat like a sheet of paper. They have at least two more dimensions; one of them is time layered within them, and the second is the value we attach to places shown on them. There are places which we cherish and want to remember and there are others that we wish to erase and forget.

Like real landscapes, the topography of maps created by our memory has folds and fissures, which the daylight of everyday life fails to penetrate. Whatever we once experienced, felt and lived, slides into these nooks and crannies requiring something akin to Marcel Proust's *petites madeleines* to drag them out but even then, whatever reappears is either excessively embellished or unduly curtailed. To reclaim them in their pristine form remains out of reach.

Something similar also happens to places, which were once upon a time etched so clearly in our mind that we never felt the need to carry a real map with us; the mind often took us there of its own volition, unprompted, unhindered.

A time comes however, when, try as we may, we fail to retrieve impressions of them, and arriving at these places we feel lost, as I was that day in Delhi. 'Hello stranger!' a voice from the memory greets us, mocking and challenging, and we accept defeat.

Luckily, the feeling of being a stranger, although unsettling at first, doesn't last long because we begin to convince ourselves that we are ready to cast off the burden of past attachments and seek new, perhaps more lasting, connections. The nostalgia that once tormented us is pushed aside, replaced by more lively engagements, and memory, like a good friend, obliges – adding fresh impressions to the map which we know will one day cheat us again. We know it and yet we continue to play the game.

Not so quiet flows the Molonglo

I live in Aranda, a leafy green suburb to the north-west of Lake Burley Griffin. Often I walk across the Black Mountain to work in one of the libraries in the Australian National University. Occasionally I change my route and follow a track along its southern slope. I have a favourite spot there: a bench-like flattened surface of a rocky outcrop looking south. The site provides a panoramic view of the lake and the Parliamentary Triangle.

I sit and watch and if I'm lucky, I enjoy the company of a few crimson rosellas, some of which nest in the hollows of scribbly gums. Quite often I hear the loud trills of white-throated treecreepers and a strange quiver runs through my body.

The lake appears quiet, laid-back. Its stillness becalms my anxiety. I watch the light bounce off the water and spread across the stringy bands of clouds streaking the sky. Sometimes I spot a few boats or ferries sail past leaving in the water arrowed trails. The autumn brings colour, and trees along the southern shores glow, irradiated by the late afternoon sun.

The lake is playing the role it was asked to and playing it well.

Edith Campbell Berry, Frank Moorhouse's fictional heroine in *Cold Light*, describes the lake as a pearly girdle around the waist of the city. For me it is just a lake, modest and graceful, adding beauty to all that exists around it.

The lake is not wholly natural but is more natural than the city for which it was planned as an adornment. The city owes its existence to the political will of Australian leaders who wanted to build an iconic capital matching the aspirations of a new federation of Australian states.

Walter Burley Griffin and his wife Marion Mahony had designed a unique city. When asked in an interview about their design, Walter Griffin said:

> I have planned a city not like any other city in the world. I have planned it not in a way that I expected any governmental authorities in the world would accept. I have planned an ideal city—a city that meets my ideal of the future.

Griffin considered himself a landscape architect and believed in the ideas of the City-Beautiful movement that emerged in response to the 1893 World's Columbian Exposition in Chicago. He and Mahony had therefore designed a city that would exist in perfect harmony with the natural landscape, taking from it whatever it was prepared to yield and returning to it whatever it was ready to accept as its meaningful elaborations.

The lake is one of them.

I have seen the lake at different times of the day and in different seasons. Sometimes it reminds me of water in the Japanese gardens, always painterly but not loud. Marion Mahony was very fond of Japanese paintings and the lake she and Walter Griffin had imagined was going to resemble them, bringing comfort to the eye by both softening the bright light in the summers and by lighting up the dim haze in the winters. Its presence, they could have thought, would mellow the effect of the heavy brick and concrete constructions which dominate most capital cities showing off the political power they host and represent.

Several times, I have watched rows of hot air balloons rise up in the early autumn sky, often drifting not too high above the water. I have also seen Patricia Piccinini's *Skywhale* sailing aloft and wondered what emotions the Griffins would have experienced seeing this imagined, and yet so real, creature trailing over the land- and the water-axis of the city they had designed. Looking at the *Skywhale*, I was reminded of Youwarkee in *The Book of Imaginary Beings* that Jorge Luis Borges describes as half woman and half bird.

The lake appears to me quite similar: half river and half lake; a river that has become a lake, and a lake which doesn't forget to remind us that it is a river.

•

The Griffins didn't know much about the site before deciding to enter the international competition and relied mainly on the wooden box they had received from the British Consulate in Chicago. The box contained a plaster model of the site that showed a large plain surrounded by hills and traversed by a meandering river in the middle. The material also included two cycloramic views of the site painted by Charles Coulter.

The river could have instantly triggered in their mind visions of the park grounds Frederick Olmsted had designed for the 1893 World's Fair in Chicago in which water had become one of the main protagonists in the urbanised landscape. The river, they could have thought, would play a similar role in the city of the future they'd design. Their city wouldn't encroach aggresively on the natural landscape but would be allowed to express itself, emphatically but gently. The symbiosis between the two would be, as far as possible, perfect.

Did they succeed?

Only partially, because as Walter Griffin had feared, the city they had planned was not the one that could have been fully accepted by any governmental authority in the world, therefore the design had to be modified to meet the financial, political, and technical constraints within which it had to be built.

To achieve perfect harmony between built and unbuilt environment is not easy because human intervention, however limited and considered, is still an intervention, and the need to produce a habitable space requires natural landscape to acquiesce and accept the order we impose on it. Even in the make-shift huts created by our hominid ancestors found at the encampment of Terra Amata, near Nice in southern France, dating back to around 400 thousand years ago, one can see how nature was made to surrender to our demands and give ground. The same is true of rock shelters and caves, where our ancestors wrested space to find a refuge from wild predators. They painted walls and roofs with figures, one of the most common elements of which are stencilled prints of human hands, to mark and assert their presence.

Sadly, domestication of nature that began so long ago didn't stop but continued at an increasing rate bringing us face to face with the existential threat of global warming.

Glenda Korporaal, Marion Mahony's biographer, writes that on her last visit to Canberra in 1938, before leaving Australia, Marion had driven to the top of Mount Ainslie to gaze at the shape of the city emerging in the Limestone Plain. She had wanted to compare the city on the ground and the city she had portrayed on her beautiful painting on silk. She was impressed by the view and optimistic that once fully built, the city would come close to what she and her husband had imagined. In 1938, the lake had yet to be built and in her opinion the city would remain unfinished without it. 'The one thing lacking to make a truly grandiose scene,' she said, 'is that waters of the Molonglo had not yet been dammed to form the permanent reflecting basin. The plan as one looks down from the heights, will not really be comprehensible till this is done.'

The permanent reflecting basin Marion Mahony had imagined emerged only in 1964, three years after her death. Walter Griffin had died in 1937, a year before her final visit to Canberra. Neither she nor her husband would come to know that their beautiful lake had been bestowed the Griffin name.

I suspect Marion Mahony would have accepted the name whole heartedly because she loved her husband and admired his work. I'm not so sure about Walter. He would have most probably regretted that the name doesn't acknowledge the contribution of Marion Mahony in designing the city and the lake because he had several times noted that 'she ought to have much more than half the credit for winning the competition'. But in the end, he would have accepted the decision almost as *fait accompli* because this was the way things were done back then.

•

In his 1970 memoir, *The Measure of Years*, Australian Prime Minister Robert Menzies mentions that there was widespread feeling amongst his supporters that the lake should be named after him, because he was its main champion, and that without his intervention, either the lake wouldn't have been built or would have appeared in a form quite different from what the Griffins had planned. Luckily, he rejected the proposal.

'I want to have the lake called Lake Burley Griffin,' he wrote because the name would give 'Griffin a memorial which no man ever so handsomely deserved.'

Walter Griffin deserved this memorial but so did Marion Mahony, his talented wife and collaborator. Like so many place names, this memorial to the designers of the city and the lake falls short. It too has become the victim of a cultural and political blind spot of its time. But isn't this the fate of most names with which we memorialise places, periods, and events? The names reflect the histories of our interaction with them mirroring our beliefs and prejudices. It doesn't require much effort to see through them and reveal what they represent and fail to represent. The same is true of the name Menzies gave to the lake he loved. Each time I read or speak it I instinctively add the name of Marion Mahony to it.

Most places we live with have layers of names, which like seams in a lithified package of sands bear in them ripples, laminations, and fossils of their past meanings and values.

The lake that Menzies named after Walter Griffin is no different. It too is layered with names and histories.

To begin with, the Lake Burley Griffin is a river that was dammed to create three large water basins. The river to its east is the Molonglo. In the west, as the water flows out through the gates of the Scrivener Dam, it turns once again into the same river meandering its way to join its larger sibling, the Murrumbidgee, a Wiradjuri word that means big water.

I have walked along the banks of the Molonglo in the east, and I have tracked it in the west reaching the point where it merges with the Murrumbidgee.

The Ngambri people who lived near the river didn't call it Molonglo. Ann Jackson-Nakano, a Canberra historian and writer, thinks that Moolinggoolah, a neighbouring group which inhabited the area in the headwaters of the river, could have used the name for the river. Her research suggests that

> Yeal-am-bidgee was the original collective Aboriginal name for the Molonglo River, at least from the upper Moolingoolah Plains to the river's junctions with Jullergung, or Queanbeyan River. From the junction of the Yeal-am-bidgee with Jullergung to its junction with the Murrumbidgee, it was known as the Ngambri (also rendered as Kembury', etc.) River ....

Jackson-Nakano believes that 'it was the early explorers who first started using the name of these plains for the river...'

It turns out that Molonglo, like many other Australian place names, is a purloined name. The settlers who intruded the area heard a name, liked it but couldn't get used to its sound. Therefore, the word was shortened and then given to the river for which the indigenous peoples in the area had more than one name. One of these names, according to Jackson-Nakano, was Ngambri, a word from which the name of the capital city could have been derived.

The river called the Molonglo starts its way in the foothills of Mount Ballard in the Tallaganda National Park at an elevation of 1,130 metres and flows in a northerly direction for several kilometres, changing its course abruptly to follow a westerly flow through Canberra, merging with the Murrumbidgee after covering a distance of 115 kilometres. During its short journey it drops close to 700 metres in elevation. From the relatively higher altitudes near the foothills it slowly descends into the flat plains.

Geologically, it is a fairly old river formed millions of years ago in the Cenozoic time (65 million to 2.6 million years ago) or even earlier, and because it is so old, it has found a state of happy equilibrium with the landscape it flows through, giving and accepting whatever it can afford and hold. Even in the relatively high elevation areas where it takes its first steps, it isn't unduly hurried but meanders at a leisurely pace throughout its course. Only in the Molonglo Gorge, located a couple of kilometres north of Queanbeyan, it appears a little more rushed, tracing a course with fewer bends.

Geologists believe that in the early Cenozoic times the area underwent tectonic upheaval along large fractures during which the region was thrust upwards. The river reacted the way most rivers do in such cases, by cutting a narrow passage through the uplifted rocks. Since then nothing dramatic has happened to the river and the land it flows through, although it did endure a succession of global warming and cooling events, the most recent of which was the Last Glacial Maximum that began around 33 thousand years ago and continued for 15 to 18 thousand years.

Roger Deakin, one of my favourite environmentalist writers, loves meandering rivers. He finds them graceful and generous ready to give away their treasures:

> Left to itself, a river will always meander. This is how rivers grow longer, and slow themselves down, and hold more water, and make themselves more interesting and pleasing to the human eye, as well as creatures that live in them. By increasing the total length and capacity ... these natural meanders, oxbows and flood meadows slow and diminish the impact of sudden storms by storing flood water. They also provide a far richer natural habitat for all the river creatures that crave the shelter.

The Molonglo is equally friendly and generous.

It meanders, forming U-shaped bends, sometimes as majestic as the horseshoe bends in many much larger and more reputed rivers in the world. The meandering, as Deakin mentions, has created a rich habitat for plants and animals in the riparian zones as well as in the broad flood plains, which, over the span of millions of years, have generated fertile ground for all forms of life to flourish.

The Molonglo was and still remains a typical Australian inland river in which the amount of water varies depending on climate and season. These changes alter its shape, size, and the rate at which the water flows.

In the book, *The Biggest Estate on Earth*, Bill Gammage paints a vivid picture of the river and its flood plain. His description is based on the notes and diaries of visitors and colonial settlers who came to the area almost two hundred years ago:

> It was a typical inland watercourse, spreading shallowly around wetlands, with a scatter of reedy pools some more permanent than it, holding fish, eel, platypus and yabbies. On each side were grassy plains ... Opposite Black Mountain a 'pebbly ford' spanned the Molonglo. East, the river divided Limestone Plains, 'extensive plains and good grazing country on each side, with a considerable portion of rich meadow land on the banks of the river'. Swampy 'alluvial flats' with reeds and lignum stretches backed by grassy downs suited emu, plains turkey, yams and native artichoke. North of the river this country continued across to the city to bellow Russell Hill, where the river looped south around an 'open plain', now East Basin, and through rich reedy swamps, perhaps the district's most extensive. Wetland tracked the river up to Pialligo, where back from the north bank long sandy rises, excellent warm-weather camps, were littered with stone tools. Within a few kilometres, closer than most supermarkets, swamps, river, plain, hill and forest were handy.

The river had created a rich habitat, a 'supermarket', for the indigenous inhabitants located within a walking distance. They lived and thrived for many thousands of years, 'farming' judiciously generation after generation, and thereby creating a particular type of landscape. Gammage uses the term 'grass-forest' to characterise it, and notes that a similar template can be seen in many other regions in Australia.

The European settlers who arrived in the Limestone Plains found the land most suitable for farming. As a result, indigenous inhabitants were forced off the land, breaking a unique kinship they had formed with it. The kinship involved not merely the ground under their feet but all the living and the non-living on earth and in the sky. It included the people themselves; together they formed a collective body that lived and survived for thousands of years. The Molonglo was part of the same body: one of its vital sources of food and sustenance.

Like many other rivers, the Molonglo and its valley provided corridors for indigenous inhabitants to move and camp. It was part of a network of passages along which they travelled searching for food and shelter, conversant with the seasonal variation of plant and animal food. In summers the warm waters of the Murrumbidgee and its tributaries, including the Molonglo, contained an abundance of fish, freshwater shellfish, tortoise, crayfish and platypus. In harsher winters they sought refuge in caves and rock shelters.

Josephine Flood, who dated material in the Birrigai rock-shelter in the Tidbinbilla Nature Reserve, notes that the indigenous peoples lived in the Canberra regions from at least 25 thousand years ago, and it's quite likely they were in the area thousands of years earlier. The sites like Birrigai were used as shelter to escape freezing conditions during the Last Glacial Maximum.

Geologists describe the presence of periglacial deposits on the slopes of the Black Mountain. These deposits are formed from periodic freezing and thawing of snow, indicating that during the Last Glacial Maximum conditions were quite cold even in areas near the Molonglo. The winters brought heavy snow falls, reducing the tree cover across the tablelands. It created areas of alpine woodlands and grassland in the Canberra region. A small pocket of the old ecosystem has survived in the Aranda snow gums. They are the remnants of grasslands which once covered the Monaro Plains. The pocket is called Frost Hollow because it is believed that the grassland was preserved because of the cold air draining from the direction of the Black Mountain. The cold air could have hampered the growth of trees and shrubs that like warmer conditions.

River corridors along which the indigenous inhabitants camped and moved have yielded rich archaeological material. Gentle slopes, spurs and alluvial flats were favourable sites for camping. Flood mentions traces of eight hundred open campsites in the region of which most are on the banks of larger rivers such as the Murrumbidgee and the Molonglo. Most campsites are located close to good fishing spots. She describes two major camping grounds in the Central Canberra area.

One of them was situated on sandhills overlooking the Molonglo at Pialligo near the airport. The second was on the Black Mountain peninsula, near Yarralumla, a camp at which in 1844 George Augustus Robinson, the Chief Protector of Aborigines, talked to the local indigenous community.

There is information about a number of shelters on the Black Mountain which were used as seasonal base camps. Some of them in time became meeting places for ceremonies and corroborees. One of them is believed to be located near the present-day entrance to the National Botanic Gardens.

This site was on the south-eastern slope of the Black Mountain not far from the western bank of the Ngambri Creek (now Sullivan Creek), a northern tributary of the Molonglo. The eastern bank of the creek, Gammage notes, was covered by undulating grass plains with tree clumps on rises:

> People burnt carefully to make this plain. It associated grass and water with shelter on an enclosing rise, which let people hunt easily. Naturally they usually kept away, harvesting perhaps once a patch-burn, but there were many such plains, each burnt in turn. Downstream the creek widened over a permanent spring, then threaded between ridges onto grassy

> flats below Black Mountain spur where another spring never ran dry, and people camped. South Oval [in the campus of Australian National University] paddock was just over the ridge, many plants including Yam Daisy were at hand, and the 'woody' spur was good winter shelter from floods and cold flats. Stone tools and chips lie there. Black Mountain was open lower down, a little thicker higher. The summit was clear.

Although no systematic survey of archaeological sites in the Lake Burley Griffin area has yet been conducted, there is information about several locations similar in significance to the one near the Black Mountain and the Ngambri Creek. The 2010 Heritage Assessment Report on Lake Burley Griffin describes several sites with ancient stone artefacts. It also suggests that many, including ceremonial ones, now lie submerged under the lake.

In a guidebook about the Heritage Trail at the campus of Australian National University, Tyronne Bell, a Ngunnawal man, recounts that 'before the lake was constructed, members of his family would play in the limestone caves along the Molonglo, where there were various rock art sites.'

The flood plain of the Molonglo, at times as wide as half a kilometre, was inundated to create the lake, under which lies a rich layer of indigenous history. It's not clear whether Walter Griffin and Marion Mahony had been informed that some of the indigenous inhabitants still lived in the areas not far from the Limestone Plain.

In her biography of Marion Mahony, Korporaal describes Mahony's trip to Tasmania in 1919. Korporaal writes that Mahony had known of the brutal treatment of indigenous peoples on the island from her reading of Mark Twain's *Following the Equator*, a book he had published after visiting Australia in the late 1890s. However, the biography doesn't mention whether Mahony and Griffin had shown interest in learning about the indigenous inhabitants in the Limestone Plain. The material the two had received in Chicago conveyed no information about them.

I sometimes wonder what effect this knowledge would have had on the design they had proposed for the city. It's hard to believe that they had not heard about places with names such as Molonglo, Yarralumla, and Yarramundi. Speaking some of these words aloud they must have, just for a moment, pondered about their meaning and provenance.

•

There used to be a sandy ridge at the site of the Old Parliament House. Walking along that ridge one could reach the Molonglo and wet one's feet. The ridge was either formed by the river itself, which frequently flooded the plains, or the wind, similar to the one mapped in the Kings Park on the opposite bank of the Molonglo. Josephine Flood believes that sandhills similar to these ridges were frequently used as campsites by indigenous peoples in the area.

H. P. Moss and W. P. Kinsella were able to find and collect numerous ancient artefacts from the sandy ridge. When the lawns of the Old Parliament House were being formed, a stone axe was retrieved from there. Kinsella collected a number of artefacts from the sandpit of the Old Parliament House. The sandy ridge was destroyed during the construction because it interfered with the line of sight between the Old Parliament House and the Australian War Memorial. In the Griffins' design, the principal land-axis coincided with this line of sight.

The sandy ridge, on which the lawns in front of the Old Parliament House are located now, became the site where in 1972 four indigenous protestors set up a temporary Aboriginal Tent Embassy. They didn't have a proper tent and decided to bring with them an ordinary beach umbrella, in front of which they sat with their banners. I don't know if they knew that they were sitting on an ancient camping ground frequented by their ancestors.

Almost twenty-five years later, in March 1999, a loud protest against the possible closure of the embassy was staged at the same site. One of the protestors was Kevin Buzzacott, also known as Uncle Kev, an elder from the Arabana nation in northern South Australia. He held in his hand an ash- and dirt-smeared Australian flag, which he pierced with a spear and raised over his head.

A few days earlier a sacred fire was lit, and wooden spears were planted around it. A photograph in *The Canberra Times* shows Uncle Kev kneeling in the circle of fire. He is watched by three policemen. The ash on the flag came from the sacred fire, and by smearing ash, Uncle Kev wanted to 'kill the evil spirit of the Federal Government'.

The protests in front of the Old Parliament House had begun a day after the Australia Day celebrations when it emerged that the National Capital Authority and the Federal Government were seriously discussing the fate of the Aboriginal Tent Embassy.

The ash-smeared and speared Australian flag in the raised hand of Uncle Kev fills the whole space of the photograph. Through a gap in the flag one can see in the far background the imposing metallic flagpole with another Australian flag flying high. The two flags, very much like the flags that draped the body of Cathy Freeman – running the winner's lap after the race in the Sydney Olympics – create warps in the space of nationhood they seem to represent. Their co-being within the same visual space of a photograph questions their presence and purpose.

When I look at the photograph of Uncle Kev it reminds me of a photograph of an Aboriginal man that appears on page 194 of Manning Clark's *A Short History of Australia*. The man is sitting on the ground and looking at the newly opened building of the parliament in Canberra. In the photograph I only see his back and a dog sleeping behind him. What catches my eye is his hat and strands of knotty hair. He occupies the foreground of the photograph, and the white building fills the far background corner.

Describing the opening ceremony, Clark writes:

> On that day thirty to forty thousand people gathered outside Parliament House in that small city of undulating plains and open sky to watch the arrival of the Duke and Duchess. As they stood on the tops of the new white building, *Dame Nellie Melba* sang God Save the King. A solitary Aborigine demanded to see the whole plurry show, but as he was deemed to be inadequately clad for the occasion, a policeman led him away.

The photograph does not show the face of the 'solitary Aborigine' and Clark does not tell his name.

An entry in the Register of the National Estate Database of the Australian Heritage Commission, however, notes that 'the first recorded Aboriginal political protest at the site was made during the opening of Parliament House in 1927 by Jimmy Clements (also known by many other names including "King Billy", "King of Canberra", and "King of the Orange Tribe").'

Mark McKenna, in his book *This Country: A Reconciled Republic?*, cites a reporter from *The Argus* in which Clements is described as a 'very old and grey and raggedly picturesque … member of the Gundagai tribe,' and 'a well-known character in the district.' A reporter of *The Canberra Times*, however, refers to him as 'a lone representative of a fast vanishing race,' who had arrived to salute the 'visiting Royalty'.

It is said that a policeman saw Clements and asked him immediately to leave. There is a photograph in the archives of the State Library of New South Wales, which shows Clements escorted by the Policeman. The photograph confirms the raggedly picturesque appearance of Clements, and one can't miss the wry smile on his face. It's the face of a proud man, a voice inside me whispers.

It seems that the crowd had noticed the smile because as McKenna writes, the people

> on the stand immediately and instinctively rallied to his side. There were choruses of advice and encouragement for him to do as he pleased. A well-known clergyman stood up and called out that the Aborigine had a better right than any man present, to a place on the steps of the Parliament in the Senate during the ceremony.

Clements didn't hesitate to show himself on May 10, a day after the opening. A report in *The Argus* stated that 'an ancient aborigine, who calls himself King Billy and who claims sovereign rights to the Federal Territory, walked slowly forward alone, and saluted the Duke and Duchess,' who 'cheerily acknowledge his greeting'.

McKenna writes that *The Argus* also printed a photograph of Clements under the headline 'Demanded his Rights'. The caption to the photograph is equally expressive: 'This is the member of the Gundagai tribe who, as representative of the original Aboriginal owners of the land, was given a prominent place at the historic ceremony in Canberra yesterday. He carried in his right hand a small Australian ensign.'

I want to peer inside the head of Clements to find out what he was thinking that day. Why did he carry an Australian flag? What did he make of the stars of the Southern Cross depicted on it?

I am here, I imagine him thinking. We are here, I hear him whisper, and we won't go away. We won't vanish, try as you may.

Clements was a proud man and so was his companion, John Noble, a Wiradjuri man, who also witnessed the ceremony and who too participated in the protest. Unfortunately, there isn't much known about him except that he and Clements had walked for nearly a week from the Brungle Mission near Gundagai.

Sorry John, I find myself saying. We need to know more about you. We definitely do.

•

In Roberta Sykes's book *Black Majority*, there is a small black and white photograph. Four young black men are standing, two on each side of a beach umbrella planted in the ground in front of the white building of the Old Parliament House. Sykes writes:

> On the evening of January 25, 1972, four black youths took a beach umbrella up to Canberra. As Australia

> Day commenced, they erected the umbrella on the lawn directly opposite, and facing, the Old Parliament House. From the umbrella they hung a sign: Aboriginal Embassy.

The four young men were Billy Craigie, Bert Williams, Michael Anderson and Tony Coorey. Each displayed a placard with simple slogans: LAND Ownership Not LEASE; LAND RIGHTS OR LEASE!; WHICH Do You Choose?? LAND RIGHTS Or BLOODSHED!; LEGALLY THIS IS OUR LAND WE SHALL TAKE IT IF NEED BE. There is a fifth placard resting against the thin plastic tent. It reads: WHY PAY TO USE OUR OWN LAND.

The first Tent Embassy was removed and re-established a number of times in 1972. The police tore it down and the indigenous protestors resurrected it. It was finally dismantled in 1975 when Charles Perkins and the Minister of the Australian Capital Territory negotiated its removal with the protestors. In January 1992, on the day of its twentieth birthday, it was re-established.

The Tent Embassy that began with a small beach umbrella has grown to include sheds, humpies, an informal camping place, and the pavement covered with murals. It now occupies most of the parkland in between the two rose gardens. The two sheds painted with slogans sit in the shadow of the memorial to King George V. One of them houses the office in front of which stands a mail box.

The base of the sandstone pylon of the memorial to King George V carries bronze portrait-plaques one of which is of Sir Henry Parkes. The memorial used to be located at the centre of the parkland, the Parkes Place, along the axis joining the seat of government with the War Memorial but was displaced to its present position in 1968 because it blocked the view to the War Memorial.

Busloads of tourists and school kids come daily to see the Old Parliament House. The buses are parked near the kerb, close to the pavement. Most tourists go to see the white building first. Some do notice the murals and sheds and walk down into the parkland.

Right in the middle of the parkland one can see a humpy-like structure, on both sides of which there are two rows of ceremonial spears. A sacred fire burns near the humpy.

In 1993, a memorial service for Kevin Gilbert was held at the embassy and his ashes were scattered in the Fire for Justice. It is interesting that this humpy-like structure occupies the space that previously housed the memorial to King George V.

The fire, I am told, is burning constantly since 4 February 1998. On the day of the protest, the healing smoke was sent into the white building where the delegates to the Constitutional Convention were meeting. Some call it the Fire for Justice, others the Fire of Peace.

There are public spaces where people gather freely because they have a right to use the place. But there are also spaces which become public, because by gathering there, people assert their right to be there.

The presence of the Aboriginal Tent Embassy within the Parliamentary Triangle creates and defines one of these forcibly acquired public spaces.

Compared to the stoniness of the white building and the copiousness of the New Parliament House on the Capital Hill, it is the frugality and thinness of the Tent Embassy that catches one's eye. If the two Parliament buildings display permanence by way of their sheer bulkiness and by their being built in stone, glass and concrete, the Tent Embassy has become an embodiment of time itself. Like time, it is transient, changing and adapting to its whims and thereby ensuring that it endures.

The politicians and the police remove it, but it reappears again. It has the swiftness and resilience of a nomad. I suspect that it's the nomadic nature of the Tent Embassy, its temporariness, which irritates the town planners and the administrators of the National Capital Authority. It is this that challenges the self-assured status of this nation of colonisers and settlers.

The Tent Embassy is presented and seen as a permanent mark of protest. It celebrates resistance and survival. It's a symbol of Aboriginal self-determination and sovereignty. Some indigenous people see in it the first signs of the emergence of Aboriginal nationhood. It is no coincidence that the Aboriginal flag was conceived and designed here.

•

On 27 January 1999, *The Canberra Times* reported that the Chairman of National Capital Authority Air Marshal, David Evans, considered the Tent Embassy to be 'an eyesore and a blight on the national capital'. He wanted the Embassy to be removed from the site. On 12 August 1999, Ian MacDonald, the Minister for Regional Services, Territories and Local Government, confirmed that the Howard Government was 'looking for alternative arrangements' for the Tent Embassy. In his opinion the Tent Embassy doesn't do justice to the proud history of Aboriginal people. 'The Government is 'very keen to see a more permanent arrangement,' something which will represent the 'best form of recognition'. He was in favour of 'a permanent memorial that all Australians would be proud of,' a memorial that 'might have more reconciliation value'.

Two days later, a report in *The Canberra Times* noted that the representatives of the Tent Embassy had rejected the offer of a 'more permanent monument,' describing it as 'some kind of dead memorial'.

It took almost three years for a permanent memorial to appear in the Parliamentary Triangle. Officially it is described as Reconciliation Place. It is located at the junction of Walter Griffin's land-axis and the pedestrian cross-axes running between the National Library and the High Court of Australia. A grassy mound dominates the landscaped walk dotted with artworks called 'slivers', showing images, text, and sounds highlighting different themes considered important for reconciliation.

I have strolled along the walkway every so often and am surprised by the lack of interest shown by visitors in it. It isn't a dead memorial, but it isn't that lively either. I have looked at the text on the slivers and haven't noticed anything that would remind visitors that it was, once upon the deepest of times, a meeting place and a campsite of the local indigenous peoples.

I am glad that the Tent Embassy continues to thrive at its own site attracting ever more visitors. It has become a place of resistance and resilience. A place created through forcible possession of the public space that also houses the seat of National Government. The forcible occupation of this space, in a strange way, underlines the history of dispossession and displacement of indigenous peoples.

This is the reason I want the Tent Embassy to remain at its current location and remain largely in its present form. Its temporariness is its most powerful attribute.

•

'Hello, my brother,' writes Paul Collis, my friend, a proud Barkindji man, a poet and a writer, but most of all a consummate yarner. 'That tree,' he continues, 'it's a marker tree, that one, a signpost.'

The message is in response to my brief note asking him about a tree on the campus of the University of Canberra; a tree I have walked past a number of times; a tree that makes me stop whenever I come near it, and I stop to look, touch and walk around it, enacting what most Hindus or Buddhists call a *parikrama* or *pradakshina*, a circumambulation, performed around anything that is sacred, in the hope that it will bring peace and consolation. The ritual stipulates that the walk should follow a clockwise direction, keeping the sacred object always to one's right, but for me the left side is as good as the right, and I allow my feet to decide which way they want to walk. And I don't utter a prayer or a chant. I prefer silence. It lets my mind follow the movement my body wishes to enact.

The tree stands alone, atop a little mound on the southern side of a tiny creek, which, once upon a time, would have run into the Ginninderra Creek.

In precolonial times the site was part of the Ginninderra Plain, which spread on both sides of the Ginninderra Creek and was covered by grassland, open woodland, and forest, similar to what used to exist in and around the flood plains of the Molonglo. Only a small patch of the original grassland has survived. It can be found in Lawson, one of the newest suburbs in Canberra, less than a few kilometres north-east of the site with the tree.

Jackson-Nakano mentions that the correct English rendition of the creek's name is 'Ghinnin-ghinnin-derra,' a word which is commonly translated as 'sparkling or throwing out little rays of light'. Peter Rimas Kabaila, a Canberra archaeologist – I particularly like his book *Belconnen's Aboriginal Past* because it has several maps, sketches and photographs – describes the creek the indigenous people in the area would have lived with. Most of the time it wasn't anything more than a chain of ponds, which turned into a rapidly flowing river only when the rains brought floods of water. Then it would have rippled and sparkled, as the name given to it suggests.

Like the Molonglo and the Murrumbidgee, the creek was an important passageway along which indigenous peoples moved, hunting and gathering food in the flood plain and the grassland. The memory of their presence survives in several archaeological sites, one of which has been found on the campus of the University of Canberra. A small ochre site has also been documented at Gossan Hill, located within a few kilometres south-east of the Ginninderra Creek.

In 1974, Ginninderra Lake was constructed in the flood plain of the creek to collect stormwater from its catchment area. Kabaila suggests that some of the sites with possible stone artefacts now lie under the lake water and its landscaped surrounds. Some also appear to be buried under the Belconnen Shopping Mall.

It's a miracle that the lonely tree has survived.

On a topographic map of the area I can spot a blue streak representing a creek, on the southern bank of which the tree, not so lonely then, would have stood. I have walked along the creek, reaching a small swampy patch after which the creek disappears buried under the landscaped ground of John Knight Memorial Park situated near the lakeside. The area surrounding the creek these days supports a small plot of woodland with yellow boxes, and red and brittle gums interspersed with wattles and she-oaks.

A couple of months after receiving Paul's message, we both walk up to the tree to sit near it and yarn about it. 'I remember the words you had written,' I tell him. 'I don't,' he says and laughs. I laugh too, and then read from memory his words:

> That Tree. It's a marker tree, that one, a signpost. That tree is coded in meaning, still standing, though broken. The branch that pointed to the East has fallen from the trunk; a hole, a borough, is what remains of its being. The branch once pointed to the East, to another Marker Tree, that in turn, pointed West to another Marker Tree, that pointed back to this tree, here. The significance of the triangle land within the Marker Trees is that it once held a Ceremonial ground – a sacred space where secrets were revealed to young initiates.

'Did I say all that?' he asks.

'You did, my friend, you certainly did.'

'Sounds like a poem,' he says and smiles.

'And a good poem it is,' I say.

'I agree,' he says after a pause, and begins to speak. I am used to his rasping voice and yet it sounds different; carried by the soft wind, it spreads around us and the tree. He speaks and I listen, keeping my interjections limited to a word here and a word there.

He holds a stick in his hand with which he draws on the rocky ground. They remind me of figures in Tyson Yunkaporta's *Sand Talk*.

I don't tell him that the tree is a yellow box *(Eucalyptus melliodora)*; that it stands between twenty and thirty metres tall; that the spread of its canopy is fifteen to twenty metres wide; that the arborists estimate that it would live for another twenty to fifty years; and that there are trees similar to it in the Canberra region, which are thought to be as old as three hundred years.

I also don't show him the topographic map of the area I have brought in my bag. All of what I know and carry with me seems superfluous, nothing other than white noise.

He soon draws a map on the ground. On it I see the creek, the lake and the triangle of an ancient ceremonial ground on one side of which stands the tree, the sole surviving witness of the sacred ceremonies.

He sits with the stick and watches me get up and walk around the tree. I pause near the carved surface on the trunk and touch its bark. A much older but similar piece of bark was used to fashion a coolamon to carry food, ochre, or perhaps a young baby. I imagine the coolamon travelling far and wide from the ceremonial place where now stands the lonely tree. With it travelled the baby carried by his or her mother, listening to songs and stories. The tree remained at the site but part of it travelled too. 'Like *warabin*, the curlew,' my mind whispers.

‘That tree, my brother,’ Paul speaks as we say goodbye to each other, ‘is in me and in you and, I hope, I am in it and so are you.’

I hope too, I want to say but keep quiet, I don’t know why.

•

One day in early September 2021, my wife Hanna and I set out for a long walk in the Aranda Bushland. This is one of her favourite walks, a bit long for me but I manage it by opting for a not-too-hurried pace and she obliges. The slow pace suits us, because it helps us to look and listen. She is more interested in plants and animals whereas I find it hard to ignore rocks and rubble.

It is a bright early-spring day and the mid-morning sun is generous, the breeze soft and not too harsh for my asthmatic lungs.

We begin at the track we have started calling the orchid trail because in the last couple of years, beginning in late September, several types of orchids have started appearing on the grassy patches along it. They continue to flower for almost eight to ten weeks and then disappear. We know it is a little early to look for them, and yet we can’t stop ourselves and, perhaps because we are so keen, a couple of nodding greenhoods reveal themselves. They aren’t the prettiest of orchids, but their arrival assures us that soon the more eye-catching ones will follow.

The orchid trail leads us to a creek which begins on the western slope of the Black Mountain and makes its way under the bridge on the Parkway. The rain in the past few years has made the creek lively with water clattering over the rocks and pebbles. It's the water and a thick canopy of trees that attract smaller birds to this place, and this is where we often stop to listen and watch noisy tree creepers, honey eaters, thornbills and my favourite, the eastern spine bills. Last year we saw a pair of mistletoe birds here. The scarlet throat of one of them sparkled.

We cross the creek, walk through an opening in the fence of an old farm, and come up to an outcrop of thick sandstones spread like a small amphitheatre. These sandstones were formed more than 440 million years ago when the area was under sea water. Standing on the sandstones one can see the creek curling around them. It is shallower and wider and appears sedate, almost pensive.

There is a track along the left side of the creek that leads to a swampy patch, the drier parts of which are covered in grass where kangaroos often gather.

Overlooking the patch is a little hill with red boxes, gums, and red stringybarks with an understorey of grasses, shrubs and herbs. Hanna loves the shrubs and herbs. One of her favourites is *Chrysocephalum apiculatum* or yellow buttons. There is a cluster growing on the rocky slope, not far from the uprooted trunk of a red box. One of them is almost half a metre tall and is flowering more lavishly than the rest. Its round, almost button-like yellow flowers – clustered as bouquets topping the long, thin stems – shine and nod.

A flock of choughs is foraging in the leaf litter, moving slowly up the slope. The litter creaks and crackles and then suddenly a branch falls off a brittle gum. Startled, the choughs break into a short, thrifty flight, exposing white patches under their wings.

The hill is just a little bump, less than twenty or thirty metres higher than the surrounding woodland and grassland. On its western and eastern sides run two creeks fed by the runoff from the Black Mountain and the hill itself. The runoff is small and intermittent, but it's enough to create and sustain a lush, swampy wetland. The two creeks run south and join a much larger one: the Black Mountain Creek that cuts through the grassland. The creek used to drain into the Molonglo where it formed a broad meandering bend, which these days has become part of the western basin of Lake Burley Griffin.

On the southern side of the hill is a patch of very old red gums. A few years ago, we found an injured kangaroo lying under one of them. Its left hip was broken, and its right arm was hanging limp. We had to call a park ranger, who arrived in less than half an hour. The ranger asked us to leave and as we were walking away, we heard a muffled shot. We turned to look and saw the ranger drive off with the dead animal.

There is a small, clean and clipped, patch of grassy land fifty or so metres to the east of the red gums. It sits surrounded by tall gums and stringybarks. The site is just a few steps away from the western bank of the creek that runs along the eastern side of the hill. Was it a meeting or a camping ground, we wonder each time we walk past it. Perhaps it was, because archaeological surveys in the Aranda Bushland have revealed several indigenous heritage sites containing various types of ancient artefacts.

The grassland and the woodland near the Black Mountain Creek would have been ideal for hunting and gathering food.

The grasslands also contain the snow gums, and the two are now included in the list of heritage sites in Canberra. Amongst the many snow gums which line the southern bank of the Black Mountain Creek, there is one snow gum that Hanna is very fond of. It's one of the largest and perhaps the oldest on the patch. Near it lies the trunk of a fallen tree. The snow gum has one solid trunk with branches spread out wide. The canopy isn't dense and yet we often see a few kangaroos resting in its sparse shade. One of its branches has dried out and will break off and fall in the coming years. This is the branch Hanna often hugs.

From here we start the return loop on the walking trail, which takes us through the Aranda Bushland. On the way we pass a few large yellow boxes and red gums, in the shadows of which squat carved wooden benches a Canberra sculptor had fashioned from the fallen trunks.

On the way back we stop near the triangulation marker planted near the spine of the Aranda Hill. This is the highest point on the spine. Not far from the triangulation mark is a bench where I usually sit to catch my breath or to do some stretching exercises.

The view opening to the south from here isn't as panoramic as the one from the Black Mountain, but it still provides a decent opening to the lake and the Scrivener Dam, just beyond which one can glimpse a hazy outline of the Molonglo.

There are noisy cockatoos nesting in the hollows of the scribbly gums. They screech loudly when they see us whereas the rosellas don't bother.

Last year at this very spot I watched a hungry currawong swoop on a bearded dragon sunning on the hollowed trunk of a fallen stringybark. Luckily for the dragon, the currawong wasn't quick, and the dragon managed to scurry inside the trunk. The currawong didn't wait long and flew off to try its luck elsewhere.

•

Hanna's favourite walk is on the Black Mountain. It loops around the summit. I have tracked along it several times but lately it has become harder for me. The path to reach the start of the walk, located close to the summit, exhausts me. These days, I look at the joggers, young and sometimes older than me, with envy. They run up the cemented path oozing health and stamina as I watch them, sitting on the side. Slowly I am getting used to the idea that I should reconcile with my predicament and tell my mind to listen to the rhythms of my tired body.

On a track near the Little Black Mountain Loop there is a creek with steep banks. Only once or twice in the last few years I have seen it gushing with rainwater. Most of the time it is dry. On the banks on each side grow large red stringybarks and scribbly gums. The rain has caused erosion and the wind brings some of them down and there is one, the fallen trunk of which lies across the creek like a bridge. Every so often I stop to look at the massive trunk. It lies uprooted and yet life around and inside it continues. Such trees don't die; they just disperse and dissipate slowly and gracefully.

'One day,' I tell Hanna, 'I'll get on top of the trunk and walk across to the other side.'

'You can if you want,' she replies, 'but stupid it would be, very stupid.'

If I slip, I'll fall two or more metres down, I estimate standing near it. Yes, it would be stupid and yet the child in me is lured by the dare.

Unfortunately, the walk in the Aranda Bushland turned out to be the last we would do together. The long trek aggravated pain in my lower back caused by pinched nerves from a bulge in the spine. The surgery, I am told, will help but I won't reach the fitness level I had enjoyed previously. The numbness in my legs and feet worries me, and my stiff ankles hurt.

Hanna walks alone these days and tells me of the plants, birds and reptiles she comes across. She shows me their photographs and complains about her failure to take a good photograph of a swamp wallaby she frequently meets. She loves watching the shy and solitary creature.

On my tablet I track her route and imagine myself tottering behind her.

We are happy that we live in Aranda in a house within a few steps of the bushland. The isolation imposed on us by the dreadful coronavirus has become more tolerable because of the forest and the woodland.

The house seems like a refuge from the virus and the illnesses we have been forced to live with. Perhaps this is the reason I have started feeling, albeit hesitantly, at home here.

It is a happy coincidence that Aranda, the suburb we live in, is named after the indigenous peoples in Central Australia. The entry in the database of the ACT Government states:

> The name of the Division of Aranda was gazetted in 1967 following a recommendation by then Senator John Gorton in 1964, who at the time was the leader of the government in the Senate and a member of the National Memorials Committee. In 1964 Senator Gorton put forward a suggestion to name Canberra suburbs to recognize the names of Aboriginal cultural groups, including 'Arunta' and 'Warramunga'.

The note also explains the significance of the name and how it should be pronounced:

> Name of an Aboriginal cultural group of Central Australia, also Arrernte and Arunta (say 'aruhnduh'). The Arrernte people of Central Australia around Alice Springs, extending from the vicinity of the Finke River in the west to the Simpson Desert in the east. The name Arrernte covers several groups, including Eastern and Western Arrernte, with some dialect variation even within these groups.

Our house is located on Noala Street. The AustLang database curated by AIATSIS states that 'Noala' is the name of the indigenous peoples in Western Australia who lived in the 'coastal plain from about Cape Preston near the mouth of Fortescue River south-west in a strip about 40 miles (65 km) wide to a line running south from Onslow, but not extending to the Ashburton River, which is held by the Talandji.' One of the alternative names for them is Nhuwala, which I like more, because of the whispering sound the word makes.

To reach our street one has to follow Bandjalong Crescent and turn onto Wangara Street.

All streets and place names in the suburb are derived from the names of indigenous peoples. As a result, a stroll in the suburb turns into a traverse on the map of indigenous geography and place-making. On my walks, I like whispering these names and carry the sounds with me, but the pleasure I get from uttering these words is always tainted with grief, for I know that the place I want to feel at home in has been stolen from the indigenous inhabitants of this land.

Mikhail Sholokhov, the Soviet-Russian writer, called the river Don, *tikhii*, quiet, because he wanted us to feel that it mourns the dead who perished in the Russian Civil War that followed the October Revolution in 1917. But it also mourns the millions, I want to tell him, who died in Stalin's famine the Ukrainians call the Holodomor, and whose stories he forgot to tell in his novels.

The rivers like the Don appear to us quiet because we fail to hear the stories they want to tell.

The Molonglo that I have come to know is not quiet. Like the Don, it mourns, but it also celebrates the resilience of indigenous peoples, their will to survive, and their determination to flower and flourish.

Listen to the Molonglo, I say to myself. Listen to the people, plants, and animals who live with it. Listen to the rocks, pebbles, gravels, and the sand which it exists in communion with.

Listen and feel. Feel and reflect. Reflect and speak.

Perhaps then, the story you want to tell will find its place in the endless symposium of voices.

Perhaps.

The Windmills of Miguel Cervantes

In the last week of March 2005 I caught a train from Madrid's Atocha railway station to go to Campo de Criptana to see the windmills Don Quixote had battled. To him, they had appeared like ominous giants a knight errant is obliged to fight and kill. Why? What was so menacing about them?

That day, I had to abandon the trip because of an accident on the railway track; the train I was travelling in had run over an old man, killing him instantly. 'A suicide,' I heard distraught passengers saying to each other.

After a delay of four hours the train was allowed to move, but I had already lost most of the day and I didn't want to stay overnight in Campo de Criptana. Therefore, I got out at the next station and found a train going back to Madrid. On the following day I boarded an early morning train and this time I arrived at my destination without any problem.

It was a nice sunny day, soft and warm. 'The spring this year is early,' I was told by the receptionist at the hotel in Madrid. 'It's the right time to go to Campo,' she said, 'because the summer in Spain is generally very hot and the light too bright to look at the white windmills.'

The train was slow, and it took almost two hours to reach Campo de Criptana. As the train approached the town, I got a glimpse of the stumpy Sierra de los Molinos, the hill on top of which stand the windmills. On the little map I had of the town, the hill is located on its northern end. At the station, Jorge, a young man at a kiosk, told me that the hill wasn't far and that I should be able to walk to the place in less than half an hour. He came out of the kiosk and pointed to me the shortest route to the hill.

I followed his instructions and after crossing the main street in the town I found myself near Plaza del Pozo Hondo, a small square with a park. There I saw a street called Calle Cervantes. It's most befitting, I thought, that a street named after Cervantes should lead me to the windmills. I walked on the footpath of the street looking at the brick and stone houses, some with white-washed walls, mostly single or double storeyed. Some had little balconies with iron railings. What caught my attention were the deep blue frames of doors and windows. The lower halves of the walls in some houses were also painted blue or bright green.

I stopped at a little café and ordered a cup of coffee. The young girl who brought me the coffee was surprised that I didn't want sugar. She offered me a little chocolate biscuit shaped like a windmill which I couldn't decline. She smiled, watching me looking at the map and waited to see if I wanted to ask her anything about her town. She was learning English at the local college, she told me, and therefore was keen to talk.

I stepped out of the café and after walking for ten or so minutes came out at Calle Don Quijote, a street celebrating the Knight of the Sorrowful Face. Standing on the street I saw at its far, northern end one of the windmills with its black sails looking in my direction. As I was about to put the map back in my bag, I noticed that a street running almost parallel to it was called Calle Dulcinea, named after the knight's beloved lady. A narrow lane off Calle Don Quijote led me to Calle Dulcinea. The hill with the windmills was also visible from there. I strode along Calle Dulcinea, side-stepping rubbish scattered around upturned bins, and after reaching the intersection with Calle Don Quijote, followed a little bend and stopped. I had arrived at the stumpy hill. On its top stood Molino de Viento Sardinero, the Windmill of Sardinero.

There used to be a cave at the foot of the limestone hill. Nowadays, Cueva la Despensa hosts a museum displaying the humble interior of the house of a seventeenth-century miller. I went up to the entrance, crossing an area paved with cobble stones and discovered that the museum was temporarily shut for renovations.

There are ten large windmills on the hill. One of them serves as the office of the local tourist bureau.

I spent most of the day exploring the hill and the windmills. One of the dirt tracks on the hills is named after Don Quixote's loyal workhorse Rocinante. Next to it is Calle Barbero; it honours the fictional barber in the book who spots in Don Quixote's library a copy of *La Galatea*, the first published novel of Cervantes.

In the evening I returned to the railway station wandering along Calle Sancho Panza. I was disappointed that it was one of the narrowest and shabbiest lanes in the town, but a few minutes later in Plaza Mayor I discovered the very impressive Hostal Sancho. In the square, not far from the hotel, on a slab of grey granite sits a bronze Cervantes. I went around the statue a couple of times and noticed embedded in the granite a scroll-shaped copper sheet scribbled with Sancho Panza's words, warning the valiant knight about the windmills: 'those things that appear over there aren't giants but windmills, and what looks like their arms are the sails that are turned by the wind and make the grindstone move.'

On the train back to Madrid that evening I played the Spanish audio recording of the windmill story on my Akai walkman. The raspy, rustic voice of the narrator was quite close to what I had imagined Sancho Panza, the peasant-squire, would have had. He read and I listened. His voice riding over the rhythmic rattle of wheels. I liked the voice. It made me feel at home just because it seemed to me the voice of a friend from my childhood.

•

The inside cover of Vladimir Nabokov's *Lectures on Don Quixote* shows the drawing of a windmill that Nabokov sketched for his students at Harvard University. Guy Davenport notes in the foreword to the book that Nabokov was keen to show his students the look of a real windmill. He drew quite a decent sketch on the blackboard, labelling each part carefully, intending to explain 'why a country gentleman might mistake them for giants'. After all, 'they were an innovation in seventeenth-century Spain, the last country to hear of anything new in all Europe.'

Nabokov's lectures were held in the grand Memorial Hall of the university in the spring semester of the academic year 1951–52. Nabokov worked hard on these lectures about a book he wasn't particularly fond of. Diligence and hard work paid off. The main beneficiaries were 'the 600 young strangers' but Nabokov too rediscovered the book. The students heard about the book and also about the way books like these have to be read. The pleasure was mutual, and it seems Nabokov didn't forget the occasion. He talked about the lectures in an interview with Herbert Gold in 1966. 'I remember with delight,' Davenport quotes Nabokov telling Gold, 'tearing apart Don Quixote, a cruel and old book, before six hundred students in Memorial Hall, much to the horror and embarrassment of some of my more conservative colleagues.'

I have read Nabokov's book on *Don Quixote* in English and in Russian translation and I agree with Davenport that Nabokov did 'tear it apart for good critical reasons but he also put it back together'.

Davenport sees Nabokov's reading as 'an event in modern criticism'. Nabokov deconstructed the book many years before the term itself was coined and reconstructed it with the love and care of an empathetic reader, critic, and a writer. The final paragraph of Nabokov's conclusion says it all:

> We are confronted by an interesting phenomenon: a literary hero losing gradually contact with the book that bore him; leaving his fatherland, leaving his creator's desk and roaming space after roaming Spain. As a result, *Don Quixote* is greater today than he was in Cervantes's womb. He has ridden for three hundred and fifty years through the jungles and tundras of human thought – and has gained vitality and stature. We do not laugh at him any longer. His blazon is pity, his banner is beauty. He stands for everything that is gentle, forlorn, pure, unselfish, and gallant. The parody has become a paragon.

Nabokov warns his students 'to avoid the fatal error of looking for so-called real life in novels. *Don Quixote* is a fairy tale, so is *Bleak House*, so is *Dead Souls*. *Madame Bovary* and *Anna Karenina* are supreme fairy tales.' But they aren't ordinary fairy tales because without them 'the world would not be real.' 'A masterpiece of fiction,' he adds, 'is an original world and as such is not likely to fit the world of the reader.'

Nabokov explores this original world of *Don Quixote*, aiming to clear some age-long misconceptions about the book. He wants his students to understand the world of the book in its totality and therefore focuses on its time and place, its narrative structure and its subtle consonances with Shakespearean texts and characters. In the later parts of his book he even analyses individual episodes, counting the number of wins and losses endured by the knight errant in his battles. He wants to tell his students that the belief that Don Quixote received drubbing in all his contests is misplaced, because in both part 1 and part 2 of *Don Quixote* the score between wins and losses is equal. There is no need to pity the Knight of the Sorrowful Face, I hear Nabokov say. But I do and this is because I look at Don Quixote through the eyes of Sancho Panza, the poor farmer who easily lets himself be persuaded to become Don Quixote's squire.

'There is not much to say for Sancho,' Nabokov writes in his concluding remarks. 'He exists only insofar as his master does. An actor of the roly-poly school can impersonate him easily and improve on the comedy.' He reminds us that Cervantes called Sancho Panza 'the pig belly on crane legs'. I know Nabokov is right and although I am dismayed, my enthusiasm for this 'rogue', 'clown' and 'tramp' doesn't diminish.

My disappointment about the treatment meted out to Sancho Panza is somewhat assuaged as soon as I see a map of Spain that Nabokov must have also sketched for his students. I love maps, and for me the reading of books can't proceed without looking at the maps of places imagined in them. They make travelling to and through those places easy and exciting.

It is a proper map that Nabokov has drawn. It has latitudes marked on it and they seem to be correct. He even shows Africa to the south, the continent from which the moors had come to Spain; the same moors without whom *Don Quixote* wouldn't have been written or would have been a different book, not the classic we read now. Nabokov intended to show his students that Cervantes was 'no land surveyor,' and his 'ignorance of places is wholesale and absolute'. That is why 'Don Quixote's excursions topographically present us as a ghastly muddle,' with 'a mass of monstrous inaccuracies at every step,' so much so that in the rambles of the knight and his squire in central Spain 'across four or six provinces, in the course of which until we reach Barcelona in the northeast one does not meet with a single known town or cross a single river.'

I don't blame Nabokov for nit-picking because his purpose is clear: he wishes to tell his students that there is little association between the story in the book and the 'real' geographical world in which it unfolds. Each road is just a road and an inn an inn; they are just backdrops for adventures to unfold.

One of the last adventures in the book is the duel between Don Quixote, the Knight of the Sorrowful Face, and Carrasco, the Knight of the Moonlike Mirrors, the mediocre usurper. The loss in the duel shakes up Don Quixote physically and emotionally and he decides to give up the role of the knight errant and changes back to Alonso Quexana, 'the fifty-year old gentleman with weathered complexion, scrawny flesh, and gaunt face'. The transformation proves fatal and after a few days the Ingenious Hidalgo of La Mancha passes away.

•

Historical records show that in the seventeenth century, Campo de Criptana, a small town in the region of Castile-La Mancha, had a population of four to five thousand. Unlike most towns in the area, which were settled on relatively flatter terrain, Campo de Criptana grew around a stumpy hill.

It is believed that the technology of windmills was introduced in the region in the twelfth century either by crusaders returning from Jerusalem or by Arabic settlers a few centuries later. The records in the Registry of the Marquis of Ensenada show that in the middle of the eighteenth century there were at least thirty-four windmills in the town. The possible contribution of Moorish settlers is supported by the presence of Albaicín Criptano, the Moorish Quarter, in the north-eastern part of the town, adjacent to the foothill area. This was the ancient centre of the village. Its network of narrow streets, historians suggest, is quite similar to Moorish towns and villages in Granada.

On my trip to Campo de Criptana I had walked along the streets of the Moorish Quarters. These days some of them have been renamed after the characters in

Cervantes's book. Calle Rocinante is one of them. It's quite likely that Cervantes had visited the seventeenth-century town because the number of windmills he mentions in the windmill story is similar to the one the historians have found in the old records. 'As they were walking,' writes Cervantes, 'they saw thirty or forty of the windmills in that countryside.'

Most windmills were owned and run by relatively poor millers. However, there were some that belonged to relatively rich people. The Infanto was one of them. Its owners rented it to poorer millers.

The millers had to be physically able to carry sacks of thirty kilograms or more. However, most people described them as rude and arrogant. Some were notorious for being outright rogues and thieves because they cheated customers and stole grain or flour. 'There are twenty-five windmills on the hill,' people often said, 'and twenty-five thieves who walk around it.'

Of the ten windmills standing on the hill now, there are three – Burleta, Infanto and Sardinero – that have been restored to their original seventeenth-century structure. The other seven have been turned into museums and galleries.

I remember going inside Burleta to learn about the way a miller's family lived and worked in the windmill. The interior of the windmill is made of three floors connected by a wooden stairway spiralling along the wall. The ground floor is called the stable. It's where the sacks of grain and flour are stored. The first floor forms the cabin where flour is sifted, and the second floor houses the grinding machinery.

The masonry wall of the windmill is generally whitewashed. The white colour reduces the summer heat. It also adds presence to the mills. One can spot them from quite a distance, standing tall on top of hills brandishing their dark sails.

The main cylindrical body of the windmill is topped by a conical wooden capping which is turned with the help of a sixteen-metre-long wooden plank called *the governor*. With the capping, the sails mounted on a shaft are rotated to match the prevailing wind direction. I asked Jordi, the guide, about the twelve small windows I had seen in the wall. They were placed just below the rotating cap. 'They match the twelve directions,' I was told. 'The miller uses them as a guide to turn the governor.'

In addition to the shaft and the main gear wheel, the sails are the most important part of a windmill. They are fashioned from cloth or tarp mounted on wooden frames. The ones on Burleta were close to eight metres in length. The whole windmill is ten to twelve metres in height and the sails attached to its top half make it appear even taller. Standing outside Burleta, I tried to move the governor and realised that it would need at least two more people of my size. 'Don't worry,' Jordi said, 'even I can't shift it.' And he was younger and much stronger than me.

We walked around Burleta, admiring the impressive sight of other windmills on the hill.

'Do they really look like giants to you?' I asked him. 'Yes,' he said, 'especially at night when the moon is nothing more than a tiny sickle, and when I have one too many glasses of local wine.' He laughed and then after a pause said, 'To me they always appear elegant and pretty like Don Quixote's Dulcinea.'

'Really?'

'Why don't you check it out yourself?' he said to me. 'I can organise a donkey for you, and you can ride on it like your friend Sancho Panza and find out.' I smiled and said that I would prefer a bike. 'Excelente!' he said. 'You are welcome to have mine.' I saw a pushbike standing near the governor of Burleta. 'Pásalo bien, have fun!' he said, watching me get on the bike and ride off.

I peddled on a track along the spine of the hill for a kilometre and a half and turned around to cycle back, keeping my sight focused on the windmills. There was wind blowing behind me, helping me to ride upslope. I watched the sails on Burleta turn, emitting the whirring sound made by the cloth that flapped and fluttered. I got off the bike after reaching Burleta and was pleased that Jordi was busy with a group of Chinese tourists, for I wasn't sure if my experiment on the bike had given me new insight into the mind of Cervantes's Knight Errant.

To enter the mind of the Knight I'll have to ask Sancho Panza, my friend, to leave me alone for a while, and that's not going to be easy.

•

On my seventh birthday my mother gave me a *gullak*, a piggy bank. It was the shape of a monkey, with a slot in its head. At the back it had a lid with a little key. She shut the lid and put away the key. She wanted me to save part of my pocket money. After a year she opened it and gave me the savings.

I used the money to buy my first book, *The Adventures of Don Quixote of La Mancha*. The large hardback was a picture book with colour plates and drawings. The text was brief, easy to read and understand. Years later I would discover that it was an abridged and simplified edition of a much larger book.

My first book had stories of two adventures of Don Quixote and one of them was about the windmills. Often, I would read the story in English and do a quick Hindi translation for my *Massi*, my aunt, the younger sister of my mother. She was only a few years older than me and liked listening to my retelling of the story. She was surprised that I liked Sancho Panza more than the Knight because to her the valiant Knight was sad but enchanting. To convince her I would show her the picture of Sancho Panza seated luxuriously on his donkey, but she would laugh saying that I was utterly silly. Perhaps I was but wasn't the knight silly too?

Jorge Luis Borges, the Argentinian writer and philosopher, would also call my fondness for Sancho Panza silly. Borges doesn't find him believable which is quite the opposite of what I feel. 'I am not sure that I can quite believe in Sancho,' he writes, 'as I believe in

Don Quixote. For sometimes I feel, I think of Sancho as a mere foil to Don Quixote.'

I believe in both Don Quixote and Sancho Panza and I am certain Cervantes believed in them too. The so-called madness of Don Quixote is real and believable. Harold Bloom in his introduction to Edith Grossman's English translation of the book notes that 'Don Quixote and Sancho really listen to each other and change through this receptivity.' Their conversation is always engaging and funny, and Don Quixote never forgets to compliment his squire. Sancho isn't a foil but a friend. 'The friendship between Sancho Panza and the Knight,' notes Bloom, 'surpasses any other in literary representation.' I feel vindicated by Bloom's assessment. I haven't wasted my time, I tell myself, by coming to know them both, and if I find Sancho Panza more endearing it is mainly because he entered my life when I was seven and therefore I consider him my childhood friend.

Since my first encounter with the book almost sixty years ago I have read Cervantes' book several times. I have with me two different English translations, and I have also read the book in Russian, Punjabi, Hindi, and Spanish. In a way I have grown up with the book and the book has grown with me, spilling outside its hard and soft covers.

The book has led me to other books and writers, poets, artists, and performers, one of which is the Belgian writer Charles de Coster whose book, *The*

Legend of Thyl Ulenspiegel and Lamme Goedzak I had read in Russian translation in 1974. De Coster published the book in 1867, and his legendry hero Thyl Ulenspiegel is based on the fourteen-century German folklore character Till Eulenspiegel. In De Coster's clever retelling the folklore hero is turned into a Flemish prankster, miscreant, and rebel rallying against the despotic foreign rule and equally ruthless and dogmatic Church. Thyl Ulenspiegel is vaguely similar to Don Quixote but his companion Lamme Goedzak is nothing but a literary twin of Sancho Panza.

I have recently discovered that there exists a Sanskrit translation of the book. It was commissioned by Carl Tilden Keller, an American businessman and book collector, and was translated by two Kashmiri pandits in 1935. One of the translators, Nityanand Shastri was paralysed by a stroke and asked another pandit, Jagaddhar Zadoo, for assistance. None of the two knew Spanish and therefore relied on an English translation done in the eighteenth century by Irish writer and painter Charles Jarvis. It took them two years to finish the project.

The translated book contains only eight chapters of Part 1, which disappoints me, but I am pleased that it does include my favourite episode, that of the windmills.

That one of the translators was paralysed and still continued his work sounds no less courageous than the bravery displayed by Cervantes's Knight Errant. And like the knight, the pandit had found himself a worthy squire in Jagaddhar Zadoo.

Borges is correct when he suggests that 'some English translators have gone wrong when they translate *El ingenioso hidalgo don Quijote de la Mancha* as *The Ingenious Knight: Don Quixote de la Mancha*, because the words "knight" and "Don" go together.' He doesn't want to emphasise the knight-ness of Don Quixote, and therefore, prefers to call him 'The Ingenious Country Gentleman'. Grossman in her translation agrees with Borges. Although the title on the front cover of her book is *Don Quixote*, the one that appears just before the prologue is similar to that which Borges prefers: *The Ingenious Gentleman Don Quixote of La Mancha.* John Rutherford's translation follows the same recipe. He also starts with the shortened *Don Quixote* on the cover page and complements it by the full title inside: *The Ingenious Hidalgo Don Quixote de La Mancha.*

I like the word 'ingenious'. My English thesaurus lists several synonyms of the word: resourceful, original, inventive, creative, nifty, inspired, imaginative, effective, and cunning. They all describe Don Quixote well. The only exception is 'cunning'. Don Quixote isn't cunning but Sancho Panza, my friend, is.

•

Cervantes begins the first part of the book by introducing his hero, the ingenious hidalgo of La Mancha:

> Somewhere in La Mancha, in a place whose name I don't care to remember, a gentleman lived long ago …. Our gentleman was approximately fifty years old; his complexion was weathered, his flesh scrawny, his face gaunt, and he was an early riser and a great lover of the hunt. Some claim that his family name was Quixada, or Quexada, for there is a certain amount of disagreement among the authors who write of this matter, although reliable conjecture seems to indicate that his name was Quexana.

I smile as I read the opening lines because I know that Cervantes, the narrator, is playing games with us. His description of the gentleman's appearance is precise, but he is uncertain about his name and age. He also doesn't want to tell us the village or town in La Mancha where he lives. Cervantes is accurate about certain things but vague about others. His intention is to keep us hoping that he might tell us more some time later.

Cervantes informs us that this gentleman from La Mancha was so caught up in the reading of books of chivalrous acts performed by knights errant 'that his brains dried up, causing him to lose his mind'. And so, either completely insane or stirred by the weird world of his imagination or perhaps both, he decides to become a knight errant himself.

The first step in this transformation is to rename his horse Rocinante, a name which suggests that the horse is nothing other than an old workhorse. The gentleman then takes another eight days to find an appropriate name for himself, settling for Quixote, which sounds similar to Quexana or Quexada, his own name.

As all knights errant have beloved ladies, he decides to rename Aldonza Lorenzo, 'an attractive peasant girl with whom he had once been in love,' Dulcinea of Toboso. The renamed lady Dulcinea (the word dulce means 'sweet') is a figment of his imagination and the real Aldonza isn't aware of the cherished place she has found inside the fertile mind of the knight errant.

Names and naming are important for Cervantes and he spends a fair amount of time and imagination in selecting them for most of his characters. The only exception is Sancho Panza who appears in chapter VII of the first part, and only after Don Quixote has undertaken his first brief sally.

If the introduction of Sancho Panza was indeed an afterthought, as suggested by Rutherford, it turns out to be a master stroke because his appearance alters the structure of the story by 'opening the way to conversations that alternate with action'. Cervantes deploys these exchanges as a device to delay, suspend or terminate action. Often the knight errant and his squire talk and tease like good friends and learn from each other. As the story unfolds 'the two clowns,' according to Rutherford, 'soon start to develop, as does the relationship between them, [and they] gain depth and complexity'. The pair turns into a 'sane madman and a wise fool'.

Cervantes was very proud of having created Sancho Panza. In the prologue of the first part he confesses:

> I do not want to charge you too much for the service I have performed in introducing you to so noble and honourable knight; but I do want you to thank me for allowing you to make the acquaintance of the famous Sancho Panza, his squire, in whom, in my opinion I have summarized for you all squirely wit and charm scattered throughout the great mass of inane books of chivalry.

Cervantes introduces his favourite character without much fanfare. After all he is just a poor peasant, a rough diamond whose brilliance is fashioned and revealed gradually:

> Don Quixote approached a farmer who was a neighbour of his, a good man – if that title can be given to someone who is poor – but without much of brains. In short, he told him so much, and persuaded and promised him so much, that the poor peasant resolved to go off with him and serve as his squire. Among other things, Don Quixote said that he should prepare to go with him gladly because it might happen that one day he would have an adventure that would gain him, in the blink of an eye, an *ínsula*, and he would make him its governor. With these promises and others like them Sancho Panza, for that was the

> farmer's name, left his wife and children and agreed to be his neighbour's squire.

Once again, I find Cervantes vague, evasive. He says that Don Quixote made many promises but doesn't elaborate. He just mentions one, confident that it would be more than enough to entice a poor peasant. The fact that Sancho Panza, on several occasions, reminds Don Quixote of the promise made to him convinces me that he doubts whether the knight errant is sane enough to keep his word.

After selecting his squire, Don Quixote doesn't honour him with a new name. He is happy with the peasant's original name although Cervantes later suggests that the peasant might have had one other name.

Cervantes reveals the second name when he comes across an Arabic book in the Alacaná market in Toledo. The book has a title similar to that of his own book, the one I am reading. The book *History of Don Quixote of La Mancha* is written by Cide Hamete Benengeli, an Arab historian. With the help of a Morisco, a Moor who had been converted to Christianity, Cervantes is able to read a Castilian translation of the text. The Arabic book carries life-like illustrations, one of which is of the squire:

> Next to him was Sancho Panza, holding the halter of his donkey, and at its feet was another caption that said: Sancho Zancas, and as the picture showed, he must have had a big belly, short stature, and long

> shanks, and for this reason he was given the name Panza as well as Zancas, for from time to time the history calls him by both these names.

Sancho Panza is a man with a big belly whereas Sancho Zancas is one with long shanks. It's quite likely they are the same person: a poor peasant with a large belly and long shanks. This is how he is portrayed in most illustrations and sculptures, and this is how I saw him in the first abridged addition of the book I had read in my childhood.

After convincing Sancho Panza to become his squire, Don Quixote can't decide if he should get a horse for him. He postpones the decision, hoping that he would be able to 'obtain an honourable mount for him at the earliest opportunity by appropriating the horse of the first discourteous knight he happened to meet'.

Don Quixote doesn't say anything to Sancho Panza about his intention most probably because he doesn't want to raise his squire's expectations, and this turns out to be a good decision because the opportunity to secure a horse from a discourteous knight doesn't arise and his squire, against all the conventions in the books of chivalry, has to make do with a donkey, 'on the back of which he rides like a patriarch, with his saddlebags and his wineskin, and a great desire to see himself governor of the ínsula his master had promised him'.

Don Quixote is pleased to see his squire happy on his dapple and when Sancho Panza reminds his master, the knight errant, of the promise to make him the governor of an island, Señor Knight Errant begins his reply by addressing his squire as his friend, which pleases the squire as well. And thus they ride, the pair of happy friends, Don Quixote on Rocinante followed by Sancho Panza on his donkey, trotting on the track that would lead them to the windmills.

Cervantes must have known that without Sancho Panza this episode wouldn't work. He needed Sancho Panza's eyes and voice to add humour and pathos to the story. The effect is dazzling. With the invention of Sancho Panza, Cervantes fashions a successful template for other adventures and gradually his presence and intervention become more emphatic, so much so that one starts to feel that the driving force behind the adventures isn't the knight errant but this worldly-wise fool.

I am grateful to Franz Kafka for revealing this uncanny aspect of the relationship between Don Quixote and his squire. I had read *The Truth about Sancho Panza*, one of his very short stories, many years ago and it's quite likely that it remained lodged in my memory, whispering to me about the significance of the unseen that lurks behind what is so immediately visible to us.

Bloom mentions Kafka's story as well and notes that 'to Kafka, Don Quixote was Sancho Panza's daemon or genius who led him unto his death'.

Kafka's suggestion in his story about the reversal of roles between the knight errant and his squire is radical:

> Without making any boast of it Sancho Panza succeeded in the course of years, by devouring a great number of romances of chivalry and adventure in the evening and night hours, in so diverting from him his demon, whom he later called Don Quixote, that his demon thereupon set out in perfect freedom on the maddest exploits, which, however, for the lack of a preordained object, which should have been Sancho Panza himself, harmed nobody. A free man, Sancho Panza philosophically followed Don Quixote on his crusades, perhaps out of a sense of responsibility, and had of them a great and edifying entertainment to the end of his days.

Kafka's story makes me think that Sancho Panza isn't a mere hapless squire, but a spectator the knight errant needs to perform for. He is one of the most important witnesses of Don Quixote, a potential chronicler of his combats and valiant deeds. This could be the reason why Don Quixote ignores his squire's warnings and launches head on into battles. To appear cowardly before Sancho Panza isn't acceptable to him. Like all performers, Don Quixote needs him because without a viewer no performance is complete.

Don Quixote, by opting to have a squire to accompany him on his sallies, hands over power to him. He might be riding ahead but it's the squire who holds the reins of his dapple and of Don Quixote's Rocinante.

•

'Every reader,' writes Bloom, 'has her or his favourite episodes in Don Quixote.' I have two: one is about the windmills, and the second recounts the story of Don Quixote's attack on a party of mourners.

I love the second episode because it shows the deftness with which Sancho Panza uses words. He can neither read nor write but possesses an intuitive feel for words and deploys them with such dexterity that even Don Quixote is ready to concede defeat.

The misadventure begins when Don Quixote decides to challenge and attack a party of twenty-six people, twenty of whom are in white shirts and are riding their mules, holding burning torches in their hands. Behind them is 'a litter covered in mourning, followed by another six mounted men draped in mourning down to the hooves of their mules'.

This is one of the few sallies in which Don Quixote scores a win over his perceived enemies, routing the whole party, which in reality is carrying a deceased man for burial in his native town.

One of the members of the party is Alonso López, a young man who first introduces himself as a licentiate but after the assault confesses that he is just a bachelor student. He informs Don Quixote about the party and the reason it is travelling from Baeza to Segovia attired in mourning. After learning the truth Don Quixote apologises for attacking and harming the party and asks Alonso López to join his companions who have run away in fear and 'on his behalf to beg their pardon for the offense against them, which it had not been in his power to avoid committing'.

This is the moment when Sancho Panza intervenes. 'If by chance,' he says to López, 'those gentlemen would like to know who the valiant man is who offended them, your grace can say he is the famous Don Quixote of La Mancha, also known as The Knight of the Sorrowful Face.'

Sancho Panza calls his master *el Caballero de la Triste Figura*. Rutherford translates it as 'The Knight of the Sorry Face'. I have also read it rendered as 'The Knight of the Woeful' or 'Doleful Countenance'. I like Grossman's version. The words 'sorrowful' sounds better than 'sorry', 'woeful', and 'doleful'. They are synonyms but like all synonyms they have different shades of meaning.

Don Quixote is impressed as well as perplexed by his squire's description of his appearance and once López has left them alone he asks Sancho Panza 'what had moved him to call him "The Knight of the Sorrowful Face" at that moment and no other.'

'I'll tell you,' responds Sancho Panza:

> I was looking at you for a while in the light of the torch that unlucky man was carrying and the truth is that your grace has the sorriest-looking face I've seen recently, and it must be on account of your weariness after the battle or the molars and teeth you've lost.

Don Quixote, although pleased by the title his squire has given him, isn't satisfied with his explanation and suspects that some other wise men he knows and had read about in various books 'must have put on' his squire's 'tongue and thoughts the idea of calling' him 'The Knight of the Sorrowful Face'. He likes the title to such an extent that he decides that he will start using it himself and will have his very sorrowful face depicted on his shield.

The response from Sancho Panza is cheeky:

> There's no reason to waste time and money making that face. What your grace should do instead is uncover yours and show it to those who are looking at you, and right away, without any images or shields, they'll call you *The Knight of the Sorrowful Face*; believe me, I'm telling you the truth, because I promise your grace, Señor, and I'm only joking, that hunger and your missing teeth give you such a sorry-looking face that, as I've said, you can easily do without the sorrowful picture.

The real is better than its picture, Sancho Panza says, and it's wise not to waste time and money in acquiring an inferior imitation. Although Sancho Panza is trying to be smart, I can't overlook the concern he shows for his master's ill health. He is so worried that as they begin the ride to their next stop, he decides to lead the way. 'And riding ahead on his donkey', writes Cervantes, 'he asked his master to follow him and since it seemed to

Don Quixote that Sancho was right, he followed him without another word.'

Sancho Panza, the squire, disregards the convention followed by knights errant and Don Quixote doesn't object. The worldly-wise fool leads and the sorrowful knight follows, proving Kafka right.

•

Most critics note the use of proverbs and sayings in the book. Some attribute this to a deliberate choice made by Cervantes to employ the everyday language of the people to tell his story. 'He wrote,' notes Grossman, 'in a crackling, up-to-date Spanish that was an intrinsic part of his time.' This could be one of the reasons why the book was popular in its time and remains so after more than four hundred years of its publication.

Don Quixote utters proverbs and sayings often, but Sancho Panza excels, surpassing his learned master. Rutherford notes that adding proverbs to the speech of Sancho Panza could have been an afterthought because in the first few chapters of the book they are absent. The main purpose, Rutherford thinks, was to make the speech and character of Sancho Panza more amusing. He speculates that Cervantes could have picked the idea from Fernando de Rojas's fifteenth-century play *Comedia o Tragicomedia de Calisto y Melibea* also known as *La Celestina*, which is 'laced with proverbs, most of which are used in *Don Quixote*'.

One of the best examples of Sancho Panza's virtuosic performance is found in Chapter XLIII of Part 2 of the book. Sancho Panza is soon going to become a governor of an island and Don Quixote wants him to know how he should govern his 'own person and home'. His first advice is:

> Do not eat garlic or onions lest their smell reveal your peasant origins. Walk slowly; speak calmly, but not in a way that makes it seem you are listening to yourself, for all affectation is wrong. Eat sparingly at midday and even less at supper, for the health of the entire body is forged in the workshop of the stomach. Be temperate in your drinking, remembering that too much wine cannot keep either a secret or a promise. Be careful, Sancho, not to chew with your mouth full or to eructate in front of anyone.

Sancho Panza doesn't know the word 'eructate' and Don Quixote explains that it means to belch, 'which is one of the crudest words in the Castilian language'.

Afraid that Sancho Panza, in his reply, will begin to string one proverb after another, he warns him:

> Sancho, you also should not mix into your speech the host of proverbs that you customarily use, for although proverbs are short maxims, the ones you bring in are often so far-fetched that they seem more like nonsense than like maxims.

Sancho Panza feels obliged to respond to his master's criticism and his reply has more than one proverb:

> By God, my lord and master. Your grace complains about very small things. Why the devil does it trouble you when I make use of my fortune, when I have no other, and no other wealth except proverbs and more proverbs? And right now four have come to mind that are a perfect fit, like pears in wicker basket, but I won't say them because golden silence is what they call Sancho.

In the exchanges that follow, Sancho Panza, to the utter despair of Don Quixote, cites scores of proverbs such as 'whether the pitcher hits the stone or the stone hits the pitcher, it's bad luck for the pitcher'; 'a fool knows more in his own house than the wise man does in somebody else's'; and 'everyone is equal when they sleep, the great and the small, the poor and the rich'.

Earlier in the conversation Sancho Panza explains why he can't resist the urge to string proverb after proverb:

> I know more proverbs than a book, and so many of them come into my mouth at one time when I talk that they fight with one another to get out, but my tongue tosses out the first ones it finds, even if they're not to the point. But I'll be careful from now on to say the ones that suit the gravity of my position, because in a well-stocked house, supper is soon cooked; and if

> you cut the cards, you don't deal; and the man who sounds the alarm is safe; and for giving and keeping, you need some sense.

I like Sancho Panza's eloquence, the alacrity of his mind, and his resolve to stand his ground. I wouldn't hesitate to have him as a companion on my travels. He would keep me amused as well as keep me on my toes. His laughter, comical and satirical, would make me laugh and ponder. Sancho Panza, my friend, is a usurper, ready to upset the apple cart of power and conventions.

•

If Cervantes rightly feels proud of having created Sancho Panza, he should also take some credit for fashioning Cide Hamete Benengeli, the Arab historian, whom Cervantes makes out to be the original author of the book. 'Though I seem to be the father,' he writes in the prologue, 'I am the stepfather of Don Quixote.'

Like Sancho Panza, the creation of Benengeli was an afterthought because his name first appears in Chapter IX of Part 1 of the book, just after the famous episode of the windmills.

Why did Cervantes create Benengeli? One possible explanation is to find someone whom he can blame for the falsehoods and other inconsistencies in his story including interruptions and abrupt endings, similar to the one we find in the story of the windmills:

> If any objection that can be raised regarding the truth of this one, it can only be that its author was Arabic, since the people of that nation are very prone to telling falsehoods, but because they are such great enemies of ours, it can be assumed that he has given us too little rather than too much.

Cide Hamete Benengeli, the name Cervantes selects for the real father of *Don Quixote* is intriguing. Grossman explains that '*Cide* is the equivalent of senőr; *Hamete*, is the Arabic name Hamid; *Benengeli* (*berenjena* in Spanish) means "eggplant", a favourite food of Spanish Moors and Jews.' She also notes that in Part 2 of the book Cervantes replaces 'Benengeli' with 'Berenjena'. Rutherford translates the second name as 'Brinjalcurry', which works equally well.

By introducing Benengeli as the real author, Cervantes wants us to believe that we are reading a Castilian translation of an Arabic book. As a translator, I am fascinated by this clever twist in the story; a twist about the book itself.

As always, Cervantes is vague in telling us about the translator, who is most probably the Morisco Cervantes had met in the Alcaná market in Toledo. Cervantes writes that

> to facilitate the arrangement and not allow such a wonderful find out of my hands, I brought him to my house, where in a little more than a month and a half, he translated the entire history, just as is recounted here.

The translation was thus carried out in his house and in his presence. Did Morisco read an oral translation to Cervantes, who wrote down and later edited and refined it to make it sound right in Castilian? I suspect that's what he did. Strangely, this is the model I follow when I undertake translation. I always have an informed and learned intermediary to help me. Morisco was also an intermediary, an interlocutor who would have explained to him the intricacies of the Arabic language.

Once Cervantes has found an intermediary or a translator, as he calls him, he shifts blame of inconsistencies and falsehoods on him and Benengeli soon transforms from a 'lying dog' to an esteemed historian, a Muslim philosopher, and 'the flower of all historians':

> Really and truly, all those who enjoy histories like this one ought to show their gratitude to Cide Hamete, its first author, for his care in telling us its smallest details and clearly bringing everything, no matter how trivial to light. He depicts thoughts, reveals imaginations, responds to tacit questions, clarifies doubts, resolves arguments, in short, he expresses the smallest points that curiosity might ever desire to know.

This is indeed high praise for the first author, an Arabic historian.

Cervantes is ambivalent on the importance of translation of literary works. He acknowledges that without translation his book wouldn't have happened, but he also suggests that translation, especially of poetry, which is near impossible, doesn't always capture the essence of the original. Quite cleverly he expresses this idea in a short speech delivered by his learned knight errant:

> It seems to me that translating from one language to another, unless it is from Greek or Latin, the queens of all languages, is like looking at Flemish tapestries from the wrong side, for although the figures are visible, they are covered by threads that obscure them, and cannot be seen with the smoothness and colour of the right side; translating easy languages does not argue for either talent or eloquence, just as transcribing or copying from one paper to another does not argue for those qualities. And I do not wish to infer from this that the practice of translating is not deserving of praise, because a man can engage in worse things that bring him less benefit.

Don Quixote, Cervantes's or perhaps Benengeli's knight errant, doesn't sound insane given the way he highlights the limitations of translation. However, this doesn't stop Cervantes from mentioning that his book is a work of translation and that he is only its stepfather.

•

In *The Childhood of Jesus*, John Coetzee describes how Simón, a refugee, selects a book in the library of a community centre. This is the book he wants to read with David, a young boy he is caring for. He finds the book lying 'flat on its face under other books, and its spine torn off'. The book appears to be reluctant to be spotted and yet Simón notices it and feels triumphant that it falls into his hands.

The book was waiting for him and David, I had thought after reading this section in Coetzee's book a couple of years after it was published and after the hype about it had subsided. That the book chosen by Simón was *An Illustrated Children's Don Quixote* surprised me, but I was pleased that David would read a book similar to the one I had read in my childhood.

Coetzee sets his novel in a fictional town called Novilla, a word that sounds like 'novel' or 'novella', located either in Spain or in a Spanish-speaking country. The name of the town is mentioned on the first page of the book and because my mind gets hooked on to places, fictional or real, I kept thinking about it, hoping that Coetzee would drop a hint later in his book about the reason why he had opted for Novilla as the setting for the story of a refugee who takes on himself the task of looking after a young boy who has lost his mother on the way to an unknown country, seeking asylum.

The name Novilla began to make some sense soon after I had read the title of the book selected by Simón. The association between the two seemed logical and believable. Perfect, I remember saying then but now as I think about it more, I feel that I made the connection because I was keen to find one, for I also know that one can't exactly ascertain how writers arrive at such decisions.

Most writers follow the narrative logic of the story, and all choices are made in consonance with it, taking care at the same time that the story doesn't trespass the threshold that would make it hard for the readers to suspend disbelief. This is essential for writers if they want to convince the reader that the world imagined and portrayed by them may not be factually true but is believable and therefore real.

It would be silly of me to suggest that because Coetzee wanted to find a place for *Don Quixote* in his book, he chose to set the book in a Spanish-speaking town because it could have been the other way around. It is likely that Coetzee's decision was intuitive because these things happen for no particular reason. However, I am certain about one thing: the introduction of *Don Quixote* in Coetzee's book invites readers to make connections, however tenuous and speculative, between the two books and their characters.

The first story Simón reads with David is about the windmills and it generates one of the many unsettling exchanges between the two. David wants to know why Sancho Panza doesn't hit the giant.

'Because Sancho knows the giant is really a windmill,' replies Simón, 'and you can't fight against a windmill. A windmill is not a living thing.'

David's reply surprises Simón. 'He's not a windmill, he's a giant!' he says. 'He's only a windmill in the picture.'

Now Simón has to find words with which to convince David and he begins by saying:

> *Don Quixote* is an unusual book. … It presents the world to us through two pairs of eyes, Don Quixote's eyes and Sancho's eyes. To Don Quixote, it's a giant he is fighting. To Sancho, it's a windmill. Most of us – not you, perhaps, but most of us nevertheless – will agree with Sancho that it is a windmill.

Simón concedes that David, like Don Quixote, might see things differently from the way others see. That David is different becomes clearer when he doesn't want to follow the common way most of us learn to read by first getting to know the letters of the alphabet. David is adamant that he wants to learn to read by recognising the words directly.

Soon we find out that David has his own, perhaps Quixote-like, way of looking at the world. Simón seeing that David is tearing at the pages of the book borrowed from the library asks him why he is handling the book so roughly. David's reply is intriguing:

> 'Because. Because if I don't hurry a hole will open.'
> 'Open up where?'
> 'Between the pages.'
> 'That's nonsense. There is no such thing as a hole between the pages.'
> 'There is a hole. It is inside the page. You don't see it because you don't see anything.'

David sees things like Don Quixote, I conclude after reading the exchange, and Simón can't get over the way most of us perceive the world as it is, without imagination. Does this mean that there is a little of Quixote in David, and something of an everyday Sancho Panza in Simón? Perhaps there is, but I find this idea crude, because the way Simón single-mindedly takes upon himself the task of looking after the young boy who is neither his son nor grandson, and to reunite the boy with his mother, whom Simón had never met, appears to me Quixote-like.

In an essay on Gabriel García Márquez, Coetzee writes about the possible lesson we can learn from Don Quixote:

> If there is any lesson he teaches, it is that in the interest of a better, more lively world it might not be a bad idea to cultivate in oneself a capacity of dissociation, not necessarily under conscious control, even though this might lead outsiders to conclude that one suffers from intermittent delusions.

To live in this world and to endure what many of us do, we need in us at least a modicum of Quixote, but this can happen only if we allow his ever-cheeky squire Sancho Panza to be with him because they need each other to be what they are. By being with each other they begin to partake some of what they both possess.

By introducing *Don Quixote* in his book Coetzee adds new layers of meaning to the two books. Coetzee's book gains a deeper, more than four hundred-year old imagined but real past, whereas *Don Quixote* extends its presence to our time and into the future. It receives a new impetus to live and endure, for it's quite likely that the readers who haven't read *Don Quixote* might be nudged to get acquainted with it.

The books I come to like tend to converse with other books of their own time and of the time gone past, and by doing so they open the possibility that they themselves will one day become part of a conversation with yet to be written books.

•

A day before leaving Madrid I went to see Monumento Cervantes at the centre of Plaza de España.

I don't regret that I saw it although I was disappointed, especially with how grandiose it looked, dwarfing almost everything else next to it. It saddened me to discover the blatant way Cervantes and his book and its characters had been incorporated into the story of Spanish nationalism and its imperial endeavours. I would have preferred something humble and delicate, cheeky and irreverent, funny and playful. I would have liked to stand in front of the monument and smile and laugh.

The project to build a monument to Cervantes began in 1915, a year before the 300th anniversary of the writer's death. It took almost fifteen years to finish the main part of the sculptural ensemble. These days the central towering monolith in stone, thirty-four metres tall, stands facing a pond at the top end of a park.

Not far from the base of the monolith sits Cervantes, in white marble, holding in his right hand a copy of the book. On a sandstone slab below him stand two bronze figures: the knight errant on Rocinante and to his left, a little shorter, his squire on his donkey. Don Quixote is upright on the horse; his right arm is raised, and he holds a lance in the other hand. Sancho Panza is emplaced a little behind. He sits sedately, with a wry smile on his round plump face. He reminds me more of Sancho Panza than Sancho Zancas, because I can't see the long shanks. There are two sandstone statutes, one each on either side of the bronze figures: the one to the left of Sancho Panza shows the peasant woman Aldonza Lorenzo and to the right of Don Quixote, her imagined incarnation, the beloved lady Dulcinea.

As I walked around the monument, I spotted on the north-east side of the monolith a woman sculpted in marble reading Cervantes's book. On the very top of the monolith sits a large globe surrounded by five women representing five continents.

I strolled around the pond and sat on the bench in the shade of olive trees waiting for something to happen. Groups of tourists arrived, Chinese, Japanese, and unusually loud Russians. They talked and took photographs, mostly selfies. An old man came and sat down on the far end of the bench, took out a newspaper and began to read. On the sandstone pedestal occupied by Dulcinea, I saw a Nazi swastika in black ink painted alongside a circle a quarter of which had been sliced. The swastika was partially smudged as if someone had tried to wipe it off.

I made a note in my diary, got up and walked up to my two friends in bronze. I stood there and stepped back as far as I could to get a good overall view, and then out of nowhere, I felt as if the knight errant had turned around followed by Sancho Panza.

'Look there,' I heard him say pointing at the monolith. 'There is a giant there holding the globe.'

Sancho Panza looked and said, 'Yes, your grace, this is a giant you need to challenge and trounce,' and then after a pause, 'I am ready to charge.'

'Let's go,' I heard the knight errant shout.

'Let's go,' said Sancho Panza.

My strange daydream lasted only for a minute and I was returned to the real world by a pigeon who decided to bless me with a decent measure of its droppings which landed on my head and the notebook.

Serves me right, I thought to myself and walked to the pond to wash off the droppings.

The next day I took an early morning fast train to Barcelona.

In the train I opened my notebook to read what I had written the night before. The note ended with the words: 'sad, no place for Cide Hamete Benengeli at Monumento Cervantes.'

Cervantes would have noted his absence as well, because for him Benengeli was the real father of the story, and when Alonso Quexana, the ingenious hidalgo of La Mancha died after refusing to act as Don Quixote, Benengeli was at his bedside. He wrote the epitaph for the Knight with the Sorrowful Face and paid him the most befitting tribute a writer could to his hero. 'For me alone was Don Quixote born,' said Benengeli, 'and I for him; he knew how to act, and I to write; the two of us alone are one.'

Benengeli can't see himself separate from his creation. They are conjoined like twins, and will live so as long as the story does. However, as Benengeli himself is a creation of Cervantes, he and Cervantes are also inseparably linked. In each statue or image I see of Cervantes, Benengeli is there with him. He may not be visible, but he is there because that's what Cervantes wants us to read and understand in the book. Without him Cervantes would find himself incomplete, wanting, insufficient.

I opened the notebook again and looked at the apple sitting on the tray table. It moved as the train suddenly accelerated but didn't fall and came to rest finding balance in its new position next to the pencil. I shut the notebook and placed it near the apple and pencil. Together they seemed happy. A perfect 'still life'. Togetherness, my mind whispered. Always together. I should remember this, and I should remind others about this simple truth. The truth of co-being, of dialogue, of translation.

The Dead Bridge of Sunil Sandhani

A few months ago my friend Sunil Sandhani sent me a book of stunning black and white photographs of bridges. The email message that came a few days later was short: 'Did you like the book? I wanted to remind you of our trip to Leningrad.'

Sunil lives in New York where he holds a senior position with a multinational computer company, heading a group on computer architecture and parallel programming. I met him aboard an Aeroflot flight to Moscow. The year was 1969 and we were both going to Moscow to study. He wanted to be a mathematician.

'Why mathematics?' I asked him, 'Why not medicine or mining?' I realised later that he was a born mathematician, with an uncanny ability to handle abstract concepts and complicated equations.

In Moscow we shared for five years a room on the third floor of a university hostel. The hostel was at the edge of a small but thick pine forest with an artificial lake. In winter the lake froze and turned into a skating rink. There we learnt to skate and play ice hockey. I enjoyed skating. It made me believe that I could control my body and make it do things that I normally couldn't. But frankly, skating was an excuse. The real reason was the large number of girls who came there to meet students from abroad. A packet of bubble gum or a Cliff Richard T-shirt was enough to tempt them. Sunil met his first girlfriend, Olga, at the skating rink.

Olga lived in Leningrad and came to Moscow to finish a course at the Moscow School of Art. She invited us to Leningrad 'to see its beautiful canals and to stroll over the bridges in the white summer nights'. I was reading Dostoyevsky those days, and walking with him the imagined walks, all the time thinking about real streets, bridges and boulevards. I wanted to see the house where Raskolnikov had murdered the pawnbroker and her sister, and to touch the stone under which he had buried the few trinkets he stole from the pawnbroker's flat. I knew that Anna Grigoryevna, Dostoyevsky's wife, had mentioned in her memoirs that once as they were wandering along Voznesensky Prospect, Dostoyevsky took her into the courtyard of a big house and showed her the stone.

We spent a whole week in Leningrad. The trip was a disappointment, not for Sunil or me, but for Olga. The first three days were all right, but soon both Olga and I noticed that Sunil was paying a little too much attention to Olga's mother, Lyubov Petrovna.

Lyubov Petrovna was an architect. 'I always wanted to be an architect,' I told her when I met her. 'An architect should have the capacity to imagine the world in five dimensions,' Lyubov Petrovna replied like an academic. 'One needs to add the axes of time and hope to the three usual spatial dimensions.' I had given up architecture after the first term because it had become difficult for me to transfer the real world onto the flat surface of a draftsman's sheet. The rules of perspective, shades and shadows remained out of my grasp.

Sunil, on the other hand, had no problem tackling the multidimensional world. He could without any hesitation or remorse reduce the 'world' to a set of polynomial equations and then play with them as if they were lumps of clay in the hands of a master sculptor.

However, the most intriguing thing about Sunil was his knack for telling stories. Stories seeped out of him. I had noticed that often he told the same story again and again, improvising with indulgence and abundance. My imagination was sluggish, but I was a good listener. I had mastered the art of quiet and patient listening and had learnt to spot the appropriate moment for monosyllabic interjections that kept the story flowing. And I was good at taking notes. 'You are a scribe,' Sunil used to tease me, 'a useless, good-for-nothing clerk.'

In Leningrad Olga showed us her three favourite bridges. 'I like small suspension bridges that hang like beautiful and delicate vines,' she told us, walking towards the Lions Bridge that spanned the Griboyedov Canal, not far from the Theatre Square. Four huge cast iron lions graced the abutments. Their forelegs were braced, heads thrown back and jaws gripping the iron chains holding the weight of the span. The canal formed a beautiful loop near the bridge. 'Wait for me,' Olga said and ran across the bridge. 'I want to draw it.'

She went into a four-storey building on the opposite bank, popped her head out of a window and waved. I followed her into the building and stood behind her. In no time the bridge, the canal and trees began to appear on the sheet of paper. Sunil sat on the granite seat, leaning against one of the lions, and waved at us.

Olga then took us to the Bank Bridge at the northern end of the same canal. Here the span was held by four golden-winged griffins.

We also saw the Egyptian Bridge that carried Lermontovsky Prospect over the Fontanka, where four sphinxes sustained the span. This was the widest of the three bridges and catered for a busy succession of trucks, cars and buses. I was disappointed with this bridge.

'Let's go and look for the pub where Raskolnikov met Marmeladov,' I suggested. 'We both are tired,' Olga replied, and I had to go on my own. I couldn't find the pub but spotted a small *pirozhnaya* café in the basement of an old crumbling building. I asked a young woman who was serving at the counter about the pub. 'Are you mad? There was never any pub around this place. I know this for sure. My *babushka* lived in that tall yellow house on the other side of the Fontanka.'

I asked Lyubov Petrovna about the pub. She didn't know much about it but told us instead the story of the Egyptian Bridge. The original bridge was built in 1826. One day in January 1905, when a string of loaded lorries and a squadron of cavalry guards were crossing the bridge, it collapsed. No one was killed. The bridge was rebuilt in 1956. From the original bridge only the four sphinxes have survived. 'I know the engineer who designed it. I worked with him as a trainee student. Do you want to meet him?' Sunil went with us.

One evening, walking through Mikhailovsky Garden, we came across a 'dead' bridge. 'The bridge,' Olga said, 'spanned a watercourse that joined the pond with the Voskresensky Canal.'

'Where is the canal?' Sunil asked.

'Disappeared, filled and forgotten,' Olga replied, and took us to another dead bridge that spanned the once living waters of the Voskresensky Canal.

Sunil asked Olga to do a sketch for him, then borrowed her FED camera and took several photographs of the bridge. I could sense a strange restlessness in him.

'What's wrong?' Olga asked him when he came and sat down with us.

'Nothing, nothing at all,' he said. I felt that there was certainly something odd in his behaviour but did not want to trouble him with questions. At that time, I didn't know that it would take me more than twenty years to solve the puzzle.

A year or so later I had to go to Leningrad again. This time I was alone with Olga, who was leaving Moscow for good. She was pregnant and wanted me to come with her. Neither of us talked. Silence, we thought, was the right bridge to carry us through the eight long hours of our journey to Leningrad. I had my Pushkin with me, and Olga was happy with her sketchbook. She sketched almost non-stop, and people in the compartment didn't mind. Some even paid her for doing their portraits.

At home I found Lyubov Petrovna very angry. She was cross at Olga, at Sunil and, God only knows why, at me. She was convinced that Olga should forget about having the child and get on with her art course. Olga, on the other hand, wanted the child, hoping it would be a dark-eyed, curly-haired boy. I returned to Moscow the same day, but before boarding the train I went once again to see the 'dead' bridge and the vanished canal.

In June the following year Olga gave birth to a girl, a carbon copy of her mother. She named her Meera.

•

The book of bridges Sunil had sent me opens with an image of another 'dead' bridge.

It's a drawing of a small wooden bridge called *A Primitive Janus.* I find the same drawing in Louise Adam Holland's book *Janus and the Bridge*. In Holland's opinion there were at least three such wooden bridges, the Jani, in ancient pre-Republican Rome. The city began on the eastern bank of the river Tiber and spread into the valleys surrounded by seven hills. Several perennial streams and brooks, small and large, ran into the river. The three Jani were located over a brook that flowed through Argiletum and Forum. The relics of only one have survived. The Janus Geminus carried Sacra Via, the sacred way, over this brook. Describing this wooden bridge, Holland writes:

> It was a wooden structure with the short span adequate for the narrow cleft of the stream bed, a 'corduroy' roadway of short legs being laid across the longer timbers beneath. A parapet of wood may also have been used. The opening of such a Janus would mean removing the roadway and allowing the water to play its natural role of divider between the settlement and the outside world, so that the function of the Janus was in its practical use comparable to the drawbridge over the moat of a mediaeval castle, but with the added element of a religious or magical protection.

The bridge was called Janus after one of the most popular Roman gods of the time. He was the god of bridges, arches and gateways, boundaries and crossings. Initially however, Janus was only associated with bridges and river crossings.

Since antiquity, societies and cultures have invested magical and divine power in rivers, streams, brooks and springs. The running water is believed to be the source of life, abundance and prosperity, and perhaps this is the reason the sites of running water were turned into places of sacrifice, propitiation, and pilgrimage. The crossing of running water came to be perceived as a special act that needed to be sanctioned by performing rituals of consecration: the *auspicia peremnia*. 'A stream is not to be crossed heedlessly,' notes the Greek poet Hesiod, 'but always with some gesture of recognition, no matter how simple. One should pause on the bank to wash the hands and say a prayer.'

The Romans instituted the presence of Janus as a benevolent god that authorised and facilitated the act of crossing, of going away and returning. He guarded the bridge and the people. His presence at the bridge turned it into a crossing point that had been permanently consecrated, making the need of performing acts of *auspicia* unnecessary, which means that Janus, the god, could be called upon or remembered occasionally, maybe once a year through festivals, fairs and sacrifices.

Like the Sumerian god Usmu, who was also a messenger of Ea the water god, Janus was imagined as a god with two or sometimes four faces. A Roman coin shows Janus with two faces looking in opposite directions. One face is bearded and old, whereas the other is beardless and young. In one of his hands he holds a key. Holland writes that the two-faced Janus

> represented the desired blessing not only on the going out but on the coming in, and the double direction of his look has in it perhaps some of the same suggestion as the dedications *pro itu et reditu*, which shows two pairs of feet – or footprints – turned opposite ways.

In modern-day Rome, you won't be able to see these Jani. This does not mean that Rome has forgotten them. They have disappeared as elements of the cityscape, but their traces remain, imprinted not only in the collective memory we call history, but also in historical maps painstakingly reconstructed by archaeologists, as well as in tourist guidebooks listing walks and bike rides.

The historians tell us that by the time Trajan became the emperor of Rome in 53 CE, the hill and the valleys of the original landscape around the river Tiber had turned into streets, palaces, markets, parks, theatres and arenas.

The Romans were, however, obsessed with running water. The city was served by eight aqueducts which brought two hundred million gallons of water every day. Water gushed into several public and private baths, fountains – some say six hundred – and gardens and gushed out through an equally elaborate system of sewers, the biggest of which, Cloaca Maxima, was built along the stream over which stood the three Jani. The stream which became part of the sewer was eventually covered by dry pavements and 'disappeared'. But the Jani survived for some years in the form of arches or gates, first as part of the real world and later in stories and fables.

A similar and perhaps more intriguing thing happened to Janus, the god. He who was known as the god of bridges, a heavenly device for easing the act of crossing and returning, metamorphosed into the god of arches and gates. The god was unable to avoid the language games we, the humans, play and thus through acts of successive metonymies was reduced to fragments. However, this displacement proved to be a blessing in disguise because, from being a god attached merely to bridges or crossing points, he turned into a god of arches and gates, beginnings and endings, comings and goings, of boundaries and thresholds and finally of time itself. It doesn't come as a surprise that the month of January in Julian and Gregorian calendars is named after him.

The water disappeared and so did the bridges but Janus the god didn't. He appeared in new sites and functions. The disappearance of this double-face god would have been a major disappointment and I am glad he survived. I like him although he has three less faces than Shiva, the Hindu god with multiple arms and eyes. I like him because he appears to be best suited for playing the role of a divine guardian of memory, without which it would have been impossible for humans to live. His two faces aptly represent the bifocal nature of memory. Like Janus, memory has two faces – one of them turned firmly to the past and the second looks to the future. Like Janus, memory, albeit metaphorically, is also a bridge spanning between the past we want to remember and forget, and the future that we look forward to, knowing that the future would soon turn into past.

•

Like Olga's favourite, the Lions' Bridge in Leningrad, my favourite bridge also sports lions. It is in Roorkee, a small Indian town about 200 kilometres north-east of Delhi and not far from Haridwar, one of the seven holy Hindu cities. I went to Roorkee in January 1980, after returning from Moscow, to take up a teaching position at the local university.

The bridge, which spans the Ganga Canal, is small and commonplace, except for the fact that it was the subject of a small and obscure watercolour by the nineteenth-century English traveller-painter William Simpson. An enlarged copy of the painting appears on the jacket of the 1996 edition of the *Cambridge Illustrated History of the British Empire*. I have walked across the bridge, been pulled in a rickshaw over it, and have carried my daughter across it on my shoulders. 'I know this bridge very well,' I tell myself, but when I look at it in the painting, it appears to me unknown, novel and attractive. It seems that the bridge, by appearing in a painting, has become special. The painting has framed it into a relatively autonomous 'reality' outside the world that surrounds the 'real' bridge over which I have walked.

The painting has also made the surrounding landscape picturesque and romantic. In the foreground, near the bank of the canal, I can see a bullock cart. The bulls are standing close to a stack of hay, munching and looking away from me. A man is sitting not far from them, cooking his food on a *chullah* from which thick streaks of bluish-white smoke are rising. A second man, standing close by, is helping him. A boat with a thatched roof is drifting down the canal. Behind the human figures stretches the stone bridge with arches curved over the canal. On the bank I can see the steps reaching up to the bridge. But the most important figure near the steps is that of a lion sitting on a sandstone pedestal.

The lion is huge. The three men, on either side of it, seem tiny. Behind the lion and the bridge, in the far background, are the three mountain ranges rising up gradually, culminating in the snow-clad peaks. The peaks are white and shining. Their glow lights up the whole painting. Streaks of bluish-white clouds dreamily spread between the ranges. There are trees on the far bank, but I am sure it is the presence of the snow-clad peaks that makes the painting novel and attractive.

The element of wonder with which Simpson has invested his view of the bridge and of the surrounding landscape now becomes apparent to me. I know that it is possible, on rare, cloudless days to see snippets of snow-covered peaks from the fourth floor of the Geology Department, but to see them as Simpson saw them or as he wanted us to see them is next to impossible. The peaks are no doubt there, but one would have to travel a few hundred kilometres upstream along the canal to see them in the glory in which they appear in the painting. Simpson saw them and wanted them to be in the painting. Their presence indicates his desire, his imagination and his creative flair. He wanted the painting and the bridge in the painting to look beautiful.

The bridge was designed and built in the late 1840s by Proby Cautley, an English military engineer. The Thomason College of Engineering, renamed Roorkee University after Indian independence, was established in Roorkee in 1848 to train the staff who were to build the Upper Ganga Canal. The college was housed in a huge white building with large circular columns, enormous domes and grand halls. It was surrounded by lush green lawns spreading over a number of terraces that overlooked the flat sprawling flood plain of the River Solani. It must have been a home away from home for many Europeans who studied and trained there. An oasis surrounded by dull, drought- and famine-prone villages. Now they are not so poor. In fact, the town of Muzaffarnagar, just fifty kilometres south of Roorkee, is known as the sugar capital of India. The canal brought water, and respite from the periodic famines.

The villagers still cherish the memory of Sir Proby Cautley, about whom stories have passed from generation to generation, making him a mythical figure, almost a Hindu god. 'He was an incarnation of Bhagirath,' an old man at a tea shop in Muzaffarnagar told me. 'Like Bhagirath he rode a beautiful white horse, his hand raised above his head, holding a sword, and the river followed him, tamed and obedient.'

The bridge at Roorkee, to be exact, is not a lion bridge because the lions don't guard its arched span. They sit on large sandstone pedestals on the embankment of the canal with their faces pointing downstream. Two similar lions also sit near a bridge a few kilometres upstream. Their faces point upstream. Between these two pairs of lions stretches one of the longest aqueducts in the world. When I look at Simpson's Roorkee Bridge and compare it with a photograph I took a few years ago, I notice that the simple, single-beam bridge in my photograph is quite different from the arched span that appears in Simpson's watercolour. The engineers in the irrigation department confirm that the bridge at Roorkee is the original one, and that the records don't show whether it has ever been rebuilt.

The bridge upstream of the Solani aqueduct, I find out later, is an arched span and carries insignia similar to those on Simpson's Roorkee bridge. It seems Simpson took the lions and the abutment of the Roorkee bridge, added them to the arched span of the other bridge, and painted a composite image. He needed the arched span to mimic the undulating peaks of the mountain ranges spread in the background.

The arched bridge upstream is located close to the famous religious shrine of a sixteenth-century Muslim fakir. I am told that the bridge came into being because of the shrine. Every year a week-long fair is held at the shrine, which brings thousands of Muslims and Hindus to the area.

It is August 1993, and I am standing not far from the arched bridge. In the past few weeks I have been visiting places where Proby Cautley lived and worked. 'What is the story of this bridge?' I ask an old man at the tea shop near the bridge. In no time a crowd gathers around us, and as I turn on my tape recorder, the story begins to emerge from several young and old voices: 'You see, when Cautley Sahib (the old man pronounces the name 'Katley', which in Hindi and Urdu means to 'cut') was cutting his canal, he discovered that the canal had to pass through this place. The villagers wanted the water and the canal to come this way but they were unhappy, because (here a teenager takes up the story) it meant that the dervish sleeping in his shrine would be cut away from his mother who is lying there, on that side of the canal. You see (the old man again intervenes) people who used to come to see the holy man also went to visit the mother for blessings. That was the tradition. The villagers and the pilgrims went to Katley Sahib and asked him to move the canal to the south. The sahib didn't agree, and the people knew that the Angrez Bahadur (the Englishman) would not change his mind easily. But then after a few days he said that he would build a bridge, right here, for the people. He went to Thomason Bahadur, the Governor Sahib, and asked for his approval. The approval was not given (a new voice breaks in and I turn to find that a policeman has joined us and taken over the story) because this would set a wrong precedent so that people in all other villages would demand bridges. But Katley Sahib was very *pukka* about his promise. He had given his word and would keep it, no matter what happened. The bridge was built, and built on Katley Sahib's own money, and that is why it carries his coat of arms.'

I go to the shrine, covering my head with a handkerchief as the rules demand, and circumambulate his grave, making a symbolic offering by throwing some coins. Outside, a group of *qawwals* are singing. I walk across the canal to see the 'mother'. A group of kids follow me around and ask me to take their photo. I oblige but ask them to stand close to the bridge so that I can snap the bridge as well. One little girl comes close to me and wants to look through the eye of the camera. I hold the camera and she tries to reach it, springing herself up like a bird. She wants to touch and hold the camera but is scared to ask. None of the kids are interested to look at the camera or the view through it. They don't want me to send the prints back to them either. They just want to be photographed, seen and shown.

A few months later when I get the film processed and look at the print, I find that the girl in the photograph has been jostled into the background by other children. I can only see her eyes, nose and a silvery nose bud. The bridge, on the other hand, is visible in its full splendour and this, I don't know why, annoys me.

•

'I have found a living bridge,' I wrote to Sunil, six months after receiving the book from him.

'Do send me photographs,' he replied the next day.

Instead of photographs, I sent him a copy of an article in the *National Geographic* with an internet link to it.

'Next time when you and I are in India, we should go there,' he said a week later.

One of the most famous of these living bridges is located in Nongriat, a little village in the East Khasi Hills of Meghalaya state in north-eastern India. It's unique because it has two stacked bridges. The tourists call it the double-decker bridge, a name the Khasi people, whose ancestors facilitated its creation, have accepted. Their own name for it is Jingkieng Nongriat.

The village of Nongriat is just 22 kilometres south of Cherrapunji, a town known to be the wettest place on the planet. In July the average rainfall recorded near the town is more than three thousand millimetres.

The subtropical highlands are densely forested with thick broadleaf trees and bisected by fast-flowing streams along gullies and ravines. Crossing these is often hazardous.

The Khasi value the rubber fig tree (*Ficus elastica*), not so much for its milky white latex fluid but the way it spreads its aerial and buttressing roots wherever it can find a niche to drop them. It grows like Shiva, the multi-limbed god, its roots resembling strands of his rough matted hair.

The life and health of the bridge depend on the tree. If the tree is healthy, the roots thrive and grow, becoming stronger. The Khasi look after them both, pruning the tree and roots, sometimes working on them like masterful masseurs to make them muscular and strong. The bridges die when the trees die but some of them can live for hundreds of years.

The art of fashioning these bridges is complex and is learnt by watching and practice. In 1844, Lieutenant Henry Yule published the story of how the bridges in Cherrapunji area were built by the Khasi.

I know Henry Yule. I read about him in one of the reports of Proby Cautley on the construction of the Upper Ganga Canal. Like Proby Cautley, he was an officer in the Bengal Engineers, a corps in the Bengal Army of the British East India Company. He served as one of the supervisors on the construction of the Upper Ganga Canal under the guidance of Proby Cautley. Prior to joining the project, he had lived and worked in the Khasi Hills. This was his first posting in India, where he had arrived at the end of 1840. The main task assigned to him was to find an easy and more practical way to transport coal from the hills to the plains.

Yule was twenty then, eager to learn and work

and possessed a keen eye. The Khasi with whom he lived fascinated him and within two short years he was able to gather enough material to write about his impressions. Walking upstream along a river he came across several root bridges. One of these was built from the roots of large trees:

> On the top of a huge boulder by the river side, grows a large India rubber tree, clasping the stone in its multitude of roots. Two or three of the long fibres, whilst still easily pliable, have been stretched across the stream, and their free ends fastened on the other bank. There they have struck firmly into the earth, and now form a living bridge of great, and yearly increasing strength. Two great roots run directly one over the other, and the secondary shoots from the upper have been bound round, and grown into the lower, so that the former affords at once a band-rail and suspending chain, the latter a footway. Other roots have been laced and twisted into a sort of ladder as an ascent from the bank to the bridge. The greatest thickness of the upper root is a foot, from which it tapers to six or eight inches. The length of the bridge is above eighty feet, and its height about twenty above the water in the dry season.

Almost one hundred and eighty years later, Paul Salopek, whose *Out of Eden Walk* is reported in the *National Geographic*, walked on some of the same bridges. Compared to the 'modern wooden or steel bridges,' he writes, which 'rot quickly into disrepair in the lush hills of Meghalaya ... the tree-root bridges endure for 500 to 600 years and grow stronger over time.'

He loved walking on them:

> The root bridges of Cherrapunji give softly, almost imperceptibly, underfoot. They cradle the body's weight in a supple way that lifeless concrete and metal never could. Underhand, through the railings made of living tissue, you feel the immense power of the joined trees. You span time.

Salopek describes them as 'bridges that breathe'. They are the 'architecture of memory, of rain and sunlight'.

In Yule's report there are no photographs, but it does include a fabulous sketch of the bridge; a sketch that I have seen reproduced in several articles about the living bridges. In the sketch, below the root bridge spanning across the river appears a small wooden log-bridge on which stands a woman carrying a bag on her back, its strap running across her forehead.

I copied the image and emailed it to Sunil, saying that Olga would have loved the sketch.

In his reply he said that he liked the sketch but didn't say anything about Olga. It was an omission I had got used to, but it still disappointed me.

•

On our trip to Leningrad, Sunil took several photographs of the 'dead' bridge, but when the prints from Olga arrived, with words Olga had scribbled on the back, he seemed to have lost all interest in them. 'They are yours,' Sunil said. I kept the photographs, but they soon disappeared in the piles of other photographs. Sunil's photobook of bridges rekindled that fascination. A bridge painted or photographed seems more real to me than a 'real' bridge. Perhaps that is why a 'dead' bridge, a bridge that was there in the past but of which nothing but a trace is left, can go on haunting us, stirring memory and allowing our imagination to take wing.

When Sunil gave me these photographs of the 'dead' bridge in Leningrad, he also gave me some photographs of Olga. In one of them she is wearing her school uniform. 'The year I left the high school,' the note at the back reads.

I have always wondered about the point of origin, if one can define such a thing, of stories. The story you are reading begins at the point where a photo-book about bridges arrives. But this is not the beginning of Sunil's, Olga's or, for that matter, my story.

Sunil, as I found later, was born in 1947, the year the subcontinent was partitioned. In August that year, as the day of Independence approached, an exodus of people began in two opposite directions: Hindus from Pakistan to India and Muslims from India to Pakistan. On the way many were robbed, raped, maimed and killed. Sunil's father owned a successful film-distribution company and two popular cinema theatres in Rawalpindi. He left them behind in Pakistan. He hurriedly packed a few things, gathered his family and boarded the refugee train. They were going to Delhi, where the parents of Sunil's mother lived. The train was slow, slower than usual, but it was the safest way to go. At night no-one was allowed to switch on the lights for fear of attack.

One night, a few miles inside the Indian border, not far from the Cantonment of Firozpur, near a bridge over a small canal, the train stopped. As the raid on the train began, Sunil's father herded his family in the direction of the bridge. His young wife was pregnant and frightened, and his mother feared that the young woman might go into labour any time.

Sunil was born under the bridge, not far from a large peepul tree. It was a starry night and a faint crescent of a young – what we call in Punjabi 'two-nights-old' – moon shone. As the new-born boy was handed to his father, the young mother, who was bleeding excessively, died. Sunil was brought up by his two grandmothers.

When Sunil was fifteen his father married Suneeta, a pretty and kind-looking seventeen-year-old girl. 'She was very beautiful, more beautiful than even Madhubala, the heartthrob of many Hindi film fans of the sixties. My friends thought she was my sister, and wanted me to introduce them to her,' Sunil told me. 'Can you imagine,' he said on another occasion, 'I have never seen my mother in my dreams? I have had dreams about her, but she has never, ever been physically present in them. Sometimes when she is about to appear, the dream abruptly comes to an end.'

Sunil mentioned that his family had once had several photographs of his mother, but they were either left behind in Rawalpindi or perished in the refugee train. Sunil's maternal grandmother had an old photograph of her when she, Sunil's mother, was a toddler. 'Did she look like me?' Sunil once asked his grandmother. 'No, not really, she resembled her father but there was a bit of me in her as well,' his grandmother replied. Sunil dug up a few old photographs of his grandfather and grandmother and took them to one of his painter friends so that he could conjure a portrait of his mother from the photographs.

His father looked at the portrait, shook his head and said, 'I am sorry, I don't seem to remember Sulakshna's face.' Suneeta saw the portrait and told him that it was time that they went in search of the old Firozpur bridge. Sunil's father let them use his air-conditioned Ambassador, chauffeured by Teja Singh, their Sikh driver, who had a cousin living in Firozpur.

In Firozpur it took them three days to find the right place. Teja Singh's cousin did most of the detective work. The Katora Canal over which the railway bridge was built had dried up because of a dam constructed upstream on the river Sutlej. The railway line had been decommissioned and the bridge declared redundant. The large peepal tree, about which Sunil's grandmother reminded them before they left Delhi, had also disappeared. In place of the canal there stood a jungle of single- and double-storey brick houses with TV antennas shooting from the roof tops. The railway bridge had been pillaged for bricks, iron and other construction material. Teja Singh's cousin told them that one of the locals, who had built his house not far from the southern bank of the canal, had reused the remains of the bridge pier in one of his kitchen walls.

In the evening as they were driving off Sunil asked Teja Singh to take him to the house that had one of its walls built from reused materials. He walked around the house and not far from its backyard found a little pile of rubble overgrown with grass and dotted with marigold flowers. There he found several broken bricks, a few of which had lumps of crumbling cement stuck on them. He picked one and put it inside his bag, hoping that it came from the Firozpur bridge where his mother had died giving birth to him on that starry, 'two-nights-old moon' night.

I have assembled this story about Sunil's Firozpur bridge from snippets of conversations we have had over the last twenty years. I know that there are several gaps in the story, but there is nothing I can do about them. I know that this story, like other stories of this type, is not finished. It still has the potential to surprise us with unforeseen twists and turns.

A twist did occur a couple of years ago when out of the blue I received a packet from Yekaterinburg, the capital city of the Urals. The packet contained a letter from Olga, a short note from Meera and an early 1970s edition of Dostoyevsky's *White Nights.* The novel was illustrated with Olga's drawings, one of which, if I remember correctly, was the sketch she did of Sunil sitting on the granite seat leaning against one of the lions of the Lions' Bridge.

Meera wrote in her note that she had just returned from India after spending a few months there, covering mass protests against the Narmada Dam project for one of the Russian national dailies. 'I am sending you some photographs which I took in India,' she noted, 'a few of which I am sure will interest you.' In one of them I can see the remains of Sunil's dead Firozpur bridge. A few others showed Meera and Suneeta, Sunil's stepmother, sitting in the veranda of a bungalow overlooking the blue span of a lake. 'Who took these photographs?' I ask myself. Did Sunil also go to India? Did he take the photograph? I want to believe that he did, for it would mean that Meera has finally met Sunil, her father, and that their story has found the closure it deserves. But I can't be sure because I have yet to hear from Sunil himself.

Will he write to me? I hope he does.

Iosif Stalin's Metro

In April 1993 I went to Moscow to research for a book about Edvard Radzinskii, one of the most popular Soviet-Russian playwrights after the Second World War. In a library, I met Leonid Vidgof, a young literary critic. He had a degree from the philology faculty of the Moscow State University and a passion for Mandelshtam's poetry. I told him how much I loved Mandelshtam's *Voronezh Notebooks* and read him some of my poems about Mandelshtam and Akhmatova. 'I know all the Mandelshtam places in Moscow,' he said, 'and if you want, I can take you on a tour.' We agreed to meet at around nine o'clock on the coming Sunday at the Mayakovskaya Metro station.

He first took me to an old house on Starosadskii Pereulok. In apartment number 3 of this house Mandelshtam and his wife Nadezhda lived for a few years with his brother. 'Here in this building Mandelshtam wrote *The Wolf Cycle*,' Leonid said and read the following poem in Russian:

No, I can't hide from this terrible ruse
Ducked behind the back of the cabbie: Moscow,
In the tram of an evil time I dangle like a noose
Why I am still alive I really don't know.

We'll take the tram A and then B
Just to see who dies first in the city
That either shrinks like a warbler
Or rises like a puffed-up pastry.

And lurking at the corner it barely manages
To threaten, you do as you please, but no,
I won't risk, my gloves are cold, so spare me
The endless ride around the whorish Moscow.

Our next stop was in front of the Herzen House on Tverskoi Boulevard. To reach it we went back to the metro, came out at the station Pushkinskaya and walked along the boulevard. Mandelshtam and his wife lived there between 1922 and 1923. They occupied a room on the first floor of the left wing. Leonid pointed out the room and read one of the many poems about Moscow Mandelshtam had written in that room.

Near the entrance to the house, on the wall close to the street there is now a tiny memorial plaque about Mandelshtam. Not far from it, there is a similar plaque for Andrei Platonov, the other famous Russian writer.

That Sunday for almost three hours Leonid and I changed metro stations, buses and trams to criss-cross Central Moscow, tracing Mandelshtam's steps. I had a feeling that I was participating in a strange act of reclaiming streets, houses, apartments, trees and pavements for Mandelshtam, his wife, 'their' poetry and their resistance. It was new for me. My first act of reclamation. But Leonid must have done it many times, physically as well as emotionally, and Leonid was not the first to do this. All those who loved Mandelshtam must have walked all these miles and many more to recreate and re-instate him.

Our 'Mandelshtam trip' ended on that Sunday. But it initiated a new one. My own journey to and away from Moscow. It is in a way a continuous process of coming and going. I go to Moscow almost every day, pick like a vulture on my memories, recreating them, making them new. The Moscow in me grows and shrinks. Like a yo-yo, we roll along the thread of time and images.

It is true that we live in cities, but it is also true that cities live in us. There is a physicality, a geographical dimension, a measurable space which we call city, but the city has an emotional, a quasi-real landscape which spreads in us. Between the city in which we live and ourselves, we erect a discourse, a way of talking and seeing, a way of looking and of being looked at. The city then exists as a space, in between us and that which we call city. A space onto which the physical and the emotive landscapes are projected, through which they meet, intermingle, and refract.

The metro in Moscow represents one such emotive landscape.

To imagine Moscow without the Metro is impossible for me. I have spent countless hours travelling in the Metro and reflecting about it, but each time I think of it I can't isolate my ideas from the feelings my memory wraps them in. They inhabit my mind like twins who rely on each other but also squabble endlessly; memory, the tricky beast, lets them play and argue like an indulgent parent. There is nothing else left for me but to accept that memories, however true or false, are what constitutes a significant part of my feeling and thinking self.

•

The Soviet Government made a decision to build the Moscow Metro in 1931. On 15 May 1935, the first two lines were opened to the public. The longer of the two had ten stations and the second, shorter one had three. The total length of the lines was more than eleven kilometres.

These days the internet site of the Moscow Metro proudly declares that in the year 2021, the system has 250 stations with a route length of almost 436 kilometres.

In April 1993, I bought a book from my favourite Moscow *bukinist*, second-hand bookshop. I used to go to the shop frequently when I was a student in Moscow in the 1970s. I had a young friend who worked there and had of his own will decided to keep aside books he thought I would be interested in; he would show them to me whenever I went there. Often, I would buy most of what he had selected. In return he would, now and then, ask for my help in identifying minerals and rocks in his collection.

In April 1993, I didn't see him in the shop and when I asked about him, a middle-aged woman behind one of the counters told me that Anatoli had migrated to Israel.

She liked the book I had chosen and showed me a few more but I was satisfied with what I had in my hand. It was an old 1958 paperback about the Moscow Metro. The book *Moscow Metropolitan Named after V.I. Lenin* was written by N. A. Pikareva, an author about whom there was no information inside. The paperback had many black and white photographs which followed a succinct description of the Metro.

Over the years I have collected a few more books and some maps of the Metro and when I look at them, I am not surprised that through them I can track many of the major events in Russia's Soviet and post-Soviet history. These are the maps on which I can also trace the shape and tenor of the nine years of my life in Moscow. Looking at them awakens my memory, which like an empathetic director begins to enact in the mind-theatre scenes of a play resonating with sounds, smells and touches; a play in which I am an actor as well as a spectator, creating thereby an uncanny experience, the authenticity of which I want to challenge but I acquiesce because the scenes appear believable. And so I watch myself reading seated and often standing in the coaches; a painter next to me begins to draw on his sketch pad as I look at his hand and fingers; on each sketch he inserts an image of a little swallow; a young musician enters the coach and starts playing on the accordion Shostakovich's jazz waltz and receives a bouquet of red carnations from an old man, a retired soldier, with medals pinned on his jacket; she bows and people including me clap; an old woman at the Kievskaya station hands me two painted Easter eggs; a militiaman, standing not far from us, watches with interest, smiles and moves away.

•

In Pikareva's book there is a 1958 map of the Metro. The Metro she describes carries Lenin's name. This is the name I also associate with the Metro I first saw in the late 1960s.

The man after whom it was originally named was Lazar Moiseyevich Kaganovich, a Yiddish speaking Jew from a village in Ukraine. He was a close comrade of Stalin and the First Secretary of the Moscow City Party Committee. Stalin appointed him to supervise the construction. He was known as 'Iron Lazar', which sounds similar to Stalin's own name, meaning 'made of steel'. The 'Iron Lazar', most historians believe, was determined, driven, and more importantly had the power of a diehard bully to finish the project on time.

Although the Metro didn't receive Stalin's name, Kaganovich would have known that it had to be a show piece to glorify Stalin and his leadership. It was going to be Stalin's Metro where his presence had to be not just visible, but omnipotent as that of any deity.

On Pikareva's map there is a station called Stalinskaya. The next station on the same line is Izmailovskaya, located near a large public park named after Stalin. The Metro has one more station named after the great leader; it's called Zavod imeni Stalina (Factory named after Stalin). However, it was at Stalinskaya station that the followers of the communist leader got the opportunity to demonstrate their unbridled admiration and devotion.

The station opened in 1944, a year before the end of the Second World War, in which the Red Army and its supreme commander prevailed over the might of Nazi Germany. This prompted the designers and artists to focus on military themes, portrayed through numerous panels with images of soldiers and weaponry. One of the prominent elements of decoration in the station was a five-metre-tall sculptural portrait of Stalin. The work *Thank you, Comrade Stalin for Our Happy Childhood* was created in 1936 and it showed Stalin holding in his arms a little girl with a bouquet. The portrait is also known by its other name, *Stalin and Gelya.* Gelya is the shortened name of a Buryat girl whose full name was Engelsina Sergeyevna Markizova. In addition to this imposing work, the upper part of the façade above the entrance to the station also carried a circular bas-relief of Stalin.

Most names changed after Nikita Khrushchev's 1956 speech denouncing Stalin's cult at the 20th Congress of the Communist Party of the Soviet Union. Even 'Iron Lazar' had to give way. The Metro once named after him was given Lenin's name. However, as a compensation perhaps, the station Okhotny Ryad received the name Kaganovich, after Stalin's 'Iron Lazar', the chief overseer of Stalin's Metro. But the new name only lasted for less than a year, and in 1957 the station was returned its original name. Stalinskaya, however, continued to exist for a few more years and in November 1961 it was changed to Semyonovskaya.

•

I remember Okhotny Ryad station as Prospect Marksa, a name it received in 1961. In 1969, when I first saw the station, the avenue running near it was also known by the same name. It was the main station in the centre of the city, a few hundred metres west of the Red Square.

Right next to one of the underground entries to the station was Hotel Moskva, one of the first grand hotels built in Stalin's time. Igor Kostenko, one of my Ukrainian-Russian friends – his father is Ukrainian and mother a Russian Jew – used to call it Stalinism in stone and glass. I recall standing with him facing the southwestern façade of the hotel, which is decorated with a large monumental portico. To get a proper view we had to move back a few hundred steps.

'What do you see?' said Igor.

I felt lost, distracted by the grand assemblage of granite, labradorite, and marble.

'Look at the two façades near the portico,' he prompted.

I looked and smiled. 'They are different,' said I.

'*Molodets*, well done,' he said and told me the story, which is repeated by Alexander Ryabushin and Nadia Smolina in their book *Landmarks of Soviet Architecture 1917-1991*:

> There is a legend that Stalin gave his approval to a project in which the towers were shown in two variants, one of which had to be selected. He approved the total project, so the towers had to be constructed as per the signed agreement, and both variations were reproduced.

On a Wednesday in the last week in April 1993 I am standing in the shadow of the grand portico. That the two variants of the façade are still there brings out a smile, as I wait for Tamrico, a researcher at the Bakhrushin Theatre Museum who has agreed to take me to the Meyerhold House Museum on the nearby Tverskaya Street.

After around fifteen minutes I see Tamrico walking briskly, almost running, and wave to her. 'Sorry,' she says after catching her breath and apologising for being late. 'The Metro train was late,' she explains. 'Hard to imagine, but these days they often are,' she says as we take the underground path to cross the avenue to reach Tverskaya.

We walk up along Tverskaya and after going past the Central Telegraph Office, we come across a small lane called Bryusov Pereulok. We turn and stop at house number 12. There is a memorial plaque with Meyerhold's portrait at the entrance of the four-storey brick house. The memorial plaque was installed in March 1968, Tamrico explains.

Between 1928 and 1939, Meyerhold and his actress wife Zinaida Raikh lived in apartment numbers 11 and 11a. This is how Konstantin Rudnitskii, the famous Russian theatre critic, describes the Meyerhold house:

> Two small and separate apartments were combined to make a four-room 'house'. It included Meyerhold's office, a drawing room which was also the dining room as well as Zinaida Raikh's room (it was also called the 'yellow' room), and two tiny rooms - one each for Kostya and Tanya (the two children from Zinaida's first marriage to the famous Russian poet Sergei Esenin). Standing on the stairwell, two separate entrances led into the house. The right-hand one opened into apartment number 11, the other into 11a. The latter was meant for people who had come to see Meyerhold only. Most often he opened the door and led the visitors into his office.

Just a block away, on the other side of Tverskaya, there is the famous Moscow Art Theatre and a studio-theatre attached to it. Not far is Kuznetskii Most, a street with bookshops. Between 1969 and 1978 I must have walked countless times along these streets. On this cobbled street Igor once took me to a spot where according to him Vladimir Mayakovskii had seen a fallen horse about whom he wrote the poem *Khoroshoe Otnoshenie k Loshadyam* (A Good Attitude Towards Horses).

Mayakovskii and Meyerhold were good friends. In 1930 Mayakovskii shot himself. Meyerhold was executed ten years later, on 2 February 1940, by an officer of Cheka, the predecessor of the dreaded KGB. He had been arrested in Leningrad in June 1939. A few weeks after his arrest his wife was murdered at night in this Moscow house.

Tamrico and I enter the house and are greeted by Maria Valentei, the granddaughter of the famous theatre director. She leads us to the small kitchen of apartment number 11 where we sit around a small table.

In a few years the adjoining 11a will turn into a Meyerhold museum. 'The work on the museum has slowed down,' complains Maria. 'There is no money and very little interest. People are so poor. They don't have time to think about museums and theatres.'

I turn on my tape recorder, and Maria begins to tell us the story of the house and its apartments. After Raikh's funeral, her children were given forty-eight hours to vacate the house. One of the apartments was allotted to a young woman in the staff of Lavrentii Beria, the KGB chief. The other went to his chauffeur. It took her more than fifty years to reclaim the apartments.

Maria pulls out a file and shows us some handwritten papers: Meyerhold's applications to the prosecutor where he talks about his torture in the Lubyanka prison. She also shows us two prints of a photograph in a book. The photograph was taken in June 1939 during the First National Conference of Theatre Directors. In one print, first from the right, one can see Meyerhold sitting on a chair. In the second print his place is occupied by another famous Russian director, Popov. 'Now we know,' continues Maria, 'that Popov's photograph was cut and pasted neatly over that of Meyerhold.' His disappearance on the photograph preceded his arrest and murder.

Maria takes us to the adjacent apartment where two young Russians are cleaning, painting and pasting new wallpaper. We finish our tea, come out of the apartment and walk to Kuznetskii Most. She takes us to a small house with an arch. 'This used to be the inquiry office of the KGB,' she says. 'Lots of people would come here in the hope of getting some news about their relatives or to hand in a parcel.'

I meet Maria again after a few days on my own and she gives me a packet of papers. It includes photocopies of Meyerhold's handwritten letters, a few theatre programs of Meyerhold plays, a tour program of the Meyerhold theatre and a four-kopeck stamped envelope issued in 1974 to commemorate the centenary of Meyerhold's birth. Maria also tells me about the crematorium and the graveyard in the Donskoi Monastery where Meyerhold is buried.

Meyerhold was shot in February 1940 and his ashes were thrown into a five-metre-deep grave. The place is marked by a stone which reads: 'Common Grave No. 1. Burial place of unclaimed ashes. From 1930 to 1942 (inclusive).' The grave also contains the ashes of another well-known Russian writer and journalist, Mikhail Koltsov, who was shot and cremated on the same day as Meyerhold. It is said that Stalin met Koltsov in the Bolshoi Theatre and congratulated him for winning the Stalin Prize for his dispatches from Spain. The next day Koltsov was arrested.

The day I went and saw the grave there were lots of roses, daisies and tulips on the stone. I sat there for a few minutes. A squirrel came, stood at a safe distance and once convinced that it was not going to get anything from this wearied foreigner, disappeared swiftly onto a nearby oak.

•

One of my favourite Metro stations is Kropotkinskaya. It is located not far from the two places I frequently visited. One of them is the Pushkin State Museum of Fine Arts, and the second, just across the street from it, an open-air public swimming pool.

Like most Metro stations, Kropotkinskaya started with a different name; a name that tells the story of one of the spectacular failures of Soviet architecture and engineering in Stalin's time.

The station was amongst the ten built in 1935, which formed the first line of the Moscow Metro. Its original name was Dvorets Sovetov, the Palace of Soviets. The plan to build the palace was abandoned but its name continued to exist for many years, until in 1957 it was given the name of Pyotr Kropotkin, a nineteenth-century Russian anarchist and philosopher. Because the station was to serve as one of the main access points to the Palace of Soviets it seemed to have received extra attention from the designers and builders of the Metro.

Pikareva describes the station as a unique achievement of Soviet architects and engineers. She hails the 'laconic style, simplicity, beauty of architectural form, and harmony of its colour scheme'. One of the most beautiful elements of the underground hall and platforms are the two parallel rows of columns. The lower half of the columns, made from siliceous marble, is topped by white marble reaching to the ceiling. Where the columns merge with the ceiling, they create a 'pattern of five-pointed stars, imitating the red-star emblem of the Soviet Union'.

Ryabuhsin and Smolina also emphasise the 'brevity of architectural solution' highlighted by 'dimly lit mushroom-shaped supports', which 'create the effect of soaring beamless ceiling'. Pikareva notes how the electrical lights hidden in small capitals at the junction between the lower and the upper parts of the columns generate an impression 'that the light is emanating from the white star-shaped forms in the roof,' and one feels 'at ease in the presence of this soft effulgence.'

I have experienced this radiance in the hall, standing near the columns. Often, returning from the university late at night, I would come out at the station to enjoy the luminous glow. The hall at that time of the night was largely empty and I was able to relish the softness with which the lights embraced the world around me. It created an atmosphere of serenity, warm, cosy, and friendly, becalming my anxious mind.

I like the underground interior but the arched pavilion at the ground level is even more impressive. Pikareva points out the simplicity and clarity of its architectural composition. It is also designed as an opening to Gogol Boulevard, one of the most beautiful in Moscow. The horseshoe-shaped vestibule is made of two chambers joined by a delicate arch through which one can view the central alleyway of the tree-lined boulevard.

Close to the entry of the boulevard there used to be a kiosk where a middle-aged woman would sell tickets for several Moscow theatres. Next to it stood a woman with a trolley who sold *pirozhki*. She worked at the nearby cafeteria and those who bought her *pirozhki* often went to get a cup of coffee in the cafeteria.

Some of the white marble that was used in the construction of the underground platform and hall came from the demolition of the Khram Khrista Spasitelya (Cathedral of Christ the Saviour) that, once upon a time, stood at the site of the open-air swimming pool Moskva. The Cathedral was detonated in 1931; its destruction was ordered by the Stalin's loyal comrade, the 'Iron Lazar'.

The decision to construct the Cathedral was made in 1812 by Tsar Alexander I to hail the bravery of Russian people in the war against Napoleon Bonaparte and to thank Christ the Saviour for protecting Russia. It took almost sixty years to build it. It was consecrated in May 1883, a day before Alexander III was crowned. The premiere of Tchaikovsky's *1812 Overture* was meant to take place in the Cathedral but in 1882 it had not been finished and therefore the overture was performed in a tent outside.

Reaching the height of more than a hundred metres and located on the higher northern bank of Moskva River, it was the tallest building in Moscow at that time. Konstantin Thon, the Russian architect, drew inspiration from Hagia Sofia in Constantinople but also followed the traditional architectural elements of Russian churches and cathedrals.

On plan it followed the layout consistent with an equal-sided cross with ledges at the four ends. The four façades were strictly symmetrical. The cathedral was topped with five onion-shaped domes, the central being the largest with a diameter of thirty metres and a height of more than twenty-seven. The copper on each of the smaller side domes as well as on the central dome was gilded. The outer smaller domes also housed the bells. There were twelve dark bronze doors, three on each side, which led people inside the Cathedral.

Marble, including five different types brought from Italy, was the dominant stone used in the construction. However, the floor and walls were covered with dark green labradorite. The twelve columns in the temple portals were made from jasper.

Sona Stephen Hoisington, an expert on Russian architecture and culture, writes that the Cathedral was often viewed as the

> personification of tsarist authority in Moscow. The link between autocracy and architecture was made more explicit in 1912, when an enormous statue to Alexander III was unveiled on the church plaza amidst great pomp and circumstance. Christ the Saviour, crowned by five cupolas covered with 1,000 pounds of gold leaf, was enormous. It stood 335 feet tall, covered an area of 8,000 square yards and could hold 10,000 people.

The Cathedral was one of those symbols the Bolsheviks would have wanted to destroy and replace it with their own, equally imposing structure. As expected, the first casualty was the grand statute of Alexander III. In the spring of 1918, a large crowd gathered at the Cathedral and brought the statue down, celebrating the triumph of Soviet power. Soon material from the Cathedral began to be removed. Russian architect Gleb Sobolev writes that by April 1922, a huge quantity of silver, diamonds and a crown with many precious stones had been removed. Some material was transferred to museums. This included bas-reliefs from the walls, which were transported to Donskoi Monastery. One of the major items of interest was more than 18 tonnes of gold on the domes. The gold was stripped and stored for potential use in the industrialisation of the country.

I have seen various photographs showing the dismantling and destruction of the Cathedral. In one of them I see ropes tied to a large cross on the dome, ready to be pulled down. Another displays rubble in front of the partially destroyed building with decapitated marble statues holding scriptures in their hands, and not far from them a rubble of severed heads. In yet another there is a group of men standing under the bell of one of the four bell towers. The camera has caught them posing just before beginning the final dismantling of the bell.

The Cathedral was detonated on 5 December 1931 at 12 o'clock. The first explosion failed to demolish it, requiring a second detonation. The temple that took close to sixty years to build was pillaged and destroyed in less than a few years.

Its demolition provided the site to build the Palace of Soviets, a project championed by Stalin. Hoisington writes that initially it was planned to locate the building, then known simply as Dom Siezdov, the House of Congresses, near Okhotny Ryad, not far from the Red Square and Kremlin but once the Cathedral was demolished, the emptied place became the preferred site for one of the most monumental of Stalin's undertakings.

The first few stages of the competition to design the building were open to the public and famous foreign architects were invited to participate. They included Le Corbusier, Gropius, Mendelsohn and Perret, and were paid a decent fee for their contributions. Hoisington publishes photographs of various designs and describes how the initial simple but aesthetically more appealing projects were replaced by grandiose and monumental proposals.

The final winning entry was submitted by Russian architect B. M. Iofan. However, it too went through a few iterations and the design that was finally approved was the one to which two other architects from Leningrad had contributed as co-authors. These changes became necessary because the Construction Council looking after the project came up with 'the idea of combining the Palace of Soviets with a striking monument to Lenin'.

A photograph of the final design was published in Pravda on 20 February 1934. Hoisington believes that 'the final design was chosen because of its dramatic appeal; highly theatrical, it has a conjuring effect.' She cites words from a report published in a 1934 issue of the magazine *Stroitel'stvo Moskvy* which notes that

> by depicting Lenin against a background of scudding clouds soaring high above the airplanes, the drawing creates a mystique of height—in effect guaranteeing that the Palace of Soviets would be the tallest building in the world, taller even than the Empire State Building.

An image of the Palace of Soviets played a prominent role in the Soviet Pavilion, also designed by Iofan, at the New York World Fair in 1939. Hoisington includes a lengthy quote from a booklet in English authored by A. N. Prokofiev, the chief of construction:

> A great edifice – the Palace of Soviets – is being built on the banks of Moscow River, near the Kremlin. This will be the highest building on earth, higher than the Great Pyramids of Cheops, higher than Cologne Cathedral or the Eiffel Tower, taller than the highest skyscraper in New York. The height of the Palace of Soviets will be 1,365 feet. ... The palace will be surmounted by a statue of Lenin, measuring 328 feet—twice as high as the Statue of Liberty at the entrance to New York Harbor. ... a colossus as high as a house of twenty-five stories, the index finger of the outstretched hand measuring 20 feet. ... Express lifts taking 30 passengers at a time will shoot up the statue of Lenin at a speed of 16 feet per second. ... The Palace and the statue of Lenin will be illuminated at night, and visible 25 miles from Moscow.

The palace was never built. By 1939, when Prokofiev wrote his booklet, only the foundation had been prepared. Soon the steel frame that had begun to rise was taken down and all work was suspended in December 1941.

I remember Igor telling me that two factors saved Moscow from inheriting this monumental monstrosity;

the first was the River Moskva and the unstable alluvial sediments over which such a gargantuan structure had to be built, and the second, perhaps more important, was Hitler, the other great dictator. The Second World War had begun, and resources, including steel from the dismantled frame, were needed for the war effort. Hoisington, however, believes that the project was discontinued because Stalin had simply got bored and lost interest in it.

The enormous hole at the abandoned site continued to exist for many years and only in 1958, during Khrushchev's rule, a large swimming pool was constructed at the site. The pool used the metal foundation of the unbuilt palace as its main basin.

I know the Moskva Pool well. I went there to swim twice a week. I remember doing laps in cold Moscow winters when the park around the pool would be covered in snow. There were evenings when the snow fell as I did my leisurely backstrokes in the warm cosy water, feeling the flakes land on my face. Whenever Igor came with me, he told me to close my eyes and lie quietly on the water. 'Why?' I would ask him. 'To hear the church bells ringing,' he would say and smile.

In April 1993 when I went to see the Pushkin State Museum of Fine Arts, I stood for a few minutes looking at the pool. It had stopped functioning two years earlier. Soon it was abandoned and the tank and the buildings servicing it were taken down. I had read about a granite foundation stone marking the beginning of the construction of a new cathedral that had been installed in December 1990. I searched for it but couldn't find it.

These days the new cathedral stands at the site where its much older predecessor used to be. It was built in less than ten years and was consecrated on 19 August 2000. The haste with which it was constructed is one of the reasons that many architects describe it as a poor, almost tasteless, imitation of the much-revered old cathedral.

I suspect that Marina Tsvetaeva, one of my favourite Russian poets, would have been disappointed looking at the new cathedral, mostly because she was a perfectionist and had watched how her father Ivan Tsvetaev had toiled hard to oversee the construction of the grand building which houses the Pushkin State Museum of Fine Arts located just across the street from the new cathedral.

I have found a brief entry in Tsvetaeva's diary dated 23 July 1919. A year earlier the statue of Alexander III had been taken down by an angry but jubilant mob. The forsaken look of the old cathedral would have grieved her. I can feel her sadness as I imagine her whispering and writing the following words in her diary:

> Just recently, in the evening I went for a walk with Charles (an anarchist, young and grey-haired, similar in appearance to Pestalozzi, a solid 'yes' to the world!). Near the Cathedral of Christ the Saviour (I carry an icon with its image around my neck, and I showed the Cathedral, the big one, my own, the smaller icon), I

glanced at the Moskva River. After absorbing the divine plumage of the sky, I looked at the Kremlin and was dumbfounded. All the domes of the cathedral were dark, black. Something hit me hard in the chest. It is the cruellest sight I have ever seen.

To imagine Moscow without churches, domes, and ringing bells was impossible for Tsvetaeva. Her Moscow 'has seven hills shaped like seven bells, and each bell is in a bell-tower, and all of them together make forty times forty'. There are, thus, sixteen hundred bells in Tsvetaeva's Moscow.

Tsvetaeva wrote nine poems about her beloved city and in six of them there are churches, domes, bells and bell-towers. One of the poems is addressed to Mandelshtam, in which she asks him to accept her city as a gift:

Iz ruk moikh – nerykotvornyi grad (From my hands – not a hand-crafted city)
Primi, moi strannyi, moi prekrasnyi brat. (Accept, my strange, my adorable brother).
Po tsirkovke – vse sorok sorokov, (Over the churches – all the forty times forty,)
I reyushikh nad nimi golubkov. (And drifting above them pigeons.)

Tsvetaeva composed these poems in 1916, not in Moscow but in St Petersburg, the city of Mandelshtam, where she had gone for a short visit. By giving her city as a gift to her friend she was also sharing with him her most intimate feelings about the city. In the final line of the poem Tsvetaeva, the poet, asks him 'not to regret that he was in love with her'.

In 1916 Tsvetaeva was twenty-four and Mandelshtam a year older. By 1919, when she went for a walk with her friend Charles and saw the Cathedral and the Kremlin, her life in Moscow had reached a point from where it would become increasingly unbearable, and three years later, she would leave the city for an extended period of exile in Paris.

Mandelshtam's life would follow a similar pattern. He too would be banished from his beloved Moscow and St Petersburg and feel forsaken and forgotten. His wife Nadezhda would share the misery of her husband's exile and become his vital connection with the lost world. She would often travel to the two cities to meet family members and friends and return with money, gifts, and kind words.

Sadly, Tsvetaeva and Mandelshtam would perish, falling prey to Stalin's brutal times, a few years short of their fiftieth birthdays.

•

That Sunday in April, Leonid took me to a house on Borisoglebskii Pereulok. Tsvetaeva lived there for a few years before and after the revolution. In recent years the Tsvetaeva Society has created a museum in this house. The society meets once every month to talk about her, her poetry and her friends. I attended one of these literary events. Two speakers addressed the gathering that evening. One of them was Sofia Bogatireva. She is a literary critic. Her father, I. I. Ivich-Bernshtein (pseudonym Aleksandr Ivich), was a literary critic and a well-known Russian writer of children's books.

In her talk Bogatireva recalled how as a teenager she witnessed the dangerous undertaking of creating, hiding, and preserving a small archive of Mandelshtam's poems. It is well-known now that Nadezhda was a living archive of her husband's poems. She knew almost every poem by heart. She would dictate these poems, which were handwritten, sometimes typed out, and checked and rechecked. After this, several copies were stored in the houses of those who loved Mandelshtam and were willing to take risks.

In her talk she described an ingenious way which her uncle employed to store Mandelshtam's poems. 'My uncle had an original way of hiding banned literature,' she noted. 'He kept them on open shelves.'

Bogatireva recalled that there were times when she felt betrayed because although she was a witness to this activity, she was not allowed to read all of Mandelshtam's poems. There was one particular collection in a box to which she had no access. One day she went to her uncle, who was an equally well-known literary critic and writer, and asked if he had a copy of the poems she wasn't permitted to read:

> Uncle heard me, carefully ignoring all my complaints against my father's despotism in not letting me read the hidden poems. He unfolded the step-ladder, silently with a supercilious gesture of his hand declined my request to help him and climbed right up to the roof. He removed a book from the shelf, came down with the book, folded the stepladder, and put it back at its right place in the far corner. He did this without any rush, carefully and neatly, holding the book under his armpit, and then gave the book to me. It was the 11th edition of comrade Iosif Vissarionovich Stalin's *Problems of Leninism*, published in 1939. I was confused and amazed. Then my uncle threw away the hard cover of the book, and I found that the entrails of the book had been removed, replaced by Mandelshtam's poems. The poems were copied on ruled pages, ripped from a school notebook.

After the talk Bogatireva gave me a reprint of her article from which she had read her address. On it she wrote the following words: 'In twentieth century Russia most talented poets had learnt how to manage without Gutenberg's great invention.'

The cover of Stalin's book, its insides ripped out to make place for Mandelshtam's handwritten poems. Can there be any more potent, visual and palpable image of Soviet life? The written book was perhaps a lesser form through which people communicated with each other. It was the oral word that ruled. The word travelled from mouth to mouth and ear to ear without any danger of being banned or burnt.

The Moscow Metro, its stations, coaches, and the parks near it, were some of the sites where such transactions occurred. The Metro didn't only transport passengers; words and memories travelled with them. I remember carrying a *samizdat*, self-published copy of Mikhail Bulgakov's *The Master and Margarita* in my portfolio bag. It was a thick bundle of unbound typed pages wrapped in the sheets of *Pravda*. I passed the packet to a young woman not far from the marble bust of Mayakovskii inside Mayakovskaya station. She was a stranger to me as I was to her, between us stretched a chain of other intermediaries.

•

Alexei Dushkin, the designer of Kropotkinskaya station, also worked on Mayakovskaya, my other favourite station.

It was one of the eight stations opened in 1938, eight years after Mayakovskii's tragic suicide in an apartment next to Lubyanka, the headquarters of Cheka, or KGB, and a year before the beginning of the Second World War.

Initially, the station was to be called Triumphalnaya after the nearby square with the same name, but in 1936 the square was renamed after the famous poet and soon the new station next to the square also became Mayakovskaya.

It is one of the first metro stations with a deep foundation located thirty-three metres under the surface, most probably intended for use as an air-raid shelter. I have seen a photograph of Stalin standing at the podium and giving a speech at the meeting of Moscow City Council held on 6 November 1941. It is said that he had travelled to the station in a Metro train. A carpet was spread on the floor of the station and a very large portrait of the commander-in-chief was hung on the wall just behind Lenin's marble bust. Victoria Ryabikova, a Russian journalist, notes that the 'speech was followed by refreshments which included beer, bread-rings and sandwiches that were served inside the coaches.' It is believed that 'women and children who normally sheltered there were cleared out for the occasion.' Most people who remember hearing Stalin on the radio thought that the speech was boring and his Georgian accent comic.

The war had reached one of its most critical stages because just a week or so later, the Nazi army would come within twenty-five kilometres of Moscow and preparations were being made to surrender the city and destroy the Metro.

As I look at the photograph of Stalin at Mayakovskaya, my eyes intuitively focus on the beautiful oval-shaped domes with lights, which the station is famous for. The thought that such a wonderful station would have been detonated comes as a shock.

Ryabushin and Smolina note that Mayakovskaya was 'the first station with a deep foundation on piers, and in its design, Dushkin made wide use of stainless steel, a new material in the Metro.' Pikareva emphasises 'the presence in the underground hall of oval arches, which were connected to longitudinal and transverse columns.' The addition of corrugated steel to the transverse arches underlined the uniqueness of the design. Jane Friedman in her study of the mosaics at the station writes that 'the polished surfaces [of steel] reflected the station's natural and artificial light, helping to create an atmosphere of *svetlost* (radiance).' She notes that Dushkin himself was impressed by the light in the hall and had said 'on the opening day, 11 September 1938: "The glint of steel as the train approached the station was stunning"'.

Referring to the work of Annie Gérin, Friedman writes that

> along with the use of steel and new style of the hall, a crowning architectural innovation at Mayakovskaya was the station's ceiling: instead of smooth continuous barrel vaults seen at many of the first- and second-line stations, the vaulting at Mayakovskaya had a succession of groin vaults pierced by oval apertures that were illuminated at the bottom edge and culminated in cupolas. These features enhanced the impression of lightness but also drew the viewers' gaze upward. These cupolas were decorated with ceiling mosaics by the artist Aleksandr Deineka, who was a close friend of Dushkin's.

Deineka's series of thirty-five mosaics was inspired by Mayakovskii's 1925 verse play *Letayuschii Proletarii*

(The Flying Proletariat) set in the year 2125. The play portrays a fictional war between the Soviet proletarian and American bourgeois air forces.

Some of the mosaics on the ceiling are accompanied by verses from Mayakovskii's play. I remember Igor pointing them out to me late one night, but the ceiling was so high above us that it was hard to read them. 'You need to fly in a plane to read them,' he had said and laughed.

The hall and the platforms employed dark and light grey marble, and the facing of the columns was done with rare semiprecious stone brought from the Urals. A unique feature of the hall were the benches in between a few arches. There was one not far from the marble bust of Mayakovskii at the northern end of the hall. I often sat on that bench and watched; once or twice I saw people, mostly women, stop near the bust, pull out a bouquet of red carnations from their bag and leave them on the granite pedestal.

Aleksandr Kibalnikov, the Soviet-Russian sculptor, finished Mayakovskii's bust in 1965, soon after which it was installed in the station. A large bronze Mayakovskii, which he sculpted in 1954, stands outside. Compared to the tall, imposing, and ready-to-take-on-the-world Mayakovskii in the square, the marble Mayakovskii in the station is more subdued, although the look of his piercing eyes is sharp and the little smile on the face is tinted with his trademark anger. Looking at him from the bench I always felt that he would suddenly break the solid, roughly chiselled marble, shake his head crowned with thick hair and begin to recite in his loud garrulous voice the lines of his unforgettable poem *An Extraordinary Adventure which Befell Vladimir Mayakovskii One Summer at the Dacha*. The trains would stop to listen, and people would gaze with their eyes wide open to find a friendly sun descend into the station and spread its sunny smile for all to share.

In April 1993, the marble Mayakovskii still stood at the same spot enjoying the company of a bunch of red carnations. Nowadays, the wall behind him has given way to the second, northern, entrance to the station and because of that 'Mayakovskii' has been moved upstairs in the vestibule. They should have kept him inside the station, for it seems that he was much happier there in a more intimate setting untroubled by people entering and exiting, and by the noise of electronic gates continually opening and shutting.

In one of the photographs of the new vestibule which opened in 2005, just above the escalators, on the ceiling I can see one of the large mosaics by Deineka with the words of Mayakovskii's verse-play scribbled around it. It isn't hard to locate them, and they are easily readable. This would definitely have made comrade Mayakovskii happy.

He loved reading and performing, especially for a large audience, and enjoyed hearing other poets and actors. He would have been flattered by poets reading standing next to his bronzy self in the square in 1958.

The poetry readings at the square seem to have begun spontaneously one evening in the summer of that year. The first followed the unveiling of Mayakovskii's statue. It was an 'official' ceremony in which the so-called established Soviet poets read and performed. However, after they had finished, the stage was opened to the public which responded enthusiastically. It was a new and exciting experience for them. Some people in the public then decided to get together in the square regularly to recite poetry. As Vladimir Bukovskii, the Soviet dissident activist, recounts, initially these meetings were thought by the officials to be quite innocuous and one Moscow daily even published an article about them.

The poetry gatherings were never advertised publicly, but the news about them began to spread. Mayakovskii Square received a new name, Mayak. 'Mayak' in Russian means a 'lighthouse' or a 'beacon'. Generally, people gathered in the evening either on Saturday or Sunday. Most participants, readers and listeners, were young students of Moscow universities and other similar institutions.

The officials tried to control and regulate the event either by placing undercover KGB operatives in the audience who instigated disturbances and clashes or by raiding the houses of the participants. In April 1961 a noisy brawl erupted during the gathering. On that day, a few hours earlier, Yuri Gagarin had returned from his space flight. A public holiday had been announced. However, this was also the day when in

1930 Mayakovskii had shot himself. The brawl ended in several arrests. This proved a fatal blow to the poetry readings which ended after a few months.

•

In January 1954 the Soviet Union began celebrations to mark the tercentenary of the 1654 Pereiaslav Agreement between the Cossack Ukrainian Hetmanate and the Russian Tsar Alexis I. For Khrushchev, who had become the First Secretary of the Central Committee of the Party after the death of Stalin in 1953, the anniversary was a special occasion to consolidate the centuries-old relationship between the Ukrainian and Russian peoples as citizens of two Soviet republics.

Most historians believe that Khrushchev had a sweet spot for Ukraine and its people, but many Ukrainian historians suggest that the sweet spot was hampered by an equally powerful blindfold that prevented him from seeing that the relationship between the two East Slavic neighbours had a torrid history of distrust, betrayals and armed conflicts. This was also the reason that he failed to understand that many nationalist Ukrainians aspired to live in a sovereign Ukrainian nation.

Khrushchev was born in the family of poor Russian peasants in a village not far from the present Ukrainian border. His father worked in the Donbas region earning meagre wages as a railwayman, a miner, and a worker in a brick factory. The Ukrainian historian Serhii Plokhy writes that Khrushchev's family were among the many

Russian peasants who migrated in the early twentieth century into cities in southern Ukraine.

Plokhy mentions that in 1938 'Stalin sent his new lieutenant, Nikita Khrushchev, to Ukraine to carry out the last repressive measures and prepare the republic for what he believed to be a coming war. Khrushchev's task was the same as that of his predecessors: to turn Ukraine into a socialist fortress.' After Kyiv was recaptured from the Nazi forces, a forty-nine-year-old Khrushchev entered the city as Lieutenant General and political commissar of the First Ukrainian Front. Plokhy describes that his main task after the victory was to streamline administration and to facilitate 'reintegration of the former Soviet territories into the Ukrainian Soviet Socialist Republic (Ukrainian SSR) and to reincorporate the lands the Soviets had not controlled before the war.'

Khrushchev had grown up in Ukraine although it's unlikely he spoke or fully understood the Ukrainian language. However, the anniversary provided him with an opportunity to support Ukraine and enhance its role in the Soviet Union, giving it the 'honorary second place in the hierarchy of Soviet republics and nationalities'. The top place belonged to Russians and the Russian Federation.

In 1953 the Moscow Metro had one Kievskaya station on the linear line and a second, Kievskaya-Koltsevaya, was being built on the ring line. Khrushchev wasn't happy with the look of either of the two. He wanted at least one of them to become a cultural symbol of the special fraternal relationship between the two peoples. A station akin to a monument where one could see and experience the true nature of the bond, which he hoped would grow even stronger.

The competition to design the new Kievskaya-Koltsevaya attracted forty entries. It isn't surprising that the project that received the approval was submitted by a team headed by E. I. Katonin, a member of the Ukrainian Academy of Architecture.

The main structural element of Kievskaya-Koltsevaya are heavy stone piers, essential to the construction of a station located at a depth of more than fifty metres. In spite of their heaviness, the marble piers transition smoothly into the three vaults which form the hall and the two adjoining platforms. There are sofa-like marble seats attached to the pedestals of the piers. The eighteen pylons are adorned with floral ornaments and mosaic panels; the panels portray important moments in the history of friendship between the Ukrainian and Russian peoples. The panel-frames bear wide stucco ornaments derived from Ukrainian traditional motifs, and under each panel a marble scroll describes the episode.

From the white vault of the hall hang large golden chandeliers, creating an impression that one is standing inside a bright gallery. To view the panels, one can sit on the marble sofas and look. Historians record that there were more than seven images of Stalin in the mosaic panels. They were later removed, including a bas-relief of Stalin and Lenin on one of the walls. The joint portrait was replaced by a smaller image of Lenin.

I recall that the old lady who gave me two painted Easter eggs in the hall of the station stood next to one of the panels. In Pikareva's book I see a black and white image of one of them. The caption of the photograph is generic. As I look at the image, my memory wants me to believe that this was the panel where I had accepted the Easter gift.

I have been able to find the full caption carved on the marble scroll underneath the panel. It reads: 'Pereiaslavskaya Rada on 8 (18) January 1654.' The second date in the parenthesis is the Georgian equivalent of the date on the Julian calendar.

In the centre of the image I spot the Ukrainian Cossack Hetman Bohdan Khmelnytsky; to his right stands Boyar Vasiliy Buturlin, the chief Russian negotiator reading from a scroll words which I presume are the oath of allegiance to the Russian Tsar Alexis I.

These days the significance of the Pereiaslav Agreement is interpreted differently by Russian and Ukrainian historians. For Russians this is one of the most significant moments in the history of the Russian empire, bringing the unification of Russia and Ukraine. Ukrainian historians downplay its significance. Plokhy describes it as the 'beginning of the long and complex history of Russo-Ukrainian relations.' He writes that

> what actually happened at Pereiaslav in 1654 was neither the reunification of Ukraine with Muscovy (which would be renamed "Russia" by Peter I) nor

> the union of two "fraternal peoples", as suggested by Soviet historians. No one in Pereiaslav or Moscow was thinking or speaking in ethnic terms in 1654.

In 1954 Khrushchev was convinced that the Soviet Union would last forever and with it also the union of the two, separate but united by history, peoples. This idea was repeatedly emphasised by most Soviet newspapers during the celebrations. For example, *Metrostroevets*, a newspaper of the builders of the Metro, published a report on 17 January 1954 with the heading: 'Together for Centuries'. Interestingly the piece is written by Katonin, the Ukrainian architect behind the winning entry. The article is followed by letters from readers, which also include a short poem by Aleksandr Timchenko from a village in Stalinskaya Oblast' in Ukraine. *Thank you, People of Russia*, it is called. Ten photographs of the panels accompany the report.

Kievskaya-Koltsevaya was one of the several monuments erected to mark the tercentenary of the reunification of Ukraine and Russia but Plokhy believes that

> the most lavish symbolic gesture celebrating the "eternal friendship" of the two East Slavic peoples, was the transfer of the Crimean Peninsula in February 1954 from the jurisdiction of the Russian Federation to that of Ukraine. Ten years earlier, the Crimean Tatars had been deported from the Crimea, as the

> entire nation was accused of collaborating with the Germans. ...The Crimea became part of Ukraine—the first and last enlargement of the republic's territory based not on ethnic but geographic and economic considerations.

The Soviet Union collapsed in 1991 followed by a gradual breakdown of the union between the two republics and peoples. Sadly, as I write this essay in June 2022, one of the bloodiest episodes of the break-up is being enacted by Vladimir Putin's Russian forces brutally attacking Ukraine, killing people, animals and plants and also destroying land, soil, rivers and lakes.

I fail to imagine what Russians who walk past the mosaic panels in Kievskaya-Koltsevaya must think and feel looking at the them in these troublesome days of Putin's war on Ukraine. Grief, shame, despair. It's likely that many have already stopped noticing them, for they know that the panels tell nothing other than lies. Some might also decide to mock them in the privacy of their homes. I hope they feel safe at home these days because I know that in Soviet times safety at home wasn't always guaranteed. Even at home one had to speak in whispers or dampen down the words with songs, poems, and guitars.

•

Six weeks after the beginning of Putin's war on Ukraine, I received an email from Igor in Canada, where he works for an exploration company. His message was brief:

> I am glad my parents aren't alive. To watch the cities and villages in Ukraine attacked by the Russian army would have been unbearable. Babushka Maria, my father's mother, lived in Podil in Kiev, which was bombed the other day. Each Russian word I speak and hear pierces my heart, but speak I must because although cursed, it is my language. My surname helps. People think I am Ukrainian, and I am not brave enough to say that I don't know who I am.

With the message he had attached two images. The first is a black and white photograph of Russian women and children sheltering in Mayakovskaya Metro station taken in July 1941. The second is quite recent. It shows Ukrainians who had taken refuge in Arsenalna Metro station in Kyiv. Arsenalna is one of the deepest metro stations in the world, built at the depth of more than 105 metres, an ideal place to hide from bombs and missiles.

I know the station. I saw it almost fifty years ago when I went to Kyiv, keen to find out more about Mandelshtam's life in the city in 1919. This was the year he had met Nadezhda Khazina at a poetry reading in a café-club, KHLAM. Their next meeting took place in a Greek café on the first floor of a building on Sofiivs'ka Street. At that meeting they decided to get married and live for each other. Nadezhda kept her promise but Osip couldn't because of Stalin's brutal intervention.

Igor's photographs aren't new to me. I have seen similar images in several books and newspapers. One of them shows a temporary maternity ward in Mayakovskaya station. I see a young mother feeding her baby and wonder with what memories of the place the two would have lived the rest of their lives.

For people at Arsenalna station the process of remembering and mourning has just begun but they, like those at Mayakovskaya, would remember them as places of fear and hope.

I imagine some of them going there either to catch a train or just to remember, grieve, and perhaps celebrate. At the station, once they feel a little settled, they start looking for traces they might have left behind: a scratch on the wall, a word scraped on the pier, an image tattooed on the floor with chalk, crayon or lipstick. Someone looks for the spot where she had stumbled in the dark, banging her head against a pier. Blood had dripped from the cut; instinctively, her hand moves to feel the wound, healed but replaced by a scar, and a smile flickers on her face.

They carry their memories recorded as if on a tape with a soundtrack of sirens, bombs, and missiles; of the ground shaking above and under their feet; of the dirt dropping from the roof, and of the songs, stories, and tunes hummed and played on an accordion, guitar or a smart phone; and intermixed with them cries, curses and sighs.

The places such as Mayakovskaya and Arsenalna stations remind me of scrapbooks in which people deposit pieces of their life. Each time they go back to the stations, the scrapbook is opened, checked, and rearranged.

There are many who, like me, remember the metro in Moscow as Stalin's Metro, although his name and images have been removed. Behind every new name of a station and the space emptied of Stalin, lurks the shadow of Mandelshtam's 'Kremlin mountaineer with cockroaches on his top lips'. Perhaps it's better that the presence of Stalin hasn't completely vanished, for each time we encounter his name, we are reminded of the brutality with which he and his regime ruled.

Nowadays, the Metro that was constructed to glorify the great dictator seems to condemn and mock him. Sadly, Stalinism hasn't been purged from the post-Soviet Russian society. The 'inner Red Man', to use the words of Nobel-prize winning Belorussian writer Svetlana Alexievich, still lives inside many Russians. Putin and people like him find nourishment in their support or in their silence. One way to cleanse the body-politic in Russia is to keep telling stories hidden in the nooks and crannies of places like Stalin's Metro.

I find one such story in an article by Oleg Yegorov published on 15 June 2018 in the Russian online magazine *Russia Beyond*. In the piece Yegorov tells the tragic tale of seven-year-old Gelya Markizova who had appeared with Stalin in the photograph that inspired the sculptural portrait which had once stood at Stalinskaya station.

Gelya's communist father gave her the name Engelsina in honour of Friedrich Engels. He called his son, the younger brother of Gelya, Vladen a word derived from Vladimir Lenin's name. In 1937, eighteen months after meeting and hugging Stalin, her father Ardan Markizov was arrested and falsely convicted of being a Japanese spy. In June 1938 he was shot. Soon after, her mother was also arrested and deported to Kazakhstan, where she was found dead later in 1938. Yegorov suspects that she was murdered by the agents of Cheka, the Soviet secret police. The orphaned nine-year old Gelya went to live with her aunt and fortunately survived to tell the story. She passed away in 2004, aged 75 in Ankara, Turkey, after a successful career as a Soviet academic and researcher.

Gelya was lucky that she survived the ordeal that many didn't. Sadly, their stories remain unknown. Like the hardback cover of Stalin's book that Bogatireva's uncle used to conceal copies of Mandelshtam's poems, Stalin's Metro might be hiding numerous stories similar to that of Gelya. Hopefully they aren't all about arrests, exiles and executions. There must be some of courage, resilience, and survival.

This may sound strange, but I have come to believe that the two painted Easter eggs I had once received from a kind woman at Kievskaya-Koltsevaya station were given to me for a reason; to remind me perhaps of Stalin's victims: the fallen and the risen.

The Old Banksia in Our Garden

There is an old banksia growing in our backyard garden. I have become used to its friendly presence and I'll miss it when it passes away. However, it's quite likely that it will outlive me. We are both old, but it appears more robust and resilient than me.

Just six months ago it endured a crushing hailstorm, battered for several minutes by hailstones as big as golf balls. It lost most of its leaves, branches and many of its candle-like flowers. But it has refused to perish, and to convince me and Hanna, who is the main carer and nurturer of the garden, that it will live for many more years, it has sprouted new spikes. In a few months the spikes will begin to flower, and birds, big and small, will come to pick and peck.

The world around it will come alive.

Keep going my friend, I say whenever I find myself standing near it.

I call him a friend because standing close to him I feel at peace with myself and with the world in which we have found ourselves together.

He is a friend, therefore the word 'it' sounds rude. I want to avoid it, but I am constrained by the straitjacket of grammar.

I like the Greek word 'philia'. It means affection or brotherly love. The word describes better the attachment I feel for the banksia. Like brothers we have grown together. He older, stronger, and luxuriant, and I older, frailer, and sparser.

We are both made of the same basic elements, I whisper to my friend.

We indeed are, and will change into them once again, I imagine hearing it murmur in reply.

As a geologist I am instinctively drawn to rocks and minerals, but now, quite late in my life I have become more aware of plants and animals. The credit for this goes to banksia, my friend. Thanks to the banksia, the connection between minerals, plants, and animals has acquired new salience for me. I no longer just know about the connection but feel its presence, its force. Knowing without feeling appears to me blind, blighted, arrogant. To know the world and be known by it requires emotional engagement, and this is what makes an object, such as the banksia, special; it no longer remains a thing but partakes of some of our humanness and we of its plant-ness.

Maybe this is why I want to write the story of our banksia; a short biography in which its presence is only a brief moment in deep time-space; the same deep time-space in which we too exist.

•

I begin the story of our banksia by returning to a fateful day in April 1770. It's the second-last day of the month, and it is Sunday.

On this day, clear with a gentle northerly breeze, James Cook, Joseph Banks and their party totalling ten people and a greyhound went ashore to make 'an excursion into the country'. This was a day after Cook and his men in the *Endeavour* had entered the bay leading to the land of the Gweagal people. In D'harawal, the language spoken by them, the place is called Gamay (also pronounced Kamay). The word means 'fresh water'.

It is obvious that no one in Cook's party could have known the name. To be honest, they had no intention, time or interest to learn its D'harawal name. Cook, impressed by the abundance of stingrays in the waters, had named it Stingray Bay but changed his mind after he noticed the number of different plants the party had collected on its excursions. 'The great quantity of plants Mr Banks and Dr Solander found in this place,' he writes on 6 May in the journal, 'occasioned my giving it the name of Botany Bay.'

I am glad that the D'harawal word for the place didn't vanish, and after almost two hundred and fifty years it has found its rightful place. It hasn't replaced the name given to the bay by Cook but it has been co-opted for a national park created in the bay area; the park is now called the Kamay Botany Bay National Park.

Cook, like most other colonial explorers, appears to be a compulsive name-giver. In part this is because the naming of geographical features was essential for him to plot them on charts and maps, recording his journey. But naming also served other important purposes: to pay tribute to his imperial masters and to acknowledge the assistance of his close friends and colleagues. After all, he was discovering new places for his monarch and the empire, opening the way for their colonisation. That he was in the process also erasing histories and cultures is clear to us now but for him the idea could have appeared fanciful, even absurd.

Cook liked the look of the south-west head of the bay and on 29 April, the second day after their arrival, he entered the name Point Solander (now known as Cape Solander) on his chart. The point located at the other, the north-east, end of the bay was equally impressive. It became Cape Banks. On 6 May, before sailing out, the party buried seaman Froby Sutherland who had died the night before, and Cook called the watering place Sutherland Point.

The entry in the *Endeavour* journal of Banks for 1 May shows that he and the party enjoyed the excursion on the land. They walked the whole day and returned to the ship in the evening exhausted but elated:

> The captain, Dr Solander, and myself, and some of the people, making in all ten muskets, resolved to make an excursion into the country. We accordingly did so, and walked till we completely tired ourselves,

> which was in the evening; seeing by the way only one Indian, who ran from us as soon as he saw us. The soil, wherever we saw it, consisted of either swamps or light sandy soil, on which grew very few species of trees, one, which was large, yielding a gum much like *Sanguis draconis*; but every place was covered with vast quantities of grass. We saw many Indian houses, and places where they had slept upon the grass without the least shelter. In these we left beads, ribbons, etc. We saw one quadruped about the size of a rabbit. My greyhound just got sight of him, and instantly lamed himself against a stump which lay concealed in the long grass. We saw also the dung of a large animal that had fed on grass, much resembling that of a stag; also the footprints of an animal clawed like a dog or wolf, and as large as the latter, and of a small animal whose feet were like those of a polecat or weasel. The trees overhead abounded very much with loryquets and cockatoos, of which we shot several [emphasis added].

The party saw animals, birds, trees and grasses and shot several lorikeets and cockatoos. However, what interests me more in the note is the word 'Indian' used to describe the D'harawal people. The word reappears several times in the next paragraph:

> Our second Lieutenant went in a boat drudging: after he had done, he landed and sent the boat away, keeping with him a midshipman with whom he set out

> in order to walk to the Waterers. In his way he was overtaken by 22 Indians who followed him often within 20 yards, parleying but never daring to attack him though they were all armed with Lances. After they had joined our people 3 or 4 more curious perhaps than prudent, went again towards these Indians who remained about ½ a mile from our watering place. When they came pretty near them they pretended to be afraid and ran from them; four of the Indians on this immediately threw their lances which went beyond our people, and by their account were thrown about 40 yards; on this they stopped and began to collect the lances, on which the Indians retired slowly. At this time the Captain Dr Solander and myself came to the waterers; we went immediately towards the Indians; they went fast away, the Captain Dr Solander and Tupia went towards them and everyone else stayed behind; this however did not stop the Indians who walked leisurely away till our people were tired of following them. The accounts of everyone who saw the Indians near today was exactly consonant with what had been observed on the first day of our landing: they were black but not negroes, hairy, naked etc. just as we had seen them [emphasis added].

The people they saw 'were black but not negroes, hairy and naked'. They were playing hide-and-seek with the new arrivals. They didn't know what to do with them. They were curious but also scared and some, as Banks notes 'threw lances which went beyond our people'. Some of them made signs which Banks in his entry for 28 April writes he interpreted as 'waving to us to be gone'. On the same day he records that muskets were fired several times, once over them and some directly at them. One shot was aimed at 'the eldest of the two' and it 'struck him on the legs but he minded it very little so another was immediately fired at him.'

Cook in his journal confirms the firing of muskets although the entry in which he mentions it is dated 29 April. However, like Banks he is of the view that the 'natives' wanted them to go away. He notes on 30 April that 'Mr Hicks, who was the officer ashore, did all in his power to entice them to him by offering them presents; but it was to no purpose, all they seemed to want [was] for us to be gone.'

Sydney Parkinson, the botanical artist on the ship, records in his journal hearing the D'harawals shout 'warra warra wai,' which he interpreted to mean to go away. 'They want us to go away,' he surmised. It appears that Parkinson misunderstood the shouts. 'Warra is a root word of either white or dead,' I read Ray Ingrey, a D'harawal man and deputy chairperson of the La Perouse Local Aboriginal Land Council, explain. 'If you are outside our community trying to look in, you will think it means "go away" but for us it means "you're all dead."' The shouts, Ingrey believes, were most probably directed at the other members of the clan, warning them about the new arrivals. The *Endeavour* appeared to them as part of 'the low-lying clouds,' and nothing but 'whiteness'. The two D'harawal men opposing the landing of the new arrivals were therefore trying to protect their people and land from the ghosts of dead people.

Cook's party, to the relief of the D'harawal people, stayed only for eight days and the *Endeavour* sailed out of the bay on 6 May.

If, for D'harawals, Banks and the party were ghosts, for Banks, D'harawals were Indians. Interestingly, both Cook and Parkinson describe them as 'natives'. It's only Banks who calls them Indians.

Is this important? Perhaps not. But because I am an Indian by birth, Banks's description fascinates me. Banks is confident that D'harawals are not negroes. On 28 April he writes:

> The people were blacker than any we have seen in the voyage though by no means negroes. Their beards were thick and bushy and they seemed to have a redundancy of hair upon those parts of the body where it commonly grows; the hair of their heads was bushy and thick but by no means woolly like that of a Negro; they were of a common size, lean and seemed active and nimble; their voices were coarse and strong.

They aren't negroes but they are also different from the indigenous peoples he meets in the Pacific islands and in New Zealand, for whom Banks employs the word 'natives'. Did he find D'harawals similar to the

Indians he might have seen and met on the south Asian subcontinent, a colony of the British East India Company at that time? He could have.

•

Banks and Dr Solander spent most of the eight days in the bay on excursions, observing and collecting samples.

Banks was pleased with the effort. The collection was substantial. On May 3 he notes in his journal:

> Our collection of plants was now grown so immensely large that it was necessary that some extraordinary care should be taken of them least they should spoil in the books. I therefore devoted this day to that business and carried all the drying paper, near 200 Quires of which the larger part was full, ashore and spreading them upon a sail in the sun kept them in this manner exposed the whole day, often turning them and sometimes turning the Quires in which were plants inside out. By this means they came on board at night in very good condition.

I read his journal carefully trying to find out if it says anything about the flowering plant which in a few years will carry his name. Not a word. The only tree he mentions by name is the one that 'bore fruit of the Jambosa kind, much in colour and shape resembling cherries'. Banks and others seem to have feasted on them although he didn't find the cherries up to scratch. 'They had little to recommend them but a little acid.'

Botanists Doug Benson and Georgina Eldershaw think that Banks was presumably describing *Syzygium paniculatum* (magenta lilly pilly or magenta cherry) which is still growing at Towra Point near the bay. In their article they recount that on his botanising excursion on 4 May in the north-west side of the bay Banks could have seen some of the Eastern Suburbs Banksias. In the journal Banks notes that

> on the NW side of the bay where we went a good way in to the country which in this place is very sandy and resembles something our Moors in England, as no trees grow upon it but everything is covered with brush of plant about as high as the knees.

Benson and Eldershaw have been able to assemble a list of floral samples collected by Banks and his party which includes nine species of banksias and one of them is *Banksia ericifolia*. In their article I also see one of the several photographs of the grassy area around Cook's monument taken between 1880 and 1905. The one shot in 1905 was captured from a ferry wharf. It shows the low scrub spotted with *Banksia integrifolia*. They note that most banksias were less than eight metres tall, but some taller single-stemmed plants were ten to twelve metres high. The same photograph also displays Norfolk and Prince's Pines near the monument. The landscape where Banks botanised in 1770 had by then been altered by farming, grazing, and replanting. The D'harawals who had lived there for thousands of years had kept it more or less unchanged. Their footprints on the land were light and humble.

The regret with which the degradation is mentioned by Benson and Eldershaw is noticeable. 'The Banksias scrub of 1770,' they write, 'has virtually disappeared, replaced by towering forest of Norfolk Island pines and Australian rainforest trees introduced during more than a century of tree planting by visiting dignitaries and well-meaning beautification projects.'

The article incudes a little map that shows the possible extent of plant communities in 1770 at the Landing Place. I look at the map and imagine the foreshore scrub and woodland on the sand knolls where banksias would have grown. Beyond the sand knolls were sturdy sandstones, which too were occupied by scrub containing banksias.

Some of the samples that Banks and Solander collected could have come from the foreshore areas shown on the map. However, it was Parkinson who would have looked at them more carefully because it was his task to draw and paint them. Unfortunately, he couldn't finish the work. He died of dysentery or malaria a few days out of Batavia and was buried at sea with fifteen other seamen. He was twenty-six.

Because he was working with such a large collection, he decided to make line drawings with black pencil first, annotating each with notes about colours to be used to finish the watercolours later. It has been suggested that he was able to finish one: a watercolour of *Banksia integrifolia*. Other watercolours were produced in 1773 for which Banks employed several artists to work on Parkinson's sketches and notes. The watercolours are presently housed in London's Natural History Museum. On their internet home page I discover beautiful images of watercolours including one of *Banksia ericifolia*. The banksia in it is almost identical to the old banksia in our backyard garden. The image shows several branches with one twenty-five-centimetre-long flower. The flower has opened at the top, its hooked styles uncurled, protruding straight, ready for birds, bees, flies, and ants to come and feed.

The botanical name of the old banksia in our garden is *Banksia ericifolia* L.f., the initials identifying Carl Linnaeus, the Younger, who described and named the genus and many of its species. He was the son of Carl von Linnaeus, the renowned classifier, who is famous for the aphorism 'God creates, and Linnaeus classifies'. The great classifier had been asked by Banks to work with him to publish the whole collection which he had called *Banks' Florilegium*. But the work got delayed for several reasons and the first description of plants appeared only in 1781 as a supplement to Linnaeus's *Genera Plantarum*, three years after the death of Carl von Linnaeus. In the supplement the plants were named by Linnaeus's son, who for reasons unknown described only four of the six banksia samples in the collection. One of them was *Banksia ericifolia*, giving the genus the name of his famous patron. It is said that his father had initially suggested to call the whole 'new' country Banksia but unfortunately or perhaps fortunately, his suggestion wasn't accepted.

Carl Linnaeus, the Younger, labelled the species *ericifolia* because of its leaves: the Latin *erica*, means 'heather' and *folium*, 'leaves'. The banksia had leaves reminiscent of heather reflected in its common name: heath-leaved banksia.

Did D'harawal have a name for it? Of course, they must have. It is quite likely they had different names for different species, based on how important they were in their everyday life. But their language has been largely lost although slowly, word-by-word, it is being resurrected. My search for indigenous words leads me to Jakelin Troy's book *The Sydney Language* hosted on the internet site of Dharug and D'harawal Resources. In the book I find the word 'wadanggari' (pronounced 'wa-tan-gre'). I smile when I discover that this is the name Dharugs use for my favourite, *Banksia ericifolia.*

I like the sound the word 'wa-tan-gre' makes in my mouth. I would have loved to hear it spoken by Dharugs to feel the syllables vibrate in my ears. I would have also loved to know the meaning of the word itself to grasp what aspect of the tree it captures. Unfortunately, in the glossary of a few hundred D'harawal words on the same internet site I don't find any for banksias. Its absence disappoints me. Perhaps one day it will reappear, I tell myself. Perhaps D'harawals trying these days to revive their language might invent a word as sonorous as the Dharug 'wa-tan-gre'.

The Ngunnawals, on the land of which I live now with my friendly banksia in the garden, have a word for silver banksia (*Banksia marginatta*). They call it *dhulwa*. The word the Gubbi Gubbi people in south-eastern Queensland use for banksia is 'wallum'. It has now become part of the common name (wallum banksia) of the species *Banksia aemula*, but the word 'wallum', I read in my reference book on banksias, is nowadays also applied to the swampy heartland community in Queensland and New South Wales.

The largest diversity of banksia species in Australia is recorded in the south-western part of Western Australia. Therefore, it doesn't surprise me that the Noongar have several different names for them. For example, the candle banksia (*Banksia attenuate*) is known as *piara* (or *biara*, *bealwara*, *peera*, *piras*), the bull banksia (*Banksia grandis*) as *mungite* (or *poolgarla*, *bulgalla*), the swamp banksia (*Banksia littoralis*) as *pungura* (or *boongura*, *gwangia*), and the parrot bush (*Banksia sessilis*) as *pulgart*. It seems there are three more species of banksia in the region for which Noongar words have not been found.

The Noongar and Dharug words are similar to common names given to plants, trees and animals. They reflect their importance in the life of people who lived with them. The botanical terms which emerged in Europe in the nineteenth century were coined for different reasons and one of them was taxonomy, aiming to identify, describe, and classify plants. As a geologist I am trained to employ a similar system for rocks. I have also learnt that such a system provides us with a means to establish links between rocks of different regions all over the earth and to some extent with rocks on other celestial bodies. Generally, the names of rocks don't signify their importance for us. They are meant to be objective and universal so that they can be applied to explore and explain their evolution in time and space.

A similar desire drives the taxonomy of plants. For example, the heath banksia is a species of the genus Banksia which belongs to the family Proteaceae that includes eighty-three genera and around 1600 species, spread across many regions in the southern hemisphere. Some of the common genera that I am familiar with are Protea, Grevillea, Hakea and Macadamia. Therefore, the heath banksia is in some way related to one of the species of Protea so widespread in South Africa.

As a geologist I understand the significance of scientific names and yet I am curious to find the origin of the Dharug word *wadanggari* or the Noongar word *pulgart.* It doesn't satisfy me that they are simply the names of two species of banksia. There must be some logic to these names, a logic derived from everyday living.

I find some answers in Myfany Turpin's article on the naming practices of Kaytetye speakers. Turpin, an anthropologist, linguist and a music scholar, spent considerable time living with the speakers of Kaytetye language, used approximately by two hundred people in Central Australia. It's a subgroup of Arandic languages, which are spoken by around four and a half thousand people.

Turpin notes that the Kaytetye name for the ironwood (*Acacia estrophiolata*) tree is *athimpe-ngkwarle* where the word *ngkwarle* is a generic term denoting sweet food. The compound name tells Kaytetye speakers that this particular ironwood is a good source of sweet sap. Like many edible tree saps, writes Turpin, the tree is referred to as a 'lolly' in Aboriginal English. The Kaytetye name *ankerre-ngke* for the heavy-soil hand-flower (*Goodenia lunata*) is related to the word used for emus. This is because the shape of its leaf is similar to that of an emu's foot. The suffix *ngke* in the name of the plant means 'foot'. Similarly, the Kaytetye call the native lemon grass *arineng-arinenge*, a compound term formed by reduplication of the word *arinenge* which signifies the euro or hill wallaroo (*Macropus robustus*). This is because Kaytetye speakers know that the lemon grass and the euros have a similar fluffy appearance.

Of the many examples discussed by Turpin in the article I find Kaytetye words for snakes the most fascinating. She lists the names of seven poisonous snakes, and each is derived from that of the plant or tree near which the snakes are commonly found. For example, the snake living in the vicinity of honey grevillea (*Grevillea juncifolia*) is called *tharrkarre-tharrkarre* where the word *tharrkarre* stands for grevillea. Thus, the name of the snake is derived by a simple reduplication of the word. The combined word spoken rapidly and loudly, suggests Turpin, should work well as a signal for the potential danger in the form of a poisonous snake.

I like the sound the word *tharrkarre* makes, and as I pronounce the three syllables the sound fills my ears. I like the feeling, and the word takes me back to *wadanggari*, the Dharug name for *Banksia ericifolia*. What does the word *tharrkarre* mean, I want to ask a Kaytetye speaker? Why do you call *Banksia ericifolia, wadanggari*, I long to find out from Dharug speakers?

It's clear from Turpin's article that names of many plants and animals are interrelated. Often, they not only describe the shape, size and appearance of a plant but also its properties. Some stress their nourishing and healing qualities whereas others warn the speakers to keep away from them or use them with caution. These names tell me that the boundaries between the three kingdoms, the animal, the plant and the mineral, that Carl von Linnaeus classified the world into are flexible and strategic, defined largely by the logic of everyday living.

As I think more about Turpin's article, I discover that I still don't know the meaning of words such as *tharrkarre* or *wadanggari*. The suggestion that they are mere sounds doesn't work for me. I doubt that Ferdinand de Saussure, the Swiss linguist, was correct when he proposed that the relation between words and objects is arbitrary and conventional. The words with which we label objects are conventional but arbitrary they don't seem to be.

It may sound mystical but often things in this world call us to be named in a particular way. Is this because they hold strange and unexplained power to attract and influence us? By giving them names we draw them into our lives, making them integral to our way of living. We can't be what we are without them. By naming them we partake of a piece of them, and they also capture a fraction of our being. Our existence in the world is nothing but an endless event of co-being in the world. We live in the world and the world lives in us.

•

The D'harawal word for the bay is Gamay which means fresh water. Assuming that its translation into English is correct I want to understand the reason why it got this name.

Is it because the water in the bay was fresh? How can the salty water in the bay be fresh? Perhaps they used the word not merely for the water but for the whole landscape: the sandstone cliffs and foreshore, the sand knolls, the sandy beach, the woodland and heathland on the cliffs, and the seawater teeming with stingrays and other fish. The location was perfect; the food was plentiful and the climate mild. The word 'fresh' was perhaps the best metaphor to describe the place.

As a writer I am happy with the idea that the word could have been a metaphor but the geologist in me wants to find something more solid and more palpable than a metaphor. Moreover, I have read the work of Luise Hercus and her colleagues who show that the names which the indigenous peoples in Australia used for places were hardly ever metaphoric. Each name was an essential part of a story embedded in the place tied up with its own and their creation; the name was as real as the place itself, reflecting its indelible presence in their lives. Hence, the word meaning 'fresh' too should have something physically real and solid to justify the metaphor.

Luckily, I uncover a clue in a scientific paper by a team of Sydney geologists and geophysicists. The article includes a map depicting topography of the seabed in the bay hidden under the water, at places greater than one hundred metres. On the map I can decipher the palaeo-channels of rivers and ridges. One of the palaeo-ridges runs north-west to south-east starting from the present-day Runway Ridge on which the airport runway of the Sydney Airport is located. The ridge divides two drainage systems. The northern system was formed by an ancient river (the present-day Botany River) and several of its short, steep tributaries. The southern was much more extensive. It was created by the precursors of the present-day Cooks and Georges Rivers and their many branches. The valleys were steep but the gradients shallow (at least at water depths less than 30 to 40 metres) generating slow and sedate flow.

'Botany Bay,' B.D. Johnson and his colleagues note, 'could not have existed until the water level in the sea had risen to the lowest part of the Runway Ridge, about 35 metres below present-day sea level.' As the sea level gradually went up the valleys were inundated by the sea leaving a *tombolo* (sandspit) formed between Cronulla and Kurnell.

The ancestors of D'harawals must have witnessed the upsurge of the sea and gradual flooding of ridges, rivers, and valleys where they fished and hunted. Before the sea rose, the present-day Towra Point was a part of a relatively wide mud and sand delta populated by mangroves; the waterways and salt marshes providing nesting and roosting sites for birds.

If the ancestors of D'harawals witnessed the surge of the sea they could have also seen a gradual drop in the sea levels thousands of years before that, a fall that led to the formation of deltaic landscape in the area. It turns out that landscape they called fresh has been made and remade by a series of melting and glacial events, one of the most significant of which is called the Last Glacial Maximum.

The scientists who study palaeoclimate and palaeoecology estimate that the last glacial period in the Earth's history began around 33 thousand years Before Present, and globally the ice sheets reached their maximum level between 27 thousand and 19 thousand years BP. This interval is defined as the Last Glacial Maximum. The maximum was followed by deglaciation and melting of ice which began in the Northern Hemisphere soon after, and at around 15 thousand to 14 thousand years BP in the Southern

Hemisphere when the West Antarctic Sheet started melting.

The Last Glacial Maximum was associated with a drop in the greenhouse gases such as carbon dioxide and methane, which based on the Antarctic ice-core data fell to around 180 to 200 parts per million for carbon dioxide and around 400 parts per billion for methane. The widespread glaciation led to a fall in the sea levels which is estimated to have stood at between 120 and 130 metres lower than today. The plunge in the sea level created a continent much larger than the present-day Australia and included Papua New Guinea and other continental islands such as Tasmania and Kangaroo Island. Archaeologists call this enlarged continent Sahul.

Estimates based on various proxies of temperature indicate that the Last Glacial Maximum was the coldest and driest phase in the past thirty thousand years. The ocean temperature around the coast of the amalgamated continent was 2 to 4 degrees Celsius lower than that of today. It was much colder on the land, probably around 6 to 10 degrees Celsius lower. Ice sheets on the Snowy Mountains and Tasmania were much larger, and persistent. The Eastern Highlands stretching from Queensland to Tasmania were transformed into a cold and arid region largely similar to steppes interspersed with sub-alpine woodland. On the west, the tablelands surrounding them were also cold and windy with slopes covered by grassland and herbs changing into forest and box woodland at lower altitudes.

Compared to the cold and arid environment on the tablelands, the eastern coastal area remained relatively mild and well-watered. It provided some of the most hospitable refuges from the harsh climate, offering food and shelter to a population that archaeologists believe was declining elsewhere on the island continent.

Radiocarbon ages at Burrill Lake and Bass Point on the south coast of New South Wales indicate occupation of the area by the ancient neighbours of D'harawal people dating back to 26 thousand and 19 thousand years BP, the years coinciding with the peak of the Last Glacial Maximum. Val Attenbrow in her review of the aboriginal prehistory in the Royal National Park and the adjacent areas rightly concludes that available archaeological ages dating back to 11 thousand years BP are much more recent than the earliest dates for occupation of Australia going back to dates older than 50 thousand years BP. There is no doubt, she notes,

> that in those earlier times people were occupying the country that is now Royal National Park and southern Sydney, and so sites older than 10 thousand to 11 thousand years BP may one day be found when further sites are investigated in these areas.

The global warming which followed the cold and arid climate during the Last Glacial Maximum must have come as a relief to the ancestors of the D'harawal and other indigenous inhabitants of the continent. But it brought unforeseen challenges as well because warming initiated the melting of ice sheets, causing an increase in the sea-level. Palaeoclimatologists estimate that the surge occurred at different rates reaching maximum values of about 15 millimetres per year (or 1.5 metres in a hundred years) first between 16 thousand and 12 thousand years BP and then again between 11 thousand and 9 thousand years BP. On the southeast coast of Australia, the general rates were comparable. The sea reached the height of 15 to 11 metres below the present-day level between 9.4 thousand and 9 thousand years BP. It went up by another 9 to 12 metres at around 8 thousand years BP. The sea reached the present-day level between 7.9 thousand and 7.7 thousand years BP. However, it didn't stop there, and kept on going up, adding another 1.5 metres in the following three hundred years. It stood at this high level until about 2 thousand years ago, after which it relatively slowly and smoothly dropped to the present-day level.

The inundation brought about by the surging sea spread across the river valleys and open ocean embayments. The sand barriers were destroyed, new bays were formed, and the freshwater river valley system was gradually replaced by the estuarine habitat of present day.

The upsurge of the sea was global and was accompanied by an increase in the concentration of greenhouse gases such as carbon dioxide and methane. Estimates show that around 11 thousand years ago (the beginning of the Holocene epoch) the concentration of carbon dioxide in the atmosphere had reached a maximum of 260 parts per million (rising from around 200 parts per million during the Last Glacial Maximum). By and large the concentration of carbon dioxide in the atmosphere remained at the same level till about the beginning of the seventeenth century when it began to grow, reaching the catastrophic level of 416 parts per million in February 2021, at least 150 parts per million higher than the levels that accompanied the sea-level increase of between 100 and 120 metres caused by global warming, which followed the Last Glacial Maximum. I call the recent trend catastrophic because if during the warming after Last Glacial Maximum, the carbon dioxide increased by 60 parts per million in around 12 thousand years (i.e. around 5 parts per million per thousand years), the recent rise of 150 parts per million have occurred in less than 500 years, with rates much higher since 1950.

The ancestors of the D'harawal people and their neighbouring clans, who witnessed the rise of the sea, couldn't have failed to notice how its fury changed over time. There were periods when it was indiscernibly slow but there were times when it was disturbingly rapid. Then it would have seemed menacing, drowning land, plants, animals and people. The people who saw and felt its rage must have fashioned stories to tell them to their children and grandchildren.

I discover brief descriptions of such stories in an article by Patrick Nunn, a geographer, and his linguist colleague Nicholas Reid. The story that catches my attention is *Kai'mia* (*The Gymea Lily*). On the internet site D'harawal Dreaming Stories, I find an unabridged version of the story. It is narrated by Aunty Fran (Frances Bodkin), the knowledge holder of the D'harawal people. It is one of the many stories which Aunty Fran describes as the 'stories my mother told me'. I soon learn that she has handed over the stories to Gawain Bodkin-Andrew, her son. Now, he is their keeper and holder.

I like the word 'holder' more than 'keeper' because it emphasises the tactile element involved in the act of holding, and because it is bodily, I imagine it to be reciprocal: he holds the stories and the stories keep a hold on him. He doesn't own them, like I own the stories I have written and published, but they own him. The obligation is mutual, and it adds to the act of holding a certain grace, a kind of blessing, which enriches them both, the stories and the holder. In time he will, like his mother, hand them over to one or more of his children, ensuring that they remain part of the collective memory of D'harawals.

On the internet site the stories are listed by their D'harawal titles. I read them aloud, unsure if I am uttering the words correctly, but this doesn't dampen the pleasure I feel, which is aural and tactile at the same time. I look for audio-recordings of the stories in D'harawal language but can't find any. A week later a book of D'harawal stories I had ordered arrives. It has fourteen stories illustrated with beautiful watercolours by Lorraine Robertson. I am impressed by the watercolours. The *wiritjiribin*, lyrebird, painted on the cover is angelic, pirouetting its dance in the company of the luscious verdure of coastal woodland.

The book doesn't include *Kai'mia*, the story of the Gymea lily, but I am delighted to find *Wattun'goori*, a story of two types of banksias and two clans of ancestor-peoples associated with them: the hairy men Wattun'goori and their little cousins Kuritjah. In five out of the fourteen stories, the focus is on the harsh, dry and arid climate. In *Wattun'goori* I read:

> there came a time when a terrible drought passed over this land. The rivers and waterholes all dried up, many of the animals died, as did many of the plants and trees. Because there was no water in the rivers or creeks, nearly all the fish died.

The opening of *Talara'tingi: How the Flannel Flower Came to Be*, on the other hand, tells of icy cold conditions:

> Once, long ago, during a time of great cold, the ground was white with ice all year round, and grey clouds covered the skies.... During this time the flowers died, and the only colour to be seen in the bushland was the green of the trees and grass, and the brown of the rocks.

If *Kai'mia* tells the story of the great flooding, the other tales are about much colder and arid times. The stories are beautiful, and I am ready to suspend my disbelief and convince myself that they truly imagine what could have happened at that time. I read them assuming that they reflect an attempt by ancient D'harawal storytellers and their listeners to come to terms with what had happened so far in deep time.

Can oral stories preserve collective memories of events buried deep in time? Can they be transmitted without corruption or embellishments? How much of the factual truth in them remains untouched and undistorted? As I ask these questions, I realise that the presence or absence of factual truth isn't important for these stories, that I make a mistake when I look for that kind of truth in them. What's more significant for me is to assure myself that they were prompted by climatic upheavals, and that I should read them in the same way as I read Ovid's *Metamorphosis,* Homer's *Iliad* or stories in Rig Vedic hymns.

Nunn and Reid also raise similar questions and conclude that indigenous stories of the flooding of the Australian coast might preserve collective memories of deep-time events largely because of the unique conditions in which they found themselves in a much larger continent 60 or more thousand years BP. They remained on the continent mostly isolated from other peoples, languages and cultures and had over time developed a deep and more meaningful attachment to the land, its animals and plants, its lakes and rivers and also with the night sky and the stars and constellations spread over them. This attachment also created experiential knowledge of the world and of themselves, which they preserved and communicated in oral stories, dances, and also in motifs they carved and drew and painted on rocks and other surfaces.

The oldest rock art found on the south-eastern coast and its hinterland is estimated to have been painted six thousand years ago, a couple of thousand years after the sea had reached the present-day level. The older rock art, if created, has either not been found or was destroyed by flooding triggered by the rising sea. However, on the western coast, archaeologists believe that they have uncovered rock art that could have been created more than 40 thousand years ago, thousands of years before the beginning of the Last Glacial Maximum. Parts of the western coast where the continental shelf is wider and slopes relatively gently, the effects of cooling during the Last Glacial Maximum were more pronounced and so were the effects of global warming that followed the cooling. The surge of the sea and the flooding were catastrophic.

For example, in Murujuga (Dampier Archipelago), the country of Ngarda-Ngarli people, the Last Glacial Maximum caused the sea level to drop 130 metres below the present-day level, and the coastline moved 160 kilometres to the west. The global warming which followed the cooling brought the sea back, and by around 10 thousand years BP it reached the outer limits of the landmass. It took another 4 thousand years for the archipelago to acquire the shape we observe now.

The ancestors of the Ngarda-Ngarli people who witnessed these catastrophic changes were forced to find new ways to live and survive. Slowly they adapted to the new conditions and recorded the changes by engraving, drawing, and painting images on rocks. The landscape began to resemble a large rocky canvas or parchment marked with stories for us to see, decode, and read.

Although much of the rock art in the area is yet to be dated, careful study of the style and of the intensity of weathering of the rocks has helped archaeologists to group them into evolutionary phases and link them broadly to major climatic events. The study suggests that as the sea level went up and the land was flooded, the older engravings of predominantly terrestrial animals such as birds, emus, macropods and pythons were replaced by the images of aquatic animals such as turtles, dugongs and fish.

Archaeologists believe that they have enough information to conclude that changing motifs in the rock art might reflect changes in the lifestyle of people who lived on the ancient land. During the Last Glacial Maximum, they lived predominantly as hunter-gatherers but altered and adapted to become an agile hybrid of hunter-gatherers and fisher-foragers.

The stories found in the rock art are literally written on stones. Unlike oral stories they can't be easily erased, corrupted or embellished although they face danger from mining activity and from future climatic upheavals.

The survival of oral stories is much more precarious. They need the written word to survive, otherwise they endure as long as the language and the speakers of that language remain alive. The D'harawal and other indigenous peoples were able to endure the catastrophic changes in global climate but couldn't withstand the onslaught of colonisation that brought disease, displacement and dispossession. In Attenbrow's review I read that by 1789, just a year after the arrival of the First Fleet, 'the Gadigal, the clan on whose land Sydney town was established, was reduced to three people.'

Just three people, I read aloud and despair because the D'harawal-speaking Gweagal people could have endured a similar tragedy. Perhaps this is one of the reasons why I cherish Dreamtime stories told by Aunty Fran. Their mere existence is a source of hope for the language and the people. If I want to speak the D'harawal words aloud this is because I naively believe that by chanting them, we will be able to find a rightful place for them in the geography of this ancient land.

From *Kai'mia*, the story of Gymea lily, I learn that the D'harawal word for the Georges River is *Kai'eemah* and the Cooks River, named after the great explorer, is called *Goolay'yari*. These words exist, and it would be appropriate to hear them each time a colonial name is uttered. These words would help the non-indigenous inhabitants of this country, and I am one of them, to experience the ripples of deep time resonating in them.

•

In 1896, during the construction of Alexandria Canal, a waterway to connect Botany Bay with southern Sydney, the digging uncovered the skeleton of a dugong. It was buried in the flood-plain sediments of Shea's Creek, a little semi-tidal stream which, before the urbanisation of the area, ran south-south-west and joined with Goolay'yari (the Cooks River).

In 2004, Robert Haworth and his team dated one of the bones of the dugong and found that it was as old as 6 thousand years. The bones rested in a layer of estuarine sediments rich in shells, and carried marks of butchering by a stone axe. The layers above and below the host sediments contained an abundance of archaeological artefacts. The sediments were made of alternating layers of estuarine sand and shell, and peat rich in plant remains. This suggested that the conditions in the flood plain fluctuated, changing from deeper tidal water to a relatively drier sub-aerial environment.

Interestingly, the basal layer of the sedimentary sequence, lying ten or so metres below the bone-bearing layer, hosted the stumps of a burnt eucalyptus forest. The team discovered that one of the logs of a eucalyptus (*Eucalyptus resinifera* or red mahogany) in the layer came from a tree as old as 8.5 thousand years. In addition to the eucalyptus they also discovered woody remains of a 9.7 thousand-year old *Angophora costata* (smooth-barked apple).

The presence of dugong bones in the flood-plain sediments of a creek, presently located outside the limits of Botany Bay, indicates that more than 6 thousand years ago when the sea was flooding and filling the old river valleys, the climate was warm and the bay was much more extensive than what we see these days. Haworth and his colleagues suggest that a shallow tidal embayment must have covered the area which is now Mascot, and that mangrove, salt marsh and other semi-saline swamp could have stretched as far north as the present-day Moore Park and Centennial Park.

The rising sea inundated and destroyed woodland and other flora in the area. The pollen record in the sediments at the eastern end of the Kurnell Peninsula reveals that the woodland at that time was populated by different species of Casuarina, Acacia, Eucalyptus, Angophora, Banksia and Monotoca. The pollens show the presence of only two species of banksia: *Banksia serrata* and *Banksia integrifolia*, but this doesn't stop me from believing that my favourite, *Banksia ericifolia*, could have been growing there as well.

The fen or wetland parts of the area were vegetated by several types of sedges, arrowgrasses, ferns and watermilfoils. The presence of some specific types of algae indicates that initially the water in the wetlands was fresh. Around 5 thousand years BP, a further rise in the sea level washed away a coastal sand barrier causing inundation and drowning of the woodland. Estimates show that around thirty percent of the land in the area could have been submerged by the rising sea. This would have been a major disaster at that time, ruining the lives of many people and forcing those who survived to find new ways to live. The sea drowned not only land and river valleys but also the footprints of people who lived there.

It is hard to imagine what the ancestors of the D'harawal people and their neighbouring clans would have felt standing on the new coastline and looking at the newly formed bay. What songs of sorrow would they have sung? What dances of mourning would they have danced? What rituals would they have performed to appease the fury of the sea?

During the periods when the sea went up slowly the people possibly had more time to escape, to salvage whatever they had and move away to safer areas and start adapting to the new conditions. However, when the rate of increase was as high as five metres every hundred years, the sea would have appeared more threatening, requiring rapid adjustments. Adjustments were made and people survived.

Before the sea level surge and flooding, the coastline during the Last Glacial Maximum was several (6 to 15) kilometres to the east of the present-day coast, but near enough for people in the area to live both as hunter-gatherers and coastal foragers.

One of the oldest dated archaeological sites along the south-eastern coast is near Burrill Lake. During the final years of the Last Glacial Maximum (around 20 thousand years BP) the cave is known to have been used as a shelter. The site is located in a relatively small wooded valley through which flowed a freshwater stream making its way through gently sloping and thickly wooded hills. Although archaeological excavations at the site didn't find any faunal material in the deepest and oldest layers, the presence of a marine shell of an estuarine species in one of the layers was enough for the archaeologists to suggest that during the cold years of the Last Glacial Maximum, people who visited the shelter could have made frequent trips to the coastline which was less than fifteen kilometres from the cave. One of the most interesting findings at the campsite came from the study of stone tools. It appears that the indigenous occupants employed fire and heat to make the rocks more amenable to cutting and grinding, so that tools could be fashioned from them.

As the sea level surged and began to inundate the area proximal to the cave shelter, the valley with the freshwater stream was replaced by the estuarine lake we see today. As the coastline moved closer, the habitat, very much like the one in Botany Bay, became predominantly estuarine. The remains of faunal material found in the youngest layer (1.67 thousand years BP) reveal that although people visiting the shelter sourced food from the lake shore, and the sea, they also obtained a significant amount from the woodland close at hand and the estuarine lake.

Archaeological studies in the Royal National Park and the nearby regions provide more information on the life and habitat of the ancestors of the D'harawal people occupying the area after the sea had risen to the present-day level (just before and after 8 thousand years BP). The remains of faunal material reveal that people consumed a wide variety of fish and land animals. Some sites contain bones of marine mammal such as fur seals and whales.

The people made tools from the Hawkesbury Sandstone and volcanic rocks which included basalts that would have been sourced from areas as far as 80 kilometres to the north. The evidence is clear that people traversed between the woodland, the coast and the estuaries, and one of the most popular marine shells that was carried furthest from the sources was Sydney cockle. The shell was valued both as food and as a good material for tools.

In Attenbrow's article I find fascinating discussion about black nerite shells discovered amongst the shell middens at a number of sites along the south-eastern coast of Australia. The shells are marked with signs of being worked on, and it was initially suggested that they could have been used to shape necklace-like ornaments. However, this interpretation was soon replaced by several intriguing ideas, one of which speculated that they were pieces from a musical instrument resembling a sistrum, often played as an accompaniment to the beating together of sticks. It was also suggested that they could have come from broken rattles for children or from water rattles used underwater to attract animals.

•

The study of pollens suggests that the ancestors of my friendly banksia were growing in the bay area at least 8 thousand years ago. However, this is just one of the many, and perhaps relatively recent, mileposts of its deep-time lineage.

It's quite likely that when the ancestors of the indigenous peoples arrived in Australia more than 60 thousand years ago, they also met banksias, which soon became part of their everyday living. The banksia was one of the most widespread plants in the south-eastern coastal area.

Palaeobotanists estimate that banksias were growing in Australia almost 65 million years ago. In the sediments of an old lake, forty kilometres south of Canberra, they have found the remains of a banksia leaf. They think that the sediments were formed in the Late Palaeocene, around 56 million years ago. It was then that a leaf blown off the tree by wind fell into the lake and was trapped forever. On the other side of the continent, sandstones in the Kennedy Ranges in Western Australia host remains of banksia fruit and flowers. The sandstone is believed to have been formed 35 million to 40 million years ago. Fossil remains of banksia of similar ages have been discovered in Tasmania, Victoria and Central Australia.

Emerging millions of years ago, banksias have become ubiquitous plants in Australia's sclerophyllous heaths, woodlands and forests. Outside of Australia a few banksia species occur in Papua New Guinea and Indonesia's Aru Islands. In Australia they seem to prefer nutrient-poor soils formed over sandstones, limestones, sand plains, and lateritic loams. They are common in most coastal and near-coastal areas and are also found on cliffs and ranges rising 1,500 metres above the sea level.

Of the coastal regions, although banksias are abundant in the south-eastern coastal areas, the main centre of diversity is located in the south-western coastal zone, the country of the Noongar people in Western Australia. It hosts more than 80% of species of banksias mostly because of its predominantly Mediterranean climate and nutrient-poor lateritic soil. Palaeobotanists believe that frequent natural fires could have created favourable conditions for rich biodiversity in this zone. Semi-arid heaths and shrublands host more diverse species than forests with relatively higher rainfall.

An intriguing feature of the distribution of banksias in Australia is that they are sparse in central Australia and completely absent in the Nullarbor Plain. Does this mean that there wasn't any floristic connection between the two coastal zones, and that the banksia evolved in them independently? This appears to be a real possibility because these zones lack species common to each other. For example, my favourite, *Banksia ericifolia,* does not grow in the south-western zone. Similarly, one of the most beautiful banksias, the parrot bush (*Banksia sessilis*), which the Noongar call *pulgart*, is not found in the south-eastern zone.

Plant ecologists Marcel Cardillo and Renae Pratt, who studied banksia evolution and diversification, suggest that there is a high probability that banksia species originated in the south-western zone and spread to other parts of Australia in two independent dispersal events. They also think that the arid limestone plateau of the Nullarbor Plain could have acted as a barrier to the dispersion of banksias from the south-western coastal zone. As banksias dispersed, they evolved to form new species more suitable for the landscape, soil and climate in the eastern coastal areas. In the process they spread widely along the coast where they didn't find an ecological opportunity or need to diversify.

I am fascinated by the story of the dispersion of banksias. Now I can tell my old friend that his ancestral lineage can be traced back to the far-flung heaths and shrublands in the south-western coastal zone in Western Australia.

•

The banksia in our backyard garden is a cultivar, bought from a nursery. Only one of the banksia species is known to grow naturally in Canberra. On an online map maintained by the Australian Native Plant Society I discover nine locations where *Banksia marginata* (silver banksia) has been sighted in the wild. The climate in Canberra is too cold for them, and the soil not hospitable.

The cultivar banksia in our garden is a hybrid of two species: *Banksia ericifolia* and *Banksia serrata*. I suspect this could be the reason it has grown so large and has learnt to bloom with unbridled splendour. It appears that it has mislaid the memory of the brutal hailstorm and has decided to grace us with many flowering spikes. A few years ago, I used to be able to count them. This year there are too many, and I have given up.

You look wonderful, I say to my friend.

Mildred, the currawong, sitting on one of the scraggy branches of the paperbark, as if responding to my thought, descends and lands near the Japanese lantern placed not far from the banksia. For the last couple of years, the currawong has taken residence in our back garden, and the paperbark is where I see her most of the time. The paperbark stands near the fence entwinned with a much larger she-oak on the other side.

In the morning as I sit down with a cup of tea, through the window I watch birds lining up to visit the banksia. The earliest to arrive is the eastern spine bill. It targets the largest flowering spike and pecks and sucks. Its stay is brief, just a minute or so. I have also seen a few willie wagtails and scarlet robins. The red wattle birds enter late. They are noisy and aggressive. They treat the banksia as if they own it. No other bird is allowed to come near. Mildred the currawong keeps her distance, watching them from afar. My favourites are crimson rosellas, but they prefer the large grevillea and the wattles with seeds.

Hanna has placed a water basin near the grevillea which the birds, especially the currawongs, love. Even in the winter they like to take a dip and wash themselves. When the red wattle birds are around, the washing doesn't last long because they swoop on the currawongs. The wattle birds don't particularly like water; they are mostly interested in showing that not only the banksia but the whole garden belongs to them. Rosellas are shy and patient. They come to the basin mainly to drink. When one of them sips, the other sits nearby keeping watch.

Mildred the currawong lets them enjoy the drink. For some unknown reason she isn't friendly to me and I can't fail to notice a hint of suspicion in her attitude. Often when she finds me standing near the banksia she swoops down from her spot on the paperbark to find a place not far from me. As if she wants to keep an eye on me. I don't mind. She watches as I walk and touch the banksia, and after a few moments busies herself foraging for insects.

When I first saw the banksia almost thirty years ago, it was less than a metre tall. Our neighbour tells me that it was planted by the previous owner of the house. Now the banksia has grown tall, more than eight metres, and has spread wide in all directions. Its roots must go deep because the soil cover in the garden is thin and it's clayey. This means that it must draw nutrients from rocks that lie underneath the soil, and the rocks are old. The sandstone, silt, and shale were formed from sediments deposited in an ancient sea more than 440 million years ago. The sea was deep and the climate warm and Australia was part of Gondwanaland, located along the northern margin of the supercontinent, just north of the Equator. Some of the chemical elements the banksia needs for its growth and survival must come from these rocks.

The roots of our banksia go very deep in the time engrained in these rocks. The birds who eat its flowers and suck its juices partake some of these elements. The deep time which feeds the banksia also nourishes the eastern spine bills, the wattle birds, and the crimson rosellas.

When I touch a spike, a flower, or a seed of the banksia, I imagine my fingers feeling the pulse of deep, very deep time. This might sound a touch romantic, but the sensation is real, similar to what I experience when I take in my hands a rock lithified billions of years ago. However, as I touch deep time in the rocks I also come into contact with deep space, for the rocks also carry in them marks of places where they were formed; the places deep in the crust or far remote form their present-day location. In such rocks the time is condensed and space compressed.

The banksia in our back garden also enjoys a tactile association, akin to a handshake, with deep time and space by letting its roots reach the rocks millions of years old.

Your roots go deeper and deeper my friend, I tell the banksia.

Yours too, I imagine hearing.

Do they? I wonder, as I watch Mildred the currawong fly off, as if bored by my silly tête-à-tête with the banksia.

And then a hesitant thought creeps in; as a migrant who has found a home in the country of the Ngunnawal and the Ngambri peoples, I haven't come empty handed. The land from where I have arrived was once upon a time a tiny segment of the Gondwanaland, a name inherited from the indigenous tribes of the Gondi people, millions of whom live now in Central India. I bring with me a smidgen of their past histories – ancient, deep, wide.

I remember reading that the Ngunnawal welcome visitors to their country by chanting: *Ngunna yerrabi yanggu* (you are welcome to leave your footprints on our land).

There are whispers of belonging in the chant; belonging to the sky, the land, the water and all else that exists with them including the banksia in our garden.

In the chant I also hear an invitation to belong, to drop roots.

Thank you, my friend, I say to the banksia.

Thank you for leading me on this walk; a walk into the deep time-space; a walk that has just begun.

Acknowledgements

Several of these essays were written during my stay at the Centre for Creative and Cultural Research, University of Canberra. I am very grateful to Professor Tracy Ireland, director of the centre, and Distinguished Professor Jen Webb for their generous support. My friends and colleagues at the International Poetry Study Institute (IPSI) offered precious advice and suggestions and were always ready to hear me talk about ideas of space, place and memories. Paul Collis, Wayne Applebee, Paul Magee and Paul Hetherington deserve special mention. Yarning with Paul Collis was humbling and rewarding. Many thanks to Dianne Firth for providing information about Walter Burley Griffin and Marion Mahony. Anna Monro, Manager of Botanical Information, Australian National Botanic Gardens, very kindly provided information about banksias. Doug Benson at the Royal Botanic Gardens in Sydney graciously shared his knowledge about the botanical collection of Joseph Banks and his colleagues on the *Endeavour*.

I am grateful to Xavier Hennekinne, the publisher at Gazebo Books, and Phil Day, the curator of the poetry imprint Life Before Man (Gazebo Books) for taking on the book and giving it a hospitable abode. Thanks to the whole team at Gazebo Books for giving the book the shape and look it deserves. Very special thanks go to Lenka Miklos in whom these essays found a critical and empathetic reader and editor. Her insightful comments have improved the content and the tone of the book.

My family offered precious support. I am grateful to Hanna, my wife, for travelling with me to some of the sites and places.

I gratefully acknowledge the support of artsACT Canberra.

Works Cited and Consulted

Serres, M 2009 *Ecrivains, savants et philosophes font le tour du monde*, Paris: Le Pommier

Serres, M 2022 *Around the World with Writers, Scientists and Philosophers*, translated by G. Walker, Sydney: Gazebo Books

George Orwell's Elephant

English translations of Sanskrit extracts from *The Bhagvadgita* are by Vrinda Nabar and Shanta Tumkur.

Abbott, G 2017 'Did George Orwell Shoot an Elephant? His 1936 "confession" – and What it Might Mean,' *The Guardian*, accessed at https://www.theguardian.com/environment/2017/mar/18/did-george-orwell-shoot-an-elephant-his-1936-confession-and-what-it-might-mean on 24 April 2022

Bowker, G 2003 *George Orwell*, London: Abacus

Crick, B 1980 *George Orwell: A Life*, London: Secker & Warburg

Eilers, R 2016 'Burmese Days: In the Footsteps of George Orwell,' *The Guardian*, accessed at https://www.theguardian.com/travel/2016/jan/17/burmese-days-george-orwell-burma-myanmar on 24 April 2022

Kosambi, DD 1987 *The Culture and Civilisation of Ancient India in Historical Outline*, New Delhi: Vikas Publishing House

Larkin, E 2011 *Finding George Orwell in Burma*, London: Granta Publications

Nabar, V & Tumkur, S (transl.) 1997 *The Bhagvadgita*, Hertfordshire: Wordsworth Editions

Orwell, G 1984 *The Penguin Essays of George Orwell*, London: Penguin Books
Taylor, RJ 2003 *Orwell: The Life*, New York: H. Holt

Thapar, R 1966 *A History of India* (vol 1), Harmondsworth: Penguin Books

With Head and Heart to the Rock (Uluṟu)
An earlier version of the essay appeared as an article in in *Axon: Creative Explorations* (2019) as *Knowing and Unknowing: An Essay in Four Maps.*

Borges, JL 1998 *Collected fictions*, London: Allen Lane

Cole, K 2010 'Long Tom Tjapanangka' in F Cubillo and W Caruana (eds) *Aboriginal & Torres Strait Islander Art: Collection Highlights*, Canberra: National Gallery of Australia, p. 78

Cumpston, N & Patton, B 2010 *Desert Country*, Adelaide: Art Gallery of South Australia

Gosse, W 1873 *W.C. Gosse's explorations, 1873: report and diary of Mr. W.C. Gosse's central and western exploring expedition, 1873*, Adelaide: South Australian Government

Hill, B 1994 *The Rock: Travelling to Uluru*, St Leonards: Rathdowne

Layton, R 1989 *Uluru: An Aboriginal History of Ayers Rock*, Canberra: Aboriginal Study Press

Lopez, R (transl. Paille, M) 2016 *Unfolding Memories*, Canberra: First Edition

Macfarlane, R 2007 *The Wild Places*, London: Granta Books

Macfarlane, R 2012 *The Old Ways: A Journey on Foot*, London: Penguin Books

Morphy, H 1998 *Aboriginal Art*, London: Phaidon Press

Nicholls, C 2014 '"Dreamtime" and "The Dreaming": An Introduction,' *The Conversation*, 23 January 2014, http://theconversation.com/dreamtime-and-the-dreaming-an-introduction-20833, accessed 6 May 2019

Sweet, I, Stewart, A & Crick, I 2012 *Uluru and Kata Tjuta: A Geological Guide*, Canberra: Geoscience Australia

Tjikatu, B (YouTube clip) https://www.environment.gov.au/resource/creation-story-uluru-kata-tjuta-national-park accessed 8 August 2019

Visitor Guide, 2002 *Palya! Welcome to Anangu Land: Uluru-Kata Tjuta National Park*, Canberra: Director of National Parks

Like a Stranger in Delhi
An earlier version of the essay appeared in Meanjin (2001) as Remembering Dehlie (Delhi).

Alexander, M (ed.) 1987 *Delhi and Agra: A Travellers' Companion*, New York: Atheneum

Benjamin, W 1986 *Reflections: Essays, Aphorisms, Autobiographical Writings*, New York: Schocken Books de Certeau, M 1988 *The Practice of Everyday Life*, Berkeley: University of California

Gole, S 1989 *Indian Maps and Plans: From Earliest Times to the Advent of European Surveys*, New Delhi: Manohar

Kaye, MM (ed.) 1980 *The Golden Calm: An English Lady's Life in Moghul Delhi*, Exeter: Webb and Bower

Minturn, R 1858 *From New York to Delhi, by way of Rio de Janeiro*, Australia and China, New York: D. Appleton

Morris, J 1994 S*tones of Empire: The Buildings of British India*, Harmondsworth: Penguin

Russell, R & Islam, K 1969 *Ghalib: 1797-1869, vol 1: Life and Letters*, London: George Allen and Unwin

Selbourne, D 1977 *An Eye to India: The Unmasking of a Tyranny*, Harmondsworth: Penguin

Singh, P & Dhamija, R (eds.) 1989 *Delhi: The Deepening Urban Crisis*, New Delhi: Sterling

Tumarkin, M 2005 *Traumascapes*, Melbourne: Melbourne University Press

Varma, P 1989 *Ghalib: The Man, the Times*, New Delhi: Viking

Varma, P & Sondeep Shankar, S 1992 *Mansions at Dusk: The Havelis of Old Delhi*, New Delhi: Spantech

Not so quiet flows the Molonglo
National Centre for Indigenous Studies 2017, *Aboriginal and Torres Strait Islander Heritage Trail*, Canberra: Australian National University

Clark, M 1986 *A Short History of Australia*, Ringwood: Penguin Books Australia

Deakin, R 2000 *Waterlog: A Swimmer's Journey through Britain*, London: Vintage Books

Firth, D 2000 *Behind the Landscape of Lake Burley Griffin: Landscape, Water, Politics and the National Capital 1899-1964*, Doctoral Thesis, University of Canberra

Flood, J 1996 *Moth hunters of the Australian Capital Territory*, Canberra: J.M. Flood

Fraser, I & Prudie, R 2020 *Black Mountain: A Natural History of a Canberra Icon*, Canberra: Friends of Black Mountain

Friends of the Aranda Bushland 2007 *Our Patch*, Canberra: Friends of the Aranda Bushland

Gammage, B 2011 *The Biggest Estate on Earth: How Aborigines made Australia*, Crows Nest: Allen & Unwin

Godden Mackay Logan 2010 *Lake Burley Griffin Heritage Assessment*, Final Draft Report, Report Prepared for the National Capital Authority

Jackson-Nakano, A 2005 *Ngambri Ancestral Names*, Canberra: Ann Jackson-Nakano & Associates

Jackson-Nakano, A 2001 *The Kamberri*, Aboriginal History Monograph 8, Canberra: Aboriginal History Incorporated

Jaireth, S 1999 'Face to Face: The Aboriginal Tent Embassy and the National Portrait Gallery,' *Australian Book Review*, December 1999/January 2000, pp. 23-27

Kabila, PR 1997 *Belconnen's Aboriginal Past: A Glimpse into the Archaeology of the Australian Capital Territory*, Canberra: Black Mountains Project

Reid, P 2002 *Canberra Following Griffin: A Design History of Australia's National Capital*, Canberra: National Archives of Australia

The Windmills of Miguel Cervantes
All quotes from *Don Quixote* come from Edith Grossman's translation.

Borges, JL 1997 'A Recovered Lecture of J. L. Borges on "Don Quixote,"' *INTI PRIMAVERA*, 45, pp. 127-133

Coetzee, J 2013 *The Childhood of Jesus*, Melbourne: Text Publishing

Grossman, E (transl.) 2005 *Don Quixote*, (with an introduction by Harold Bloom) London: Vintage

Instituto Cervantes (Nueva Delhi) 2022 'El Quijoe en Sancrito,' accessed at https://cultura.cervantes.es/nuevadelhi/es/el-quijote-en-s%c3%a1nscrito/152927 on 6 July 2022

Kafka, F 2005 'The Truth about Sancho Panza,' *The Complete Short Stories* (transl. Willa Muir and Edwin Muir), London: Vintage, p. 430

Nabokov, V 1983 *Lectures on Don Quixote*, San Diego: HBJ Books

Rutherford. J (transl.) 2005 *The Ingenious Hidalgo Don Quixote de La Mancha*, London: Penguin UK (ebook)

Tourist Information Office, Poyatos Windmill 2005 *Windmills from La Mancha*, accessed at www.campodecriptana.info on 12 March 2022

Valle, A & Romero, M 2009 'Don Quixote's Countenance before and after Losing His Teeth,' *Journal of Dental Research*, vol. 88, 2, pp. 101-104

The Dead Bridge of Sunil Sandhani
An earlier version of the essay appeared in Meanjin (2003) as 'Bridge Near Firozepur'.

Brown, J 1980 'A Memoir of Colonel Sir Proby Cautley, F.R.S, 1802-1871, Engineer and Palaeontologist,' *Notes and Records of the Royal Society of London*, vol. 34, 2, pp. 185-225

Dhillon, A 2022 'The Knowledge of Our Elders: India's Living Root Bridges Submitted to UNESCO,' *The Guardian*, accessed at https://www.theguardian.com/world/2022/apr/01/india-living-root-bridges-submitted-to-unesco on 12 May 2022

Dupré, J 1998 *A History of the World's Most Famous and Important Spans*, Köln: Könemann

Holland, LA 1961 *Janus and the Bridge*, Michigan: University of Michigan Press

Salopek, P 2019 'Living Tree Bridges in India Stand Strong for Hundreds of Years,' *The National Geographic*, accessed at https://www.nationalgeographic.com/history/article/india-living-tree-bridges-stand-hundreds-years?loggedin=true on 15 January 2022

Yule, H 1844 'Notes on the Kaisa Hills, and People,' *Journal of Asiatic Society of Bengal*, vol. 14, 152, pp. 612-631

Iosif Stalin's Metro

The Cathedral of Christ the Saviour, Moscow, Official website (in Russian), accessed at http://new.xxc.ru/about/istoriya_hrama/istoriya/postroenie_hrama in May 2022

Friedman, J 2000, 'Soviet Mastery of the Skies at the Mayakovsky Metro Station,' *Studies in the Decorative Arts*, vol. 7, 48-64
'History of the Cathedral of Christ the Saviour: Project of Palace of Soviets' (in Russian), 2016, accessed at https://stroi.mos.ru/unikalnaya-arhitektura/... on 6 June 2016

Hoisington, SS 2003, '"Even Higher": The Evolution of the Project for the Palace of Soviets,' *Slavic Review*, vol. 62, pp. 41-68

Katering, KL 2000, 'An Introduction to the Design of the Moscow Metro in the Stalin Period: "The Happiness of Life Underground,"' *Studies in Decorative Arts*, vol. 7, pp. 2-20

Naumov, MS & Kusyi, *IA 2005, Moscow Metro: A Guidebook* (in Russian), Moscow: Vokrug Sveta

Pikareva, NA 1958, *Moscow Metropolitan named after V.I. Lenin* (in Russian), Moscow: Isskustvo

Plokhy, S 2015, *The Gates of Europe: A History of Ukraine*, London: Penguin Random House

Ryabushin, A & Smolina, N (transl. Gerard Magennis) 1992 *Landmarks of Soviet Architecture 1917-1991*, New York: Rizzoli

Ryabikova, V 2020, 'Rave Wake and Stalin's Speech: The Most Unusual Events in the Moscow Metro,' *Russia Beyond*, accessed form https://www.rbth.com/arts/333370-the-most-unusual-events-in-the-moscow-metro on 10 July 2022

Tsvetaeva, M 1919, 'Diaries and Notes' (in Russian), accessed on http://www.tsvetayeva.com/prose/pr_iz_zap_knon10July2022

Zveriov, V 2008, *Moscow* Metro (in Russian), Moscow: Algoritm

The Old Banksia in Our Back Garden

Attenbrow, V 2010 *Sydney's Aboriginal Past: Investigating the Archaeological Records*, Sydney: UNSW Press

Attenbrow, V 2010 'The Aboriginal Prehistory and Archaeology of Royal National Park and Environs: A Review,' *Proceedings of the Linnean Society of New South Wales*, vol. 134, pp. B39-B64

Austlang AIATSIS Collection: Information about Aboriginal and Torres Strait Islander Languages, https://collection.aiatsis.gov.au/austlang/language/A14 accessed 10 November 2021

Banks, J 1962, *The Endeavour Journal of Sir Joseph Banks, 1768-1771* (ebook), accessed from http://gutenberg.net.au/ebooks05/0501141h.html on 12 July 2021

Benson, D 2020 'Joseph Banks and Daniel Solander at Botany Bay: How Serious was the Science in 1770; where did they actually go?' *Australian Plants*, vol. 30, pp. 258-273

Bodkin, F & Robertson, L 2019 *D'harawal Dreaming Stories*, Sussex Inlet: Envirobooks
Bodkin, F & Robertson, L 2019, *D'harawal Climate and Natural Resources*, Sussex Inlet: Envirobooks

Cane, S 2013 *First Footprints: The Epic Story of the First Australians*, Crows Nest: Allen & Unwin

D'harawal *Dreaming Stories*, https://dharawalstories.com/ accessed 30 October 2021

Carpenter, RJ, Jordon, GJ & Hill, RS, 1994 'Banksieaephyllum taylorii (Proteaceae) from the Late Palaeocene of New South Wales and Its Relevance to the Origin of Australia's Scleromorphic Flora,' *Australian Systematic Botany*, vol. 7, pp. 385-392

City of Joondalup 2020 *Plants and People in Mooro Country: Noongar Plant Use in Yellagonga Regional Park* (4th ed), Perth: City of Joondalup

Cook, J 1893 *Captain Cook's Journal: First Voyage* (ebook), accessed from http://gutenberg.net.au/ebooks/e00043.html#ch8 on 12 July 2021

Cooks River Alliance 2020, *Aboriginal History along the Cooks River*, Sydney: Cooks River Alliance

Greenwood, DR, Haines, PW & Steart, DC 2001, 'New Species of Banksieaeformis and a Banksia "Cone" (Proteaceae) from the Tertiary of Central Australia,' *Australian Systematic Botany*, vol. 14 (6), pp. 871-890

Hanckel, M 1985 'Hot Rocks: Heat Treatment at Burrill Lake and Currarong, New South Wales,' *Archaeology in Oceania*, vol. 20, pp. 98-103

Heap, AD & Harris, PT 2008 'Geomorphology of the Australian Margin and Adjacent Seafloor,' *Australian Journal of Earth Sciences*, vol. 55, pp. 555-585

Hercus, L & Koch, H (eds.) 2009 *Aboriginal Placenames: Naming and Re-naming the Australian Landscape*, Aboriginal History Monograph 9, Canberra: ANU E Press and Aboriginal History Incorporated

Hill, RS, Truswell, EM, McLoughlin, SE & Dettmann, ME 1999 'Evolution of the Australian Flora: Fossil Evidence,' *Flora of Australia* (2nd ed), vol. 1, pp. 251-320

Howarth, RJ, Baker, RJV & Flood, PJ 2004 'A 6000 Year-Old Fossil Dugong from Botany Bay: Inferences about Changes in the Sydney's Climate, Sea Levels and Waterways,' *Australian Geographical Studies*, vol. 42, pp. 46-59

Johnson, BD, Albani, AD, Rickwood, PC & Tayton, JW 1977 'The Bedrock Topography of the Botany Basin, New South Wales,' *Journal of the Geological Society of Australia*, vol. 24, pp 403-408

Lambeck, K, Yokoyama, Y & Purcell, T 2002 'Into and Out of the Last Glacial Maximum: Sea-Level Change During Oxygen Isotope Stages 3 and 2,' *Quaternary Science Reviews*, vol. 21, pp. 343-360

Lampert, RJ & Hughes, PJ 1974 'Sea Level Change and Aboriginal Coastal Adaptations in Southern New South Wales,' *Archaeology and Physical Anthropology in Oceania*, vol. XI, pp. 226-235

Lewis, SL & Maslin, MA 2015, 'Defining the Anthropocene,' *Nature*, vol. 519, pp. 171-180
Lampert, RJ 1971 *Burrill Lake and Currarong*, Canberra: Australian National University

Manne, T & Veth, PM 2015 'Late Pleistocene and Early Holocene Exploitation of Estuarine Communities in Northwestern Australia,' *Quaternary International*, vol 385, pp. 112-123

Mast, AR & Givnish, TJ 2002 'Historical Biogeography and the Origin of Stomatal Distributions in Banksia and Dryandra (Proteaceae) Based on Their cpDMA Phylogeny,' *American Journal of Botany*, vol. 89, pp. 1311-1323

Martin, ARH 1994 'Kurnell Fen: An Eastern Australian Coastal Wetland, its Holocene Vegetation, Relevant to Sea-Level Change and Aboriginal Land Use,' *Review of Palaeobotany and Palynology*, vol. 80, pp. 311-332

McDonald, J 2015 'I must go down to the seas again: or, what happens when the sea comes to you? Murujuga rock art as an environment indicator for Australia's north-west,' *Quaternary International*, vol. 385, pp. 124-135

McDonald, J & Berry, M 2017 'Murujuga, Northwestern Australia: When Arid Hunter-Gatherers Became Coastal Foragers,' *The Journal of Island and Coastal Archaeology*, vol. 12, pp. 24-37

McKenna, M 2004 *The Country: a reconciled republic?* Sydney: University of New South Wales Press

Mulvaney, K 2003 'Iconic Imagery: Pleistocene Rock Art Development Across Northern Australia,' *Quaternary International*, vol. 285, pp. 99-110

Mulvaney, J & Kamminga, J 1999 *Prehistory of Australia*, Crows Nest: Allen & Unwin

Ngunnawal *Plant Use: A Traditional Aboriginal Plant Use Guide for the ACT* Region, 2014, Canberra: ACT Government

Nunn, PD & Reid, NJ 2016 'Aboriginal Memories of Inundation of the Australian Coast Dating from More than 7000 Years Ago,' *Australian Geographer*, vol. 47, pp. 11-47

Parkinson, S 2004 *A Journal of a Voyage to the South Seas, in his Majesty's Ship, The Endeavour* (ebook), accessed from https://webarchive.nla.gov.au/awa/20100622043717/http://southseas.nla.gov.au/journals/parkinson/title.html on 12 July 2021

Rawson, A 2020 'Sydney Parkinson, Botanical Draughtsman to Banks,' *Fronds*, vol. 95, pp. 12-13

Sloss, CR, Murray-Wallace, CV & Jones, BG 2007 'Holocene Sea-Level Change on the Southeast Coast of Australia: A Review,' *The Holocene*, vol. 17, pp. 999-1014

Troy, J 1993 'The Sydney Language', Canberra: Aboriginal Studies Press

Turpin, M 2013 'Semantic Extension in Kaytetye Flora and Fauna Terms,' *Australian Journal of Linguistics*, vol. 33, pp. 488-518

www.ingramcontent.com/pod-product-compliance
Lightning Source LLC
LaVergne TN
LVHW041111080826
845145LV00007B/1763

* 9 7 8 0 6 4 5 6 3 3 7 9 5 *